Trust in the European Union in Challenging Times

Antonina Bakardjieva Engelbrekt
Niklas Bremberg
Anna Michalski
Lars Oxelheim
Editors

Trust in the European Union in Challenging Times

Interdisciplinary European Studies

palgrave
macmillan

Editors
Antonina Bakardjieva Engelbrekt
Department of Law
Stockholm University
Stockholm, Sweden

Anna Michalski
Department of Government
Uppsala University
Uppsala, Sweden

Niklas Bremberg
Uppsala University
Uppsala, Sweden

The Swedish Institute of International Affairs
Stockholm, Sweden

Lars Oxelheim
University of Agder
Kristiansand, Norway

Research Institute of Industrial Economics
Stockholm, Sweden

ISBN 978-3-030-08872-9 ISBN 978-3-319-73857-4 (eBook)
https://doi.org/10.1007/978-3-319-73857-4

Cover illustration: daitoZen

Printed on acid-free paper

This Palgrave Macmillan imprint is published by the registered company Springer International Publishing AG part of Springer Nature.
The registered company address is: Gewerbestrasse 11, 6330 Cham, Switzerland

Contents

Notes on Contributors

Antonina Bakardjieva Engelbrekt is Professor of European Law and *Torsten och Ragnar Söderberg* Professor of Legal Science (2015–2018) at the Faculty of Law of Stockholm University. She chairs the Swedish Network for European Legal Studies. Her research interests are directed at processes of Europeanization and globalization and their influence on national law and institutions, as well at interactions between legal systems (legal transplants). She has been Fernand Braudel Fellow at the EUI, Florence, Global Research Fellow at NYU Law School, and Visiting Professor at Bond University, Chicago Kent College of Law and Keio University, Tokyo.

Linda Berg is Senior Lecturer in the Department of Political Science and Director of the Centre for European Research (CERGU) at the University of Gothenburg. Her main research interests are European parliament elections, political attitudes (specifically towards the EU) as well as identity and policy in a multi-level setting.

Andreas Bergh is Associate Professor at the Department of Economics, Lund University, and a researcher at the Research Institute of Industrial Economics in Stockholm. His main research interests are public and institutional economics, trust, corruption, sharing economy and development economics.

Niklas Bremberg (PhD in Political Science) is research coordinator for the Swedish Network of European Studies in Political Science (Department of Government, Uppsala University) and senior research fellow at the Swedish Institute of International Affairs. His research focuses on international practice theory, security communities, and EU foreign and security policy. He has been visiting researcher at the University of Toronto, the University of Liverpool, and Universitat Autònoma de Barcelona.

Anna Felländer is Digital Economist with extensive experience in analysing how digitalisation is affecting organisations, society and the economy. She is affiliated to the Swedish Royal Institute of Technology and advisor to the Swedish Minister of Digitalisation. Felländer has a Master of Science degree in International Economics from the Stockholm School of Economics.

Ester Herlin-Karnell is Professor of EU Constitutional Law and Justice and University Research Chair at VU University Amsterdam. She is also the co-director and founder of the VU Centre for European Legal Studies. Her main research interest is European criminal law and she is working on a monograph on EU Justice and Home Affairs.

Håkan Holmberg is Data Scientist specialising in the fields of psychometrics and blockchain technology. He is presently involved in projects at Uppsala University as well as the National Board of Health and Welfare. Holmberg holds a master's degree in Mathematics from the Stockholm University.

Sarkis J. Khoury is retired from the University of California at Riverside. During his academic career, his works on issues related to banking and finance had been published extensively. Khoury holds a doctoral degree in International Business from the Wharton School, University of Pennsylvania.

Anna Michalski is Associate Professor of Political Science and at the Department of Government, Uppsala University, and associate research fellow at the Swedish Institute of International Affairs. She is Chair for the Swedish Network for European Studies in Political Science (SNES) and member of the Swedish Foreign Policy Society. Her research focuses on European foreign policy, EU-China relations, strategic partnerships and socialization in international organizations. She has held academic positions at Fudan University, Shanghai, and The Europe Institute, Auckland University, New Zealand, as well as at several European policy research institutes and the European Commission.

Joakim Nergelius is Professor of Law at Örebro University. He has served on numerous occasions as expert and legal advisor to, inter alia, the European Commission and the Swedish government. His research interests include EU law and constitutional law.

Lars Oxelheim is Professor of International Business and Finance at the University of Agder, Kristiansand, Norway, and professor emeritus at Lund University, Lund, Sweden. He is affiliated with the Research Institute of Industrial Economics (Institutet för Näringslivsforskning), Stockholm, Sweden, and is honorary professor at the Fudan University, Shanghai, China. Oxelheim's research interests are in the area of the interplay between the firm and its macroeconomic environment encompassing economic and financial integration as well as managerial aspects, corporate governance, and risk management. He is a delegate of the Royal Swedish Academy of Engineering Sciences (IVA), the Royal Society of Letters at Lund and is elected fellow of the European International Business Academy (EIBA).

Bo Petersson is Professor of Political Science and IMER (International Migration and Ethnic Relations) at Malmö University. He is also Director of the research platform Russia and the Caucasus Regional Research (RUCARR). His special areas of interest include nationalism, legitimacy, and political myth.

Eva Storskrubb is Associate Professor of Procedural Law and a researcher at Uppsala University. She also works as a practising lawyer at Roschier in Stockholm. Her research interests include EU procedural law, civil justice and transnational dispute resolution on civil and commercial matters including private international law.

Robin Teigland is Professor of Business Administration and Co-director of the Centre for Strategy and Competitiveness at the Stockholm School of Economics (SSE). She is Fellow of the KIN Centre for Digital Innovation at VU University Amsterdam. Her research interests reside at the intersection of strategy, technology, innovation, and entrepreneurship.

Göran von Sydow is Deputy Director and Senior Researcher in Political Science at the Swedish Institute for European Policy Studies (SIEPS). His main research interests are political parties, Euroscepticism, European integration, and constitutional change. He holds a doctoral degree in Political Science from the Stockholm University.

Clas Wihlborg is the Fletcher Jones Chair in International Business at Chapman University and a visiting professor at the University West, Sweden. He is a member of the Royal Swedish Academy of Engineering Sciences. His research interests include financial institutions, and international and corporate finance.

List of Figures

List of Tables

Trust in the European Union: What Is It and How Does It Matter?

Antonina Bakardjieva Engelbrekt, Niklas Bremberg, Anna Michalski, and Lars Oxelheim

Trust is an elusive concept. We can have it without being able to see or touch it. It takes a long time to build up, but it can be demolished in an instant. The paradoxical thing about trust is that it can be said to be present as long as we take it for granted, but as soon as we need to demonstrate its existence, it tends to disappear. The motto of President Ronald Reagan regarding relations between the US and the Soviet Union during the Cold War—that they ought to be based on the principle of 'trust, but

A. Bakardjieva Engelbrekt
Stockholm University, Stockholm, Sweden

N. Bremberg
Uppsala University, Uppsala, Sweden

The Swedish Institute of International Affairs, Stockholm, Sweden

A. Michalski (✉)
Uppsala University, Uppsala, Sweden

L. Oxelheim
University of Agder, Kristiansand, Norway

Research Institute of Industrial Economics, Stockholm, Sweden

A. Bakardjieva Engelbrekt et al. (eds.), *Trust in the European Union in Challenging Times*, https://doi.org/10.1007/978-3-319-73857-4_1

verify'—illustrates this paradox rather well. Yet many of the institutions of society—not least the judiciary, the market, and the welfare state—cannot function without a certain measure of 'unverified trust'.[1] This means that trust is one of the main ingredients of a system of democratic majority rule, wherein representatives are chosen from a set of political parties in general elections to form a government and lead the country and in that capacity rule in the name of all.

Not least for its role in facilitating collective action has trust figured centrally in the European project, often as an unspoken but virtually unattainable precondition for integrating different states, political systems, and peoples in Europe (cf. Haas, 1958). One scholar who took an interest in European integration early on, political scientist Karl W. Deutsch, envisaged that trust would play a decisive role in the process. He believed that if citizens of the different member states started to see themselves as belonging to the same community, and came to trust and understand the citizens of the other member states to essentially the same degree that they trust and understand the citizens of their own country, the prospects for successful integration would be greatly enhanced (Deutsch et al., 1957).

This is the first book in the Interdisciplinary European Studies series. It is published at a time when the project of European integration is facing many serious crises. The unity of Europe is put under stress by the migrant and refugee crisis, the lingering euro crisis, a multitude of security crises, and not least 'Brexit'. It must also be acknowledged that the US administration under President Donald Trump has taken a much more critical stance towards the European Union than under any of his predecessors and the level of trust in transatlantic relations is at a record low. Recent studies on euroscepticism and populism in Europe have highlighted the role of popular distrust of elites in order to explain the high level of social contestation of the EU in many member states (see e.g. Abts, Heerwegh, & Swyngedouw, 2009; Harteveld, Meer & Vries, 2013; Hobolt & Tilley, 2016; Kriesi, 2014; Scharpf, 2014). In contrast, transnational trust among political leaders, civil servants, and officials is often assumed to be of great importance for the EU's ability to respond to current challenges. Despite the importance of trust in complex political and social systems, there are few works in the field of EU studies that address comprehensively the issue of trust in the light of recent developments. This book, therefore, contributes to fill this void by investigating through an interdisciplinary perspective the importance of trust for the EU in meeting the internal and external challenges it is facing.

When EU leaders must find solutions to difficult problems, trust among them is central in their capacity to reach an agreement and make decisions. This can be seen when the Union's ability to act must be strengthened to improve the implementation of common policies; trust between officials in different national and European agencies is invaluable. This is because trust and consensus, particularly between the member states and their representatives in the EU's institutions, is in many ways the glue that enables the EU to hold together and its policy processes to work. Similarly, democracy in the Union will remain incomplete, unless and until the question of solidarity among the peoples of Europe is addressed which in itself is dependent on a degree of mutual trust among the citizens of different EU member states taking hold as this is a basic precondition for common democratic processes.

Scholars have described how trust and the ability to solve problems have grown at the elite level in the EU as a result of years of more or less constant negotiation (see e.g. Checkel & Katzenstein, 2009; Favell, 2011; Fligstein, 2008). However, it is also clear that nothing similar has taken place among the broader population, whose sense of European identity is often weak. Undoubtedly, the ongoing crises and myriad challenges are eroding, rather than building up, trust among the EU's member states, public agencies, economic and social actors, and populations. Therefore, the importance of trust seen from different perspectives urgently needs to be discussed in depth in relation to the EU as well as European cooperation more broadly.

Trust, as noted above, is an elusive concept, and this is reflected also in the research that focuses on the matter. In part this has to do with how trust is conceptualized: as a condition among actors; as a notion held by one person about the behaviour and actions of another; or as an independent factor facilitating collaboration, exchange, and joint decision-making. It also has in part to do with where we look to find trust: at the interpersonal level; within institutions, systems, and procedures; or at the interchange between peoples and states. The contributors to this book analyse the prevalence of trust from the vantage point of law, economic, and political science, and they consider the consequences for the EU at both the national and European levels when trust is lacking. In this introduction, therefore, we set out to discuss the importance of trust within the EU as a constantly evolving political system and to shed light on where and when trust plays a critical role in managing this multi-level system with an uneven distribution of competences and without a sense of self-evident legitimacy.

Trust Within the EU in Historical Perspective

In light of the ongoing crises in the EU, it is worth emphasizing that, historically, the emergence of European integration and the creation of the EU's predecessors in the 1950s were something remarkable from the standpoint of trust.[2] The European Coal and Steel Community (ECSC) was founded in 1952, followed by the European Economic Community (EEC) in 1958. This begs the questions how six West European states were able to create these institutions so soon after the Second World War, when trust between political elites must have been at an absolute low in Europe? The literature on European integration often highlights the heroic efforts of far-sighted political leaders, working together with high-level civil servants. To be sure, the convictions of leading politicians, based on their personal experience of one or often two world wars, were critical in this context. Central figures here included Robert Schuman, French Foreign Minister; Konrad Adenauer, German Chancellor; Jean Monnet, President of the High Authority of the ECSC; Paul-Henri Spaak, Belgian Prime Minister; and Altiero Spinelli, prominent leader of European federalism. Still more important for the integration effort was the capacity of these individuals to see beyond selfish nationalism and destructive competition between neighbouring countries. It is clear, however, that such qualities would never have sufficed had a number of background conditions not been present at the time the EEC was created. These conditions played a decisive role in enabling trust to be created among political elites, and in making it possible for a broad albeit vague support among the peoples of the member states to be mobilized.

Among these external conditions, American hegemony was extraordinarily important. The US aided economic reconstruction and supported the democratic consolidation of weak political regimes in Western Europe that were threatened by communist takeover and revanchist forces. A further factor, and at least as important, was the overarching security umbrella which the Americans provided through the North Atlantic Treaty Organization (NATO), which furnished protection against external powers and embedded the remilitarization of (West) Germany in joint structures. The emerging liberal order and US support for reconstruction laid the foundation for intra-European free trade. The rules governing the disbursement of Marshall Plan aid forced the Western Europeans to trade with each other without erecting undue trade barriers. In various ways, then, the economic interchange among the countries in question, together with the military and security cooperation in NATO, made it possible to create a security community in Western Europe.[3] The different political elites learned to work together to overcome real barriers through negotiation and compromise, rather than by issuing threats or resorting to coercion. Furthermore, the opportunities for mobility and exchange which the internal market afforded to economic actors (companies, investors, and workers) reinforced the feeling of belonging to a security community. The ground rules established for interaction among the member states, and the perception that war was henceforth impossible between them, strengthened trust and promoted confidence, ensuring development along democratic and market-based lines.

A further precondition for the West European experiment in building a political order based on voluntary integration was the long period of economic growth following the Second World War. Without rising prosperity in the West, it would have been much more difficult to carry out the structural changes required for modernization of the economy and it would not have been possible to gain widespread acceptance for far-reaching free trade. The association of the EEC, in the minds of people in most of the member states, with social and economic progress and with greater material wealth laid a foundation for trust and helped to ensure popular support.

The internal conditions for European integration were based on the arrangements that political elites in the original six member states laid down for the EEC. These regulated relations of power between the participating states on the institutional, economic, and political level. It was established early on that, despite their differences in terms of geographic area, economic scale, and population size, the member states would be regarded as functionally equal in the treaties. Later, after decision-making by majority vote was introduced through the adoption of a weighted system for voting in the EU, the smaller member states still held a disproportionately large share of the votes. In addition, a supranational body, the European Commission, was set up and tasked with presenting legislative proposals, further protecting the smaller countries from dominance by the larger ones. These arrangements helped endow the EU, in comparison with other international organizations, with a stronger capacity for action but without jeopardizing the interests of its smaller members.

Where economic integration was concerned, necessary structural reforms were embedded in an agreement between the member states on shared costs, in exchange for free trade and the dismantling of non-tariff barriers to trade. The EEC thus promoted economic modernization, helped to equalize the costs entailed, and held out the promise of prosperity based on market integration (without, however, establishing a common economic policy). It was in this context of close cooperation and rising trust among political, economic, and bureaucratic elites that the term 'permissive consensus' was coined, to describe the confidence felt by the peoples of the member states in the efforts of the European elite to achieve integration (cf. Hooghe & Marks, 2009).

The State of Trust in the EU at Challenging Times

A great deal has happened, of course, in Europe and the world since the second half of the twentieth century. The conditions reviewed above, however, long remained the linchpin for dealings between the Union's member states and between them and the EU's institutions. Nonetheless, it cannot be denied that the situation in the Union 2018 is different and that the habitual patterns of cooperation have changed. The crises of recent years serve to highlight several ways in which trust within the EU has eroded. In September 2016, in his annual address to the European Parliament in Strasbourg, the President of the European Commission, Jean-Claude Juncker, vented his frustration:

> I have witnessed several decades of EU integration. There were many strong moments. Of course, there were many difficult times too, and times of crisis. But never before have I seen such little common ground between our Member States. So few areas where they agree to work together. (Juncker, 2016)

The President of the European Council, Donald Tusk, spoke along similar lines in May 2016, on the 40th anniversary of the founding of the Conservative Party group (the European People's Party) in the EP:

> Obsessed with the idea of instant and total integration, we failed to notice that ordinary people, the citizens of Europe do not share our Euro-enthusiasm. Disillusioned with the great visions of the future, they demand that we cope with the present reality better than we have been doing until now… [t]he spectre of a break-up is haunting Europe and a vision of a federation doesn't seem to me like the best answer to it. (Tusk, 2016)

Between the two of them, Junker and Tusk paint a picture of a serious shortage of mutual trust between the elites of the different member states as well as of public trust in the EU today. The euro crisis, especially the way the Greek debt crisis was handled, offers a particularly illustrative example. The eurozone debt crisis is often thought to encapsulate an insurmountable ideological conflict between North and South, between lenders and borrowers, and between German 'ordoliberalism' and Greek 'neo-Marxism'. But as Christopher Bickerton points out, the ideological conflicts in this case are easily exaggerated. There was and is in fact a far-reaching consensus, in terms of both objectives (keeping Greece in the euro) and means (loans plus de facto debt forgiveness, in exchange for tough economic reforms). What was seen as unacceptable, however, was the way in which Yanis Varoufakis, the Greek Finance Minister, openly criticized his peers, thereby breaking the informal norms and rules by which the Eurogroup operates (Bickerton, 2015). This highlights the crucial role that expectations of proper behaviour still play among elites in the EU. At the same time, it lays bare the problems to which an approach of this kind gives rise when the legitimacy of decisions is being challenged by significant parts of the population.

The refugee situation in Europe and its neighbourhood is another indicator of the lack of trust among EU elites today. In 2015, as the number of refugees arriving in Europe was sharply increasing, the European Commission proposed a quota system for the number of refugees that each member state would take in, based on a range of indicators such as the size, population, and economy of the country in question (European Commission, 2015). On this basis, in September, a majority on the Council of Ministers decided—in the face of opposition from several Central and East European states—to reassign 120,000 refugees who had come to Italy and Greece and to other member states. Among others, Viktor Orbán, the Prime Minister of Hungary, refused to accept the decision which had been taken by the majority. This demonstrated the profound differences in views between the member states and showed how collective decisions within the Union are undermined when portions of the political elite fail to respect the common rules of the game. When member states act in a self-willed fashion and call into question decisions made to address common problems, it is a very serious matter. Such behaviour is more to be regretted if the historian Hartmut Kaelble is correct in his contention that EU citizens, while displaying but a weak European identity, increasingly expect the Union to find solutions to common challenges in regard to, for example, security policy, foreign affairs, and climate change (Kaelble, 2009).

'Brexit' too has sharply posed the issue of trust between member states, as has the question of the terms for the UK's withdrawal. Negative perceptions of EU membership have been a regular feature in British debate for a number of years. They were accentuated during the government of David Cameron, culminating among other things in a symbolic but substantively meaningless renegotiation of British participation in the EU's arrangement for the free movement of labour and the role of national parliaments. Harsh and uncompromising rhetoric filled the air as the referendum of June 2016 approached, further undermining prospects for an objective examination of the merits and drawbacks of British membership of the EU. The debate also demonstrated, with salutary clarity, the belief among advocates of British withdrawal in the possibility of securing an agreement on unhindered access to the internal market, coincident with an end to the free movement of labour (notwithstanding repeated declarations by European political leaders that such a settlement will never be allowed).

Over one year into the negotiations between Britain and the remaining 27 member states, it is something of a truism to state that trust between the two sides has reached a record low. The negotiations have been severely delayed due to a lack of common appreciation of the ground rules for a member state leaving the EU. With the British government being under the illusion that the terms of 'Brexit' are negotiable and the remaining 27 refusing to give any ground before the British accept the principles on financial compensation, the UK-Irish border, and the status of EU nationals in the UK, the talks are stalling. This does not bode well for the EU and the UK to move on to discussions about the future relationship between them. Various extreme scenarios, such as the UK crashing out of the EU, are obviously to the detriment of both sides, but with the Brexiteers refusing to fully understand the implications for the UK and the EU of Britain leaving the Union without working arrangements, there is virtually no fertile ground in the circumstances of early 2018 to build fruitful future relations between the two.

How Does Trust Matter Within the EU?

Political scientists have long taken an interest in situations where sovereign states voluntarily relinquish formal decision-making power to a political union, wherein decisions are made together with other states with the help of independent institutions (see e.g. Milward, 1992; Rosamund, 2000; Tallberg, 2004). In particular, the issue of the autonomy of the member states and their need to protect their national interest have stood at centre.

Several explanations have been advanced: that the states of Europe, due to their vulnerability and small size, have had no other choice than to seek out common solutions to challenges and cross-border threats; that recurrent negotiations give rise to a logic of give and take, because 'the shadow of the future' rewards those who play by common rules and who look to more than just their self-interest; and that the EU's supranational institutions have served to even out the informational asymmetry that normally besets efforts at international cooperation. Social-psychological theories have also been cited to explain such outcomes (Haas, 1992). These fasten on the tendency among officials and experts not only to form knowledge communities on the premise that threats and challenges are best confronted jointly but also to form common conceptions on appropriate solutions. Consensus thus arises, and new forms of trust and loyalty emerge—as do common notions of appropriate behaviour and shared ideas about how political problems ought to be addressed (Lewis, 2005).

Predictability, a shared worldview, and a knowledge of national conditions create the kind of trust the EU needs to be able to make necessary decisions on a daily basis. This dimension, which encompasses the executive direction of the Union, is important, but it can no longer contain the tensions which the EU's deepening and enlargement have entailed. Efforts to democratize the EU have enhanced the position of the European Parliament, but without strengthening either the parliamentary or the party-political dimension of the Union. Political parties are still mainly anchored in national arenas, and transnational ties between them are relatively weak. National parliaments show no interest in cooperating more closely with the EP within the framework of a multi-level parliamentary system. The diversity of political values and experiences has increased as a result of the EU's enlargement to the east. Increased politicization has taken place, but the multi-level political system that distinguishes the Union has not put down robust roots. The executive direction of the member states at the Union level has been strengthened, but stronger bonds have not been established either with national parliaments or with the various national populations. At the popular level, finally, the permissive consensus, a kind of passive confidence in the Union among the public, has given way to a growing mistrust of the exercise of power at European level, nourishing a rising populism both nationally and centrally.

One key dimension of trust in the Union is the assumption that its legal order is based on the rule of law. Under the treaties, the member states are obliged to grant EU law precedence in the event of a conflict with national law. This does not alter the fact, however, that the EU system is based essentially on international law. In the end, therefore, it is up to the government of each member state to choose a posture towards the Union and up to the national courts to interpret national law in conformity with EU law. This underscores the vulnerability of the Union from the standpoint of the rule of law. A member state may decide, namely, not to apply EU legislation, either on account of political considerations or because it opposes the precedence of EU law in principle. In either case, trust in the Union is undermined. If political considerations are allowed to trump solidarity with the other member states, the effect will be to destroy the trust upon which effective EU action is based: trust that agreements will be followed, that EU law will be respected, and that the member states will act together to uphold the Union's legal order. A strict adherence to principles of national sovereignty, self-determination, and defence of the national interest comes at the expense of the common interest. Trust must therefore be seen by all member states as a common asset, which each of them has the responsibility to maintain.

The principle of 'sincere cooperation' has been enshrined in the EU treaties since 2009, when the Treaty of Lisbon entered into force (Article 4(3) TEU). Principles for the conduct of state administration are often regarded as a national competence, although there are relatively well-developed common legal principles of good administration which are applied by the European Court of Justice. But a lack of trust between national agencies undermines prospects for cooperation, reduces the interest of member states in agreeing on common policies, and ultimately erodes the confidence of the larger population in the Union as a collective actor. Trust between the member states at the administrative level is therefore of crucial importance for the EU. The underlying reason for this is that, notwithstanding its adoption of a great many laws and regulations, the Union as an organization has virtually no administrative resources to implement and enforce them. In a vast number of policy areas, the implementation of EU laws and regulations is therefore directly dependent on the expertise of national agencies, their financial and human resources, and their willingness to implement the provisions in question. Yet uniform implementation would seem to be a fundamental condition for the maintenance of fair competition on the internal market and ultimately a prerequisite for the rule of law within the Union. The problem is accentuated by the fact that there are relatively few guidelines for cooperation between agencies in the different member states. This despite the fact that coordination between national policies, for example, in the economic field, is being recommended more and more.

Different Dimension of Trust and How to Achieve It

The following chapters in this book consider the importance of trust for the EU in a variety of ways. How, for example, is trust in the Union as a political system affected by the fundamental conflict of values expressed in the debate over the EU's handling of the refugee crisis? How has confidence in the Union's institutions evolved over time in the different member states? How has interpersonal trust been affected by migration within the Union and by the influx of people from outside its bounds? What sort of regulatory framework for economic affairs promotes confidence in European cooperation in currency and banking? Can we presume that national bodies in the area of civil and criminal law have confidence in their counterparts in other EU countries? These are some of the issues addressed in this book.

In the second chapter, Joakim Nergelius considers various crises and challenges facing the Union: the refugee crisis, Britain's imminent withdrawal, the risk of state bankruptcy in Greece, and the lack of clarity over sanctions against Russia. These crises ought not to be seen, Nergelius argues, as just political in nature: they are eminently constitutional as well. This is evident not least from the conflict of values which has been exacerbated of late by the actions of the Hungarian and Polish governments. Why have these problems and crises emerged in recent years? One reason emphatically stressed by the author is that the Union has taken its requirements for membership, and its criteria for admission to various cooperative arrangements, too lightly. States which are already members of the Union need closer oversight as well, particularly where the protection of rights is concerned. Another basic cause highlighted by the author is the distrust of the entire EU project evinced by large portions of the population in several member countries.

In large parts of the Union, we may now speak of an ongoing conflict of values between a liberal model of society and various conservative, authoritarian, and nationalist ideals that were long thought to be obsolete. Nationalist parties in a number of European countries are exploiting the lack of trust in the EU within broad sections of the population. Here, Nergelius contends, we can identify both a popular suspicion of political elites in general and a distrust of the essentially supranational, cosmopolitan, and rule of law-based EU project as such. This conflict of values was exacerbated by the refugee crisis in 2015, which opened up a gulf between (North)Western Europe and most of the Eastern member states, which have refused to accept refugees from Africa and the Middle East. Moreover, the EU's agreement with Turkey in March 2016—on returning refugees from Greece—is problematic in several ways, both juridically and politically. As of 2017, however, a fundamentally liberal majority of the EU's member states are calling continuously—as are the European Commission and the European Parliament—for a continued acceptance of refugees, assuming the question of their distribution can be solved. The more liberal states, the author argues, should make use of the mechanisms set out in the treaties to force recalcitrant states to adopt more liberal policies on refugees, on rights and freedoms, and on matters of tolerance generally.

In the third chapter, Bo Petersson looks back at the great eastward enlargement of 2004. Ten countries joined the Union in that year, eight of them located in Central and Eastern Europe. Enlargement was seen at the time as a huge gain for Western liberalism and democracy, even if certain problems were anticipated, primarily in connection with labour markets and social safety nets. It has since become clear, however, that enlargement has led to tensions within the Union—and in a way that few predicted. The EU incorporated states whose political life and civil society were marked by the experience of the Cold War and of long-term membership in the Soviet-dominated Eastern bloc. This has given rise to serious tensions. Over the course of the last decade, governments have taken power in Central Europe which have their own notions of what the core values of the Union consist of. These governments, particularly those of Hungary and Poland, seem most inclined to heed the siren call of authoritarian powers outside the Union. A serious challenge has been mounted to the interpretation of the Copenhagen criteria (regarding democracy, human rights, and the rule of law) which had earlier been taken for granted. This has badly undermined trust and confidence in the Union.

The growing public support for populist parties across the Union poses another serious challenge to the EU's core values, Petersson points out. A good many voters find simple solutions to complex problems attractive. This is taking place as the EU shows increasing signs of weakness on both economic and identity-related issues. The repeated and long-standing economic crises from 2007 onwards is testimony to this, as is the imminent withdrawal of Britain from the Union. A unifying vision and a common identity are needed to give the member states and their populations the motivation to keep moving forward together. A common identity based on shared values is essential for trust within the Union and for the EU's influence and reputation in the world. For such a thing to be possible, there must be internal unity on the interpretation and implementation of core values. Democracy, human rights, and the rule of law must never become beautiful phrases without concrete content.

In the fourth chapter, Linda Berg looks at trust between citizens on the one hand and the EU's political system on the other. Her chapter deals in part with people's general attitude towards the EU and in part with their trust and confidence in the Union's institutions. She discusses various models for explaining the variation in levels of trust between countries and between people. On the one hand, the results show relative stability over time in people's general attitude towards the Union or in their views on the desirability of their country's membership therein. The years of crisis have seen a certain decline in this regard, but public opinion is still supportive overall. On the other hand, trust in the EU's institutions more specifically has fallen sharply during the crisis years. This accords with what we might expect, that is, that attitudes of a more specific type (e.g. regarding EU institutions) will change more rapidly than attitudes of a more general kind (e.g. regarding the EU as a whole).

A closer look at variations between countries and over time reveals a similar pattern. A majority of citizens in most member states remain well disposed to the Union, even after the years of crisis. The exceptions here are Greece, Cyprus, and Austria. When it comes to confidence in the EU's institutions, on the other hand, the variation between countries is greater. Confidence is greatest in countries that are politically and economically stable or where the comparison with domestic political institutions comes out in the Union's favour. Variations of this kind, according to Berg, can be understood on the basis of such factors as the following: self-interest; the influence of different national political actors; political and economic developments (both in the EU and in the country in question); and perceptions of how EU membership has affected the country and its identity. While feelings of affiliation with Europe remain important for trust in the EU, Berg's chapter shows that such feelings today—in the wake of the recent crises—are not able to the same extent as before to offset opposing views and feelings of dissatisfaction. In light of this, Berg argues, basic civics training in all member states must be devoted to deepening the public's understanding of how the Union works as a multi-level system, how decisions within it are made, and how citizens can influence the policies pursued.

In the fifth chapter, Andreas Bergh discusses the relationship between migration and interpersonal trust in the Union. Interpersonal trust, Bergh avers, is an important foundation for a well-functioning society. A society where people trust each other works better—economically, politically, and socially. The research shows, moreover, that variations in trust are great within the EU, both between different member states and within the same country. Trust between people is high in the Nordic member states and low in such countries as Poland, Portugal, and Hungary. But no clear trend up or down is apparent; the proclivity to trust people (or not to) seems in general to be stable over time. The challenge for Europe in coming years will be to make the most of the opportunities arising from increased migration, both between member states and from outside the Union.

One central issue in this context is how interpersonal trust is affected by increased migration between countries with differing levels of trust. New research shows that migrants from low-trust countries who move to high-trust ones tend to show higher trust than those who remain in the former lands. Their trust is not as high, however, as that displayed by persons who have always lived in countries with higher trust. Bergh also considers the reverse question: what happens to the trust shown by emigrants from a high-trust country when they have lived for several years in a low-trust one (with high levels of corruption, for instance)? Reviewing research on trust shown by Swedish expatriates, Bergh notes that the high-trust level seems very robust, except to some degree in the case of persons who were younger than 30 when they moved to a low-trust country. Trust is an attitude, research shows, which is largely shaped by the influence of parents and the impact of events during youth and which remains very stable throughout the later stages of life. Thus, while corruption and defects in the rule of law in Europe need not have an immediate negative impact on trust, today's crises in the EU can nonetheless—by affecting trust in the younger generations adversely—cause damage in this area which will be very difficult to repair later. It is therefore of utmost importance, Bergh contends, that the Union continue to act to strengthen the rule of law and that it makes greater efforts to combat economic and social inequality as well.

The sixth chapter, authored by Clas Wihlborg, concerns the EU's common currency and banking union. The question here is whether greater institutional flexibility would strengthen confidence in the Union's common efforts in these areas. In the matter of currency, Wihlborg notes,

EU member states which are outside the Economic and Monetary Union (EMU) already enjoy considerable flexibility; by contrast, the states taking part in the common currency have no discretion in monetary matters. As for banking, the regulatory framework for it was flexible and nationally oriented until the debt crisis broke out in the eurozone in 2010. Banks were allowed to operate throughout the Union with a 'single licence', while supervision and regulation were mainly the responsibility of national agencies. This, Wihlborg claims, made for institutional competition, which was reinforced by the mobility of services, capital, and labour. The EU's banking union was created in order to strengthen confidence in the monetary union. The idea was that harmonizing supervision, crisis management, and deposit insurance would break the link between the sovereign debt crisis and the banking crisis. Other financial activities in the EU would still be carried out on the basis of a 'single licence'. This is the background to the controversial question of whether British financial firms will be able to continue operating in the EU on the same terms after 'Brexit'.

In his chapter, Wihlborg highlights the costs and benefits of harmonization as compared with those arising in a system of competing national regulatory frameworks. He attaches particular importance to analysing the conditions under which institutional competition would result in an improvement in member states' regulatory systems over time. One conclusion highlighted in his chapter is that greater trust requires either that a number of EU member states abandon the euro as their currency or that they affect far-reaching structural reforms. For political reasons, the author believes, it may be advantageous to divide up the eurozone into two different currency areas. As to the EU's banking union, Wihlborg contends that a high degree of market discipline with regard to banks' risk-taking will be necessary if institutional competition is to produce an improvement in national regulatory frameworks over time. Mutual recognition between different national supervisory authorities thus requires a degree of harmonization in terms of effective rules for dealing with troubled banks. Finally, Wihlborg argues, harmonization on such a basis will be necessary if conditions for increased flexibility are to be created for other aspects of banking regulation and supervision as well.

In the seventh chapter, Ester Herlin-Karnell discusses the importance of trust for cooperation within the Union in the area of criminal justice. The Treaty of Lisbon, she points out, holds out the creation of an area of 'freedom, security and justice' in Europe. What, she asks, does this commitment really mean? Due to cooperation in connection with Schengen, Europe's passport-free zone, freedom of movement on the one hand, and the fight against crime and terrorism on the other hand sometimes end up in conflict with one another, since greater security for one person can mean less freedom for another. This area of law and policy may thus be described as one of Europe's most dynamic but also as one of its most sensitive of late.

However, due to the tough political climate in the EU in recent years, it is first and foremost mutual recognition—whereby member states recognize judgements and decisions deriving from other member states—that figures in criminal-justice cooperation within the Union today, rather than harmonization of national laws and regulations. This form of cooperation is also thought to accord well with the EU's principle of subsidiarity: that is, the view that national laws and regulations can be maintained to a great extent, inasmuch as decision-making is supposed to take place at the lowest possible level within the EU's multi-level system. In Herlin-Karnell's view, the challenge for the EU is to increase trust between its member states. This can be difficult, however, when it comes to criminal law. This is because criminal-justice systems, notwithstanding influence from both international law and EU law, have remained nationally anchored—in theories that set out the obligations of the state and the rights of the individual. The author accordingly recommends, on the basis of reasoning presented in her chapter, that the EU give greater weight to the proportionality principle within its system for cooperation in the area of criminal justice. She calls as well on the European Court of Justice to apply a proportionality test in its interpretation of the concept of mutual recognition, thereby making it clear to the member states that the EU Charter of Fundamental Rights and the European Convention on Human Rights always represent the minimum requirements for legislation in this area.

The eighth chapter, by Eva Storskrubb, looks at trust and confidence between the different national legal systems in light of the EU's scheme for judicial cooperation in civil matters. She focuses particularly on how such trust finds expression when judgements in this area cross national borders. The question of how the principle of mutual trust is to be interpreted, and what it de facto means, has emerged in recent years as one of the most important challenges for judicial cooperation within the Union in civil matters and for the EU's project of creating an area of 'freedom, security and justice'. The overarching question raised by this principle is whether legal protection for individual parties can be sacrificed in order to sustain (in some cases no more than) a presumption of mutual trust. The answer to that question, as the author sees it, has implications for the legitimacy of the Union in a broader perspective. The chapter deals with a part of the judicial system—that deals with civil matters—which affects an extremely broad group of actors in society and which is fundamental for the functioning of the EU's internal market.

Storskrubb stresses that it takes time for legal cultures to meet and for confidence to arise between institutions and actors. If, as a method for driving developments forward, confidence is simply presumed to exist, the effect will be to corrode trust in the EU and to undermine the Union's legitimacy. Paving the way for real trust requires taking supportive measures, in the form of education, collaboration, and e-justice. Legal actors in the member states must also be involved to a greater extent. Patience is needed, as are resources and systems for evaluation. Critical safeguards must be retained in the rules governing the cross-border circulation of judgements. It is true, Storskrubb grants, that the member states are not yet ready for a thoroughgoing harmonization of legal procedures. Nevertheless, she contends, it is critical that a dialogue be started at EU level about how effective legal systems can be established that will contribute to mutual trust.

In the ninth chapter, Håkan Holmberg, Anna Felländer, and Robin Teigland discuss the challenges and opportunities that digitalization and the sharing economy involve for the Union and its member states. The Union ought, the authors argue, to engage more intensively in issues relating to digitalization of European societies. It can promote economic growth in the EU thereby and help to enhance the member states' capacity for innovation. They also deem it essential that the Union develop a 'digital presence', in order to prevent the European perspective on issues dealing with democracy and freedom of expression from being lost in a technological trend which is greatly influenced by actors elsewhere in the world. It is therefore important that the EU work to strengthen public trust in digital environments.

As the authors see it, the spread of the sharing economy in the EU and other parts of the world offers people new opportunities for value creation. With the help of so-called digital platforms, participants in the sharing economy are able to cut out traditional intermediaries—something which may be assumed to make a cheaper exchange of goods and services possible. Digitalization enables more people to produce and consume more cheaply and to use existing resources more efficiently. At the same time, a vacuum of responsibility tends to arise in the wake of digitalization, which makes it difficult to uphold the provisions of labour law and consumer law in a variety of industries. Creating trust in the digital environment is thus one of the sharing economy's biggest challenges. The authors believe that the technology of so-called blockchains—digital ledgers where all actors have access to an identical copy of the transactional history—can provide part of the solution to the problem of inadequate accountability that attends digitization. They propose among other things that the EU's 'Horizontal Task Force' be made into a laboratory where different blockchain actors are given space to develop, so as to answer the question of whether a standardized blockchain should apply in all of the member states or whether different countries and industries should develop their own instead.

In the final chapter of the book, Göran von Sydow depicts an EU in crisis, wherein trust between the member states themselves, on the one hand, and between the member states and the Union, on the other hand, is under heavy strain. Are the problems with trust linked to the question of loyalty between the member states and the Union? The basic problem, according to von Sydow, is that the EU is a system which profoundly affects its member states, at the same time that the legitimacy of its central organs is in dispute. The absence of full-scale democracy at the level of the Union means that the EU still acquires its legitimacy largely from the willingness of its member states to show loyalty to the joint project. The question is what happens when such loyalty falls short. With the aid of Albert O. Hirschman's classic concepts of 'exit', 'voice', and 'loyalty', von Sydow identifies three different systemic crises the Union is now undergoing. These are 'Brexit', the euro crisis, and the conflict between EU member states over the refugee situation. All three crises turn on highly contentious issues.

The author calls our attention to research which shows that, as the process of integration becomes more and more politicized, new demands are placed on the legitimacy of the Union. The requirement that the member states behave loyally towards the Union becomes more palpable when the issues are of a politically sensitive nature. As a result, national resistance to the Union is plainly growing in many parts of Europe. Eurosceptic parties, usually on the populist right, are becoming stronger. This undermines trust in the system still further. The author analyses such disaffection in light of the lack of arenas within which representative democracy can address conflicts and disagreements over European policy. Finally, he argues, the faltering trust in the Union requires that a wide-ranging debate now be joined on a fundamental question: Should the EU take a stride towards a strictly federal system? Or ought it instead to return to a more intergovernmental form of legitimation, where EU member states can choose more freely which cooperative schemes they wish to take part in?

The Way Ahead

What, then, can the Union do to remedy the lack of trust in its institutions felt by many citizens across the member states? How can trust and confidence between the member states be strengthened in the wake of 'Brexit', the euro crisis, and the refugee crisis? How can confidence between different national agencies be sustained and deepened, so as to ensure the EU's ability to implement joint decisions? Judging from the contributions to this book, which span over the disciplines of law, economics, and political science, the Union must above all stand up for basic principles of democracy and the rule of law. Many of the crises the EU has recently faced involve more than just conflicting economic and political interests; increasingly, they have taken on the character of a challenge to the Union's community of values. Regaining the confidence of citizens in the Union and its institutions requires not just that the EU 'deliver' concrete outcomes in terms of economic growth or a functioning European policy on asylum and migration; it is just as much a question of defending the idea that open, democratic, and at the same time integrated societies and economies are what best serve the mass of citizens.

It is also abundantly clear, however, that confidence in the EU is something of a double-edged sword. On the one hand, the EU's development into the multi-level political system that exists today—one with significantly greater economic and juridical powers than any other international organization—would not have been possible without a relatively high degree of trust and confidence between its member states. On the other hand, this trust has not been so great as to prevent the Union from being characterized by apparently contradictory arrangements in several policy areas. Two examples are particularly striking in this regard: the EU has a common currency but no common fiscal policy and it has a common security and defence policy but no mutual-defence guarantees or common army.

Future crises are likely to be exacerbated rather than solved if we act as if a higher degree of mutual confidence prevails between different member states and national agencies than it actually does. It takes time to reconcile the economic and legal systems of different states—systems that in turn rest on institutions and practices which have evolved over long periods. The Union must constantly strive to achieve the right balance between harmonization at European level and respect for distinctive national characteristics. It is not impossible that the EU, as a consequence of the crises it is now undergoing, will have to do less in a range of areas in future if it is to recover the confidence of both member states and citizens. On the other hand, it may need to do more in areas where citizens expect it to play a role, such as foreign affairs, security policy, and climate change. Indicating clearly where the limits of the Union go may prove to be, paradoxically enough, an effective way to strengthen trust in it.

Notes

1. The academic literature on social and political trust is vast and it spans several fields ranging from sociology, economics, political science, and psychology; see, inter alia, Easton (1965), Norris (1999), Mishler and Roses (2001), Tinggaard Svendsen and Lind Haase Svendsen (2009), Algan and Cahuc (2010), and Schlössers, Fetchenhauers and Dunning (2016).
2. For a comprehensive historical overview of European integration, see Urwin (2014).
3. On the concept of security community and European integration, see Deutsch et al. (1957), Adler and Barnett (1998), Bremberg (2018).

References

Abts, K., Heerwegh, D., & Swyngedouw, M. (2009). Sources of euroscepticism: Utilitarian interest, social distrust, national identity and institutional distrust. *World Political Science Review, 5*(1), 1–26.

Adler, E., & Barnett, M. (1998). *Security communities*. Cambridge: Cambridge University Press.

Algan, Y., & Cahuc, P. (2010). Inherited trust and growth. *American Economic Review, 100*(5), 2060–2092.

Bickerton, C. (2015, July 9). The real sins of Varoufakis. *Le Monde Diplomatique*. Retrieved from http://mondediplo.com/outsidein/the-real-sins-of-varoufakis

Bremberg, N. (2018). The EU and the European security community: History and current challenges. In A. Bakardijeva Engelbrekt, A. Michalski, N. Nilsson, & L. Oxelheim (Eds.), *The European Union: Facing the challenge of multiple security threats*. Cheltenham: Edward Elgar.

Checkel, J., & Katzenstein, P. (Eds.). (2009). *European identity*. Cambridge: Cambridge University Press.

Deutsch, K., Burrell, S., Kann, R., Lee, M., Lichterman, M., Lindgren, R., et al. (1957). *Political community and the North Atlantic area: International organization in the light of historical experience*. Princeton, NJ: Princeton University Press.

Easton, D. (1965). *A systems analysis of political life*. Chicago, IL: University of Chicago Press.

European Commission. (2015, May 13). A European agenda on migration, COM(2015) 240 final, Brussels. Retrieved from https://ec.europa.eu/home-affairs/sites/homeaffairs/files/what-we-do/policies/european-agenda-migration/backgroundinformation/docs/communication_on_the_european_agenda_on_migration_en.pdf

Favell, A. (2011). *Eurostars and Eurocities: Free movement and mobility in an integrating Europe*. John Wiley & Sons.

Fligstein, N. (2008). *Euroclash: The EU, European identity, and the future of Europe*. Oxford: Oxford University Press.

Haas, E. (1958). *The uniting of Europe: Political, economic, and social forces, 1950–1957*. Stanford, CA: Stanford University Press.

Haas, P. (1992). Introduction: Epistemic communities and international policy coordination. *International Organization, 46*(1), 1–35.

Harteveld, E., Meer, T. V. D., & Vries, C. E. D. (2013). In Europe we trust? Exploring three logics of trust in the European Union. *European Union Politics, 14*(4), 542–565.

Hobolt, S. B., & Tilley, J. (2016). Fleeing the centre: The rise of challenger parties in the aftermath of the euro crisis. *West European Politics, 39*(5), 971–991.

Hooghe, L., & Marks, G. (2009). A postfunctionalist theory of European integration: From permissive consensus to constraining dissensus. *British Journal of Political Science, 39*(1), 1–23.

Juncker, J. C. (2016, September 14). Speech on the State of the Union, Strasbourg. Retrieved from https://ec.europa.eu/commission/state-union-2016_en

Kaelble, H. (2009). Identification with Europe and politicization of the EU since the 1980s. In J. Checkel & P. Katzenstein (Eds.), *European identity*. Cambridge: Cambridge University Press.

Kriesi, H. (2014). The populist challenge. *West European Politics, 37*(2), 361–378.

Lewis, J. (2005). The Janus face of Brussels: Socialization and everyday decision making in the European Union. *International Organization, 59*(4), 937–971.

Milward, A. (1992). *The European rescue of the nation-state*. London: Routledge.

Mishler, W., & Roses, R. (2001). What are the origins of political trust? Testing institutional and cultural theories in post-communist societies. *Comparative Political Studies, 34*(1), 30–62.

Norris, P. (1999). *Critical citizens: Global support for democratic government.* Oxford: Oxford University Press.

Rosamond, B. (2000). *Theories of European integration.* New York: St. Martin's Press.

Scharpf, F. (2014). Political legitimacy and in a non-optimal currency area. In O. Cramme & S. Hobolt (Eds.), *Democratic politics in a European Union under stress.* Oxford: Oxford University Press.

Schlössers, T., Fetchenhauers, D., & Dunning, D. (2016). Trust against all odds? Emotional dynamics in trust behavior. *Decision, 3*(3), 216–230.

Tallberg, J. (2004). *European governance and supranational institutions: Making states comply.* London: Routledge.

Tinggaard Svendsen, G., & Lind Haase Svendsen, G. (Eds.). (2009). *Handbook of social capital.* Cheltenham: Edward Elgar.

Tusk, D. (2016, May 30). Speech at the 40th anniversary of the European People's Party, Luxembourg. Retrieved from http://www.consilium.europa.eu/en/press/press-releases/2016/05/30-pec-speech-epp/

Urwin, D. W. (2014). *The community of Europe: A history of European integration since 1945.* London: Routledge.

What Explains the Lack of Trust in the EU Among Its Member States? A Constitutional Analysis of the EU's 'Value Crisis'

Joakim Nergelius

Over the last few years, the European Union has been shaken by a great crisis which is political in character but could to a certain extent also be described as constitutional, at least in the broad sense of the word. This crisis has several different underlying causes and has expressed itself in many different ways, for instance, through the refugee crisis in 2015, the problems related to Brexit, the risk of a Greek bankruptcy and Greece's forced withdrawal from the euro zone ('Grexit') and, not least, the crisis of values related to authoritarian and illiberal tendencies in certain EU member states, chiefly, but not exclusively, Hungary and Poland.

This begs the crucial question why all these various crises occurred, possibly peaked more or less at the same time between 2015 and 2016. One important, general reason is probably that the EU was not strict enough concerning the conditions for entry into different parts of the integration process. This is, for instance, an obvious fact as far as the Greek membership of the euro zone is concerned, but it is probably also a fair assessment of the somewhat forced, probably premature, accession of Bulgaria

J. Nergelius (✉)
Örebro University, Örebro, Sweden

A. Bakardjieva Engelbrekt et al. (eds.), *Trust in the European Union in Challenging Times*, https://doi.org/10.1007/978-3-319-73857-4_2

and Romania as members to the EU in 2007, which took place despite doubts that these two states most likely did not meet the necessary requirements in relation to the rule of law and the fight against corruption and organized crime.

Furthermore, as will be discussed below, the supervision of existing EU member states, which met in principle all the relevant criteria for membership at the time of joining the EU (the so-called Copenhagen criteria, which include among other aspects, issues relating to democracy, rule of law and human rights), may need to be strengthened. The member states' continued fulfilment of the criteria for EU membership seems to be among the most important prerequisites for the future development of the EU. When Hungary, Poland and eight other states joined the EU as members on 1 May 2004, no one could anticipate that these states which had suffered many decades under communist dictatorships would once again be tempted to regress into authoritarian forms of government (see e.g. von Bogdandy & Sonnevend, 2015). Thus, the backslide into authoritarianism which began in Hungary in 2010, spread to Poland in 2015 and was accompanied by similar tendencies in many other EU member states, mainly in Central and Eastern Europe took the EU by complete surprise. The ensuing situation, in which we now find ourselves, is exacerbated by a lack of legal as well as other measures in the hands of the EU leaders and does not bode well for the Union's future (see e.g. Habermas, 2012, 2015).

Another, quite different reason for the crisis, which without doubt influences the assessment of various governments of the range of possible political measures, is the widespread lack of confidence and trust vis-à-vis the EU project as a whole expressed by substantial parts of the population in many EU member states. The events leading to the 'Brexit' referendum in June 2016 and their aftermath constitute perhaps the most obvious example of this. At the same time, we may also point to the fact that newly elected governments sometimes try, through nationalistic rhetoric, to explore national sentiments in the population. In such a context, criticism towards the EU project as a whole and its deep-seated aims and purposes may then easily become part of authoritarian and populist political programmes. This tendency has been especially striking in Hungary and Poland and has engendered particular problems related to constitutional reforms in these countries aiming, for instance, at curtailing the independence of the judicial system.

Against this background, it is today appropriate to say that a widespread, general conflict of values, between a liberal model of society and conservative, authoritarian and national ideals, which most observers thought were part of a bygone era, is now playing out in the EU, and indeed perhaps in the whole Western world. Nationalist parties have encountered unexpected success in Austria, France and Sweden in the second half of the 2010s, to give but a few examples. In September 2017, an extreme right-wing party, *Alternative für Deutschland*, became the third biggest party in a general election in Germany and is now holding a substantial number of seats in the *Bundestag* for the first time since the Second World War. Such parties try to explore the general, popular lack of trust towards the EU. It is clear that the popular distrust of political elites in general, at the national level as well as vis-a-vis the EU, seems to be merging with a conservative and nationalistic inclined distrust of the supranational, liberal and cosmopolitan EU project as such. Populist parties seem to know how to explore both these sentiments.

This rather deep conflict of values, forming the core of this chapter, is centred on but not limited to Eastern Europe. The refugee crisis escalating rapidly during 2015 has contributed to a deep feeling of malaise and has led to a clear division between Northern and Western EU member states, on the one hand, and a majority of the Eastern European member states, on the other hand, who simply refused to accept or host refugees from Africa and the Middle East. In 2015, Hungary and Slovakia brought a case to the European Court of Justice (ECJ) to this effect, questioning the legality of an EU decision on the redistribution of refugees according to a quota system which was eventually struck down by the court in a ruling in September 2017 (cases C-643/15 and 647/15). Pending the outcome of these cases, the EU was not able to advance in this area. The relative calm and order that has characterized the refugee situation since 2016, compared to the chaos of late 2015, is entirely due to the rather peculiar agreement between EU and Turkey signed in March 2016, which itself is highly controversial. Thus, the situation is complicated, to say the least.

Nevertheless, a majority of the member states, along with the European Commission and the European Parliament (both of which passed a vote reconfirming their stance on this matter as recently as 19 October 2017), still advocate receiving refugees into the EU, provided that adequate mechanisms for redistribution may be found. This same majority of states, led by Germany, is, incidentally, also critical towards the authoritarian tendencies in other member states, chiefly Hungary and Poland. A crucial question for the future, then, is whether they should use the existing mechanisms of the EU treaties, such as qualified majority voting (QMV) in the Council and increased control of member states, to enforce more liberal values on these reluctant states which seem to ignore the rule of law and prefer an authoritarian model of society. And should authoritarian states even remain members of the EU under the current treaties?

Thus, this chapter addresses the following questions: What possibilities do the EU treaties offer for a qualified majority of EU member states to 'curb' a minority of reluctant member states who seems to question and openly challenge the basic democratic ideals of the Union? And what measures will, in the long run, strengthen the trust between member states, as well as between them, the citizens and the EU institutions? In the following section, the existing rules and agreements concerning human rights and treatment of refugees, including the granting of asylum, are described. Following that, the reasons behind the current crisis are further explored. At the end of the chapter, some solutions are presented, based on the assumption that in the long run, it will be better for the EU to stick to its basic idea(l)s of democracy, rule of law and human rights than to yield to populist temptations and allow member states a wide discretion in such crucial matters.

The Current Legal Framework in the EU

One undeniable aspect of the crisis in values that distinguishes it from other current crises besetting the EU, not least the refugee crisis, is its highly legal nature. This prompts us to clarify some legal issues before moving on. Moreover, the toxic mix of legal and political measures in this area became clear when Hungary announced in 2015 that it would refuse to take part in the common asylum policy and then brought a case to the ECJ together with Slovakia, a move which was reinforced by a referendum in October 2016, itself called for on legally dubious grounds.

Thus, in order to understand this complex situation, it is necessary to look closer at some of the important decisions, rules and documents that are at the origin of this situation and which will have a decisive impact on its outcome. In a way, then, the first formal document of importance is the decision of the Council of the EU of 22 September 2015, establishing provisional measures in the area of international protection. This decision, with a legal basis in Article 78(3) of the Treaty on the Functioning of the

EU (TFEU), was enacted on the basis of QMV on a proposal from the Commission and with support from the European Parliament and should be seen as a response of the EU member states to the urgent refugee crisis that had been escalating in the late summer of 2015, due primarily to the civil war in Syria. It was also this decision, encompassing a total number of 120,000 refugees, that was formally approved by the ECJ in September 2017 (C-643 and 647/15). More specifically, the decision states that 66,000 persons out of the total number of refugees who had arrived in Europe at the time were to be redistributed immediately to other EU states, from the two most severely affected Mediterranean member states, Italy and Greece, subsequently followed within a year by another 54,000 persons. The refugees would be resettled with the assistance of a special mechanism of redistribution (which also includes a financial compensation of no less than €6000 for each relocated person to be paid from the common EU budget to the receiving state).

However, despite the financial generosity of this decision, it turned out to be surprisingly difficult to implement, due to resistance of a number of member states, which included not only the notoriously difficult ones in Central and Eastern Europe but also, for example, Denmark and the UK. The degree of reluctance to accept and host refugees was in effect much stronger in many member states than their sense of loyalty to assist in finding a common solution to a serious problem notwithstanding the prospect of a substantial financial compensation.

This situation must, when viewed in conjunction with the thwarted legal action against the decision of the European Council brought by Hungary and Slovakia and the shift towards a more restrictive refugee policy which swiftly followed in other EU states, be considered to amount to a basic challenge against the supremacy of EU law and against the principle of solidarity and loyalty that follows from Article 4(3) of the Treaty of the European Union (TEU). It also revealed a fundamental lack of trust between the EU member states, as well as between at least some of them and the EU institutions. How can we today, approximately three years later, understand the consequences of this unpredicted, unforeseen and deeply problematic situation?

To begin with, we note that this sudden crisis led to the controversial agreement between the EU and Turkey of 18 March 2016, according to which Turkey undertook to take back a huge number of refugees from Greece and prevent continued mass migration to the same country, through the means of a restored border control at the Aegean Sea.

Simultaneously, the EU offered to pay Turkey no less than €3 billion and to receive refugees currently in Turkey, through a scheme that would guarantee that the overall number of refugees residing in Turkey remain constant. However, apart from the financial compensation that Turkey has enjoyed since early 2016 for strengthening the control of its border(s) with Greece, other aspects of the agreement have not been fulfilled, which could in a paradoxical way explain why it is formally still in force. However, that issue is not further dealt with here.

In April 2016, the European Commission (2016) presented a proposal for a new EU asylum system, that outlines a new common asylum policy for the whole EU, to be realized through a reform of the so-called Dublin Regulation (604/2013), further strengthened by a new regulation governing the whole asylum process, with the aim of clarifying which individual member state in any given situation is responsible for specific, individual requests for asylum. In the wake of this proposal, which has yet to be enacted, a discussion ensued on the economic responsibilities for EU member states which refuse to accept refugees. Discussions on these, and a host of related matters, have taken place since then, and have for obvious reasons become increasingly vivid.

The Refugee Crisis as Part of the Greater Conflict of Values Within the EU and the Western World

If we view the situation in a somewhat wider context, however, it is obvious that what is here centred on the refugee crisis is in fact a part of a much wider crisis, one which may be referred to as a crisis of values, characterized by fundamental conflicts of values between EU member states and, even more, between different ideologies and ideological camps in the EU along with the whole of the Western world. In this wider conflict reigns a general distrust of the EU and its institutions, which many actors may believe to be in their interest and therefore promote further.

The crisis or clash of values within the EU started probably as early as 2010 on the back of the electoral victory of the *Fidesz* party in Hungary, which came to power through a landslide that saw it win a two-thirds majority of the members in Parliament. Once in power, the party immediately made use of its huge majority in Parliament in order to appoint new judges and chief executives to various public bodies. These moves were followed by a new media law as well as a new constitution in 2011 and subsequently a decision to force all judges of 62 years of age and above into retirement.

These (and other assaults on the rule of law and other fundamental values stated in Articles 6–7 TEU) gave rise to a number of reactions on behalf of the EU. Among the more noteworthy actions initiated by the EU is the case brought by the Commission against Hungary to the ECJ concerning the forced retirement of judges older than 62 years. The Court ruled in 2012 that the actions of the Hungarian government amounted to unlawful discrimination on the grounds of age (C-286/12). However, it seems that the Commission deliberately chose a technical approach, claiming an alleged treaty violation according to Article 258 TFEU rather than arguing that a basic, fundamental principle of the rule of law was violated. In fact, the EU refrained until very recently from invoking Articles 6–7 TEU, according to which a member state that does not respect the rule of law and/or other fundamental values of the EU (such as democracy, human rights, human dignity, freedom and equality as stipulated in Article 2 TEU) may temporarily lose some of its rights as a member, including the right to vote in the Council of the EU. Metering out such a harsh measure against a member state, upon the decision by all the other member states, would of course be controversial for a number of reasons, but in the long run it may be hard to avoid, should one or more member states continue to repeatedly, almost provocatively—as has been the case in recent years—demonstrate that they do not want, and have in fact no wish whatsoever, to respect the EU's fundamental values.

In this context, it may be added that a widespread discussion on the application of Article 7 TEU (previously Article 6 TEU) already took place in 2000, when a majority of EU member states was willing to introduce informal sanctions of a mild and in reality informal sort against Austria, as a consequence of the right-wing populist party, Freedom Party Austria (FPÖ), joining the Austrian government (as it did again after the general election in October 2017). For a number of reasons though—the most important of which being that Austria had in fact not violated any of the fundamental values—the rather bizarre measures thus initiated, such as the refusal to shake the hands of Austrian ministers or let them join common photo sessions, were quickly abandoned.

However, the discussions that have occurred since 2010 concerning the situation in Hungary, at times also in regard to Romania and since early 2016 not least in relation to Poland, have taken place against a somewhat bleaker and more sinister background. In these EU member states, and in others, such as Slovakia, ruling governments have expressed profound doubts concerning the very validity of the EU's fundamental values. Probably the most noted statement to this effect was made by the

Hungarian Prime Minister, Viktor Orbán, who in 2014 advocated in favour of 'illiberal democracy', a political system that would in his view better respond to contemporary challenges, such as migration and terrorism, than liberal democracy and pluralism (see also Bo Petersson's chapter in this volume).

It is thus no wonder, that, ever since 2010, Hungary has been the focal point of this conflict or crisis, which has been steadily escalating since 2011, in parallel to but with less media coverage in comparison to the euro crisis. At the same time, an intense legal debate has taken place regarding the accession of the EU to the European Convention on Human Rights, further fuelled by the Opinion of the ECJ in December 2014 that such an accession is not possible on legal grounds (Opinion 2/13). Still, when the majority of the EU member states would wish to react against one or more members which blatantly violate fundamental rights is a wider and more dramatic question, and probably is also a more urgent one.

Should a decision to react against a failing member state eventually be forthcoming, it would, according to Article 7 TEU, have to be carried out in two steps. First, the Council of the EU must establish, with a majority of four-fifths of its member states (the failing state not counted), that a clear risk exists that this member state is violating the basic values of Article 2 TEU. Upon the confirmation of such a risk of violation, the Council may unanimously (the failing state in question is again not allowed to participate) declare that the member state in question is found in serious and systematic breach of these values.

Ever since 2011, legal experts have been discussing when the threshold, in respect to the violation, will have been considered broken in Hungary or, in other words, that, when Article 7 should be activated if it is to have any real significance at all (see e.g. Hillion, 2016). Since 2015, the resistance of Hungary and a few other members in regard to both the proposed and the existing EU policy on refugees has added fuel to the fire, at a time when the conservative government of Poland seems bent on repeating what happened in Hungary a few years earlier. In hindsight, the EU certainly took its time before reacting sharply to what happened in Hungary. Today, the Union may regret having reacted (too) slowly. Concerning Poland, on the other hand, the European Commission already initiated a dialogue in January 2016. This dialogue is still going on, as will be further explained below.

Since March 2014, the European Commission has at its disposal a new instrument for its dialogues with member states at risk of breaching the

EU fundamental values, namely the so-called *Rule of Law Framework* (COM 2014/158). The main purpose of this instrument is to make it possible for the European Commission to engage in dialogue with EU member states, based on a careful observation of an unfolding negative development in the country in question, without having immediately to resort to the controversial and politically difficult procedure envisaged in Article 7 TEU. In fact, the practical use of Article 7 now seems more remote than ever, since Hungary has promised to use its veto in case of a vote against Poland and Poland has made a similar declaration concerning a vote in regard to Hungary.

The surveillance mechanism envisaged in the Rule of Law Framework states that the European Commission shall assess the situation in a member state where problems in relation to the rule of law have been observed, which in turn shall be followed by recommendations to redress the situation as well as a follow-up in the form of an evaluation of the measures taken by the state in question. It is hard to say whether the rather speedily use of this mechanism in regard to Poland, as opposed to the quite passive attitude initially shown towards Hungary, is due to the simple fact that this framework did not exist in 2011 or if the Commission in fact believes that the Polish government will be more inclined towards constructive dialogue than the Hungarian government. However, in the latter case, there seems to be a risk for disappointment, as discussed below.

Once again, it may be wise to underline that these conflicts are in fact part of a very serious international clash between liberalism and conservatism that became evident in 2016 with 'Brexit' and the election of Donald Trump as US President, and which is likely to prevail and possibly dominate the Western world for many years to come. In the field of political science, this situation is often referred to as a new ideological conflict between GAL (i.e. Greens, Alternatives and Liberals) and TAN (i.e. Traditionalists, Authoritarians and Nationalists) which is replacing the old cleavage of right-left ideologies in Western politics in general, with a clear focus on cultural values rather than economic interests (Hooghe, Marks, & Wilson, 2002). This may of course be a true depiction, but it is equally possible to view the current crisis as merely the latest outburst of the long-standing conflict between liberalism and conservatism, which dates all the way back to the debates between Thomas Paine and Edward Burke in the 1790s on the long-term consequences of the French Revolution and whether it is at all possible to proclaim such a thing as universal human rights.

What can we learn from this, then, except the fact that many political or ideological phenomena are not quite as new as we sometimes tend to believe? In the remaining discussion, I make the argument that although fewer things than we tend to believe are in fact really new, we must take into account that the current discussion occurs in a totally different context than the corresponding ones in 1793, when of course no political union such as the EU existed. The global development is not entirely cyclical after all. This also means that the response(s) of the EU to this specific crisis must be adequate and apt to address the problem we are currently facing today. Against this background, I intend to discuss more in detail what has caused the crisis on the one hand and how to solve it on the other hand, with a focus on the rule of law and human rights, but perhaps with more far-reaching repercussions.

How to Explain the Clash of Values in the EU?

A basic condition when recommending certain measures in order to prevent or stop a crisis is to be able to identify the factors that led to the crisis in the first place. Here, I stress two reasons in particular that seem to have caused the value crisis in the EU. The general lack of trust from EU citizens towards the EU and its institutions constitutes one of these factors (see also Linda Berg's chapter in this volume). Societal phenomena and attitudes of this kind, which tend to shift over time, are usually explained by experts as depending on whether the EU will 'deliver' in terms, for instance, of economic growth and a well-functioning internal market. Now, at this moment of time, there are clear signs that the current distrust held by large sways of citizens throughout Europe is aimed equally—perhaps even more intensively—at national politicians and domestic political institutions than towards the EU, a circumstance that populist parties in a number of countries have exploited skilfully. Thus, this tendency can hardly be seen as a purely EU problem, although the distance between voters and decision-makers may be perceived as wider in relation to the EU institutions than in relation to the national political institutions. Still, as such this problem is not new and it has, as far as the EU is concerned, hardly grown worse in recent years, barring a possible reservation for the euro crisis, when the so-called troika, consisting of civil servants from the European Commission, the European Central Bank (ECB) and the

International Monetary Fund (IMF), played a decisive, but strongly contested, role.

Another factor, however, that seems to be somewhat underestimated when discussing the roots of the crisis, is the tendency to view the performances and prospects of (new) EU member states with a somewhat exaggerated optimism, as mentioned above. As far as the euro crisis and its roots in Greece is concerned, this phenomenon is quite obvious. It is clear that Greece overestimated its future economic prospects while it underreported dire figures in the national accounts during the 1990s in order to qualify for membership of the euro zone. However, it would hardly have been able to get away with the cosmetic gilding had the EU bodies in charge, notably ECB and the European Commission, carried out a more thorough control and review.

Nevertheless, the general problem of excessive optimism concerning the development in individual EU member states has also contributed to the exacerbation of the value crisis, though in a quite different way. Here, the problem is rather the opposite, since the European Commission does in fact carry out a rather strict survey of the progress that candidate states to EU membership have achieved in areas such as democracy, the rule of law and the protection of minorities, as well as in the fight against corruption and organized crime. In addition, the candidate state's national administration and the legal system must possess the capacity to implement, enforce and correctly apply EU law. The European Commission's assessments are carried out in accordance with the so-called Copenhagen criteria of 1993. It should therefore be realistic to assume that the ten new member states who joined the EU in 2004 actually did meet these requirements at that time of accession (whereas doubts in this respect linger concerning the state of preparedness of Romania and Bulgaria at the time of their accession to the EU in 2007).

The real problem, however, is that once a state has joined the EU, this control ceases to exist (which incidentally is not the case as concerns financial controls). Here, the EU seems to rely on the assumption that states will continue, once they have acquired the status of EU member, to behave in a decent manner, according to general conventions of civilized behaviour. Now, with hindsight, this has simply turned out to be too optimistic, a fact that provides a lot of food for thought in relation to the future for the EU.

Ever since the developments in Hungary began to seriously worry the EU in early 2011, the main attention has been drawn to the ever more authoritarian tendencies of the Hungarian government, which were followed in late 2015 by a very similar development in Poland. Still, this is only one side of the coin. Tendencies to allow corruption continue unabated as well as the persistence of authoritarian attitudes in general among politicians and civil servants seem to have been totally underestimated by the EU. Examples from countries such as Bulgaria, Romania, Slovakia, Slovenia and the Czech Republic are too numerous to be ignored and this makes the situation for the whole EU quite puzzling. On top of this, the refugee crisis has provoked an unexpected degree of xenophobia in several of these countries that will not be easily dealt with. Other divisive issues concern the attitudes towards homosexuals and authoritarian regimes in the neighbourhood of the EU, for instance, Russia, contrasted with the general necessity of pluralism in today's societies. The question is how will the EU manage to overcome the conundrum of addressing all these issues?

The EU Must Protect Its Core Values

The main concrete lesson that the EU needs to draw from the value crisis is of course to avoid making similar mistakes in the future. Thus, the EU needs to be much more cautious in its negotiations with the current candidate states Albania, Serbia and, possibly, Turkey than was the case in the run-up to the accessions in 2004 and 2007, also with a view to somehow ensure a continued surveillance once membership has been achieved. In the case of Croatia, which joined the EU in 2013, it is probably too early to make a comprehensive evaluation of the situation.

Now, it seems clear that a very tough position from the EU during the membership negotiations, in relation not least to the Copenhagen criteria, will not be enough to prevent problems of this kind from occurring in the future. Therefore, the EU badly needs some kind of surveillance mechanism for existing members—old and new. One such possibility, should the Rule of Law Framework not prove to be enough, is to lower the threshold for deciding on punitive measures against failing EU member states in Article 7 TEU, perhaps by enabling other member states, minus two or three, to initiate such sanctions. Should such a future treaty reform turn out to be impossible, other measures will definitely have to be discussed.

In a future discussion on new measures, the need for the EU to uphold its basic values, such as those stated in Article 2 TEU, but also other values such as free trade, free movement of people, services and capital, prohibition against state aid and an effective European competition law, is crucial for a number of reasons (see e.g. Müller, 2015). To a certain extent, it is understandable that the EU refrains from getting entangled immediately in disputes with a newly elected government in a democratic member state which has expressed more or less controversial views on democracy, pluralism, human rights or refugees in the preceding electoral campaign. But, at the same time, the EU needs to show that there are clear limits for unacceptable behaviour or, put in legal terms, for what the treaties will allow. A government, such as the Orbán government in Hungary, which has gradually and purposefully torn down the rule of law in the classical sense of the word over a period of five years, must be aware that the EU will, in the end, reach a point where decisive action is necessary to the effect that the country in question will end up losing its right to vote in the Council of the EU (not to mention some of the many economic subsidies that it has enjoyed for so long). This should be the consequence not only because the rule of law and human rights count among the EU's core values but also, more importantly, to safeguard the general legal culture and traditions of the EU, whose evolution has always been characterized by a great respect for written rules in general and treaties in particular.

The fact that these core values are enshrined in the Treaties is therefore crucial. The same can be said about the decisions of the Council on the EU's refugee policy, which have their legal base in Article 16 TEU, regardless whether the decisions were taken unanimously or by QMV. Signals from a number of member states which simply do not wish to be part of EU policy in this area stand in clear contrast to everything that EU membership signifies as it cannot solely be a matter of receiving benefits but also involves contributing to and working for the interests of the Union, as stipulated in Article 4(3) TEU. Other treaty-based rules, such as those stated in Article 80 TFEU, also stress the need for solidarity and loyalty between the EU member states. Hungary, Slovakia and some other member states which do not wish to be part of this community of rules and values have through their actions, to put it mildly, challenged some very crucial pillars of European integration.

Against this background, my advice to the EU and its leaders is as follows: in order to solve the value crisis, the EU must stick to its core values, not least in relation to those member states which do perhaps not wish to adhere to them. This must be the way forward even though being tough to certain member states may in the short run increase the risk for internal division. The Union should take this course of action despite the fact that it may challenge, even provoke, a large number of voters in many member states, not only in Central and Eastern Europe. At least as long as a qualified majority of the member states—amounting to no less than 55 per cent of the states of the EU, representing at least 65 per cent of its population, as stipulated in Article 16(4) TEU—still believes in upholding in the Union's core values, it is in my view, a good idea for the EU to protect and promote these values in an ever more turbulent world in spite of the short-term costs involved. In the long run, a steady and consistent stand in regard to reigning value conflicts will pay off and lead not only to greater respect worldwide but also to the EU finding itself—its own soul so to speak—which will make it easier for the Union to deal with future conflicts of the same kind.

The EU will quite simply be stronger and enjoy more 'soft power' in the world if it does not lose sight of its core values. Such a stand is also likely to promote unity among those member states which will now find strength not to back down in this crucial conflict. And, finally, this majority of states may also reflect upon the fact that it may now be the moment to make extended use of the QMV mechanism, in order to stand up for what is right and thus, eventually, achieve greater global success.

On a more practical level, the forthcoming negotiations on a new long-term budget of the EU, running from 2020 onwards, may offer a good opportunity for the until now rather 'silent majority' of EU member states to put pressure on those members that refuse to host refugees and/or refuse to follow EU decisions taken within the common asylum policy. As stated above, the co-operation among member states is and must be based on solidarity and loyalty (cf. Article 4(3) TEU). Member states, which obstruct EU decisions, and in the process act according to a spirit contrary to the Union values, simply cannot expect to receive benefits, subsidies and contributions from the cohesion and regional funds or from the agricultural funds indefinitely. It is hardly a coincidence that politicians in many of the 'net contributing' member states are now increasingly stressing this linkage, for which there are both financial and moral reasons. Cutting down on the subsidies to member states which refuse to take part in the quite costly refugee policy is also an effective sanction that may be imposed without any treaty change, which is of course a huge advantage in a situation where treaty changes seem very difficult to bring about as they must be approved by all member states (cf. Articles 48–49 TEU). Politically, it is an issue that is logically connected to the 'Brexit' negotiations and that needs to be discussed soon in any event. Thus, this is an area where some developments can be expected, quite separate from what happens in the sometimes complicated legal arena.

Concluding Remarks

These reflections, along with the string of suggestions made above, do not, of course, give the full picture of the value crisis within the EU. Nor is it possible to anticipate here the possible developments in all key member states, which are all more or less likely to become affected by the crisis. For instance, who knows where Austria and the Czech Republic will be heading after their respective parliamentary elections in the fall of 2017, which in both cases led to considerable successes for populist parties. Will Austria once again cause controversy in the EU in the same way as in 2000—but this time for more 'real' reasons? And which consequences may then follow for the rest of the EU? Once again, Austria may turn out be a key player in the area of human rights and for the rule of law regime of the EU.

What we do know, however, is that the European Commission declared in July 2017, after having sent a Rule of Law Recommendation to Poland in line with the Rule of Law Framework, that it is ready to 'trigger' the procedure under Article 7(1) against Poland should the country refuse to improve the conditions in the judicial system and go ahead with certain proposed reforms in that area. Poland replied to that letter in October 2017 but the Commission has gone on to suggest a so-called reasoned proposal for a Council Decision under Art. 7(1) TEU in December 2017. It should of course also be stressed that the final decision concerning sanctions against a member state is made by the other states—which, should it come to that, will have to take the opinion of the Commission into account when considering their response.

At the same time, there are a number of infringement cases pending before the ECJ concerning Hungary and Poland. The outcome of those proceedings will of course be interesting to follow, but at the same time it remains to be seen what consequence a ruling of the Court in these matters will actually have. In 2012, Hungary repealed its retirement scheme for judges as a direct consequence of the Court's ruling, but there are no guarantees that Hungary, Poland, Slovakia or other EU member state might be as obedient this time, about six years later. It is thus likely that other punitive measures on behalf of the EU will have to be added to the traditional infringement procedures in order for any real change to come about.

References

Council of the European Union. (2013). Regulation (EU) No 604/2013 of the European Parliament and of the Council establishing the criteria and mechanisms for determining the Member State responsible for examining an application for international protection lodged in one of the Member States by a third-country national or a stateless person (recast), Brussels, 26 June 2013.

Council of the European Union. (2015). Council decision (EU) 2015/1601 establishing provisional measures in the area of international protection for the benefit of Italy and Greece, Brussels, 22 September 2015.

European Commission. (2014). Communication from the Commission to the European Parliament and the Council. A new EU Framework to strengthen the Rule of Law, (COM 2014/158 final 2), Brussels, 19 March 2014.

European Commission. (2016). Communication from the Commission to the European Parliament and the Council. Towards a reform of the Common European Asylum System and Enhancing Legal Avenues to Europe, (COM (2016) 197), Brussels, 6 April 2016.

Habermas, J. (2012). *The crisis of the European Union: A response*. Cambridge: Polity Press.

Habermas, J. (2015). Democracy in Europe: Why the development of the EU into a transnational democracy is necessary and how it is possible. *European Law Journal, 21*(4), 546–557.

Hillion, C. (2016). Overseeing the rule of law in the European Union: Legal mandate and means. *SIEPS European Policy Analysis, No. 1*. Stockholm: The Swedish Institute for European Policy Studies.

Hooghe, L., Marks, G., & Wilson, C. J. (2002). Does left/right structure party positions on European integration? *Comparative Political Studies, 35*(8), 965–989.

Müller, J.-W. (2015). Should the EU protect democracy and the rule of law inside member states? *European Law Journal, 21*(2), 141–160.

von Bogdandy, A., & Sonnevend, P. (Eds.). (2015). *Constitutional crisis in the European constitutional area: Theory, law and politics in Hungary and Romania*. Oxford: Hart Publishing.

Perspective on the Eastern Enlargement: Triumph of the EU or Seed of Its Destruction?

Bo Petersson

The Eastern enlargement of the European Union in 2004, when ten countries joined the Union at one go, was in many ways the peak of the euphoria that had prevailed in Europe since the end of the Cold War. Although there had been fundamental setbacks, especially in relation to the Balkan Wars in the early 1990s, this Big Bang of EU enlargement evinced the belief that Europe was finally united, or at least well on the way. Most of the new member states belonged to the former Eastern Bloc. Now they would be embedded in a structure that, once and for all, would heal the old antagonisms generated or exacerbated by the Cold War. All of them would now be part of a community informed by adherence to the central values of the EU: democracy, human rights and the rule of law, as formulated in the European Council's Copenhagen criteria of 1993 (European Council Conclusions, 1993–2003). Poland, Hungary, Czech Republic, Slovakia, Slovenia, Estonia, Latvia, Lithuania, Cyprus and Malta became full members of the EU family. This was the great triumph of the

B. Petersson (✉)
Malmö University, Malmö, Sweden

A. Bakardjieva Engelbrekt et al. (eds.), *Trust in the European Union in Challenging Times*, https://doi.org/10.1007/978-3-319-73857-4_3

EU. Or was it really? As this is written, well into the second decade after the Eastern enlargement, there is an opportunity to discuss the issue with distance and perspective. Was the enlargement the EU's shining moment, or was it the beginning of the end of its success story? How did it actually affect the development of a common identity and trust within the Union?

These questions are the subject of this chapter, which is arranged as follows. After a background discussion of the dilemma of the Eastern enlargement, the issue of a common identity for the EU and where this might reside is addressed. The argument is that the existence of a common identity based on shared values is critical to trust within the Union, as well as to its influence and standing in the world. The discussion then turns to the challenges now being directed at the shared fundamental values of the EU: from the 'illiberal democracies' of Hungary and Poland; from authoritarian states outside the EU, such as Russia and Turkey; and from populist currents across the entire EU and outside it. The chapter ends with a summation and recommended action to safeguard shared values, common identity and trust within the Union.

The Dilemma of the Eastern Enlargement

Ahead of the Eastern enlargement of the EU in 2004, there was certainly awareness in some quarters that fundamental problems remained unsolved. The main worry among the old EU countries was that far too many citizens of the new member states would take advantage of the free movement allowed by the EU to seek better lives in their countries. There were serious concerns that the social security systems in the established EU countries would be overused. It was also feared that low-wage competition from the new member states would distort labour markets in the old ones. By way of example, an intense and poisonous debate was sparked in France about the invasion of the 'Polish plumbers', spreading anxiety that cheap labour from the new EU countries would push the people in their own country out of jobs at home.

There were, however, others who pointed out problems of a different magnitude that might eventually ensue. Among those who expressed themselves most presciently was former Czech President Václav Havel. In an address to the European Parliament in Strasbourg, a good four years before the Eastern enlargement, he expressed apprehensions about the consequences of the inadequately developed civil societies in the new prospective member states:

> If the European Union is shortly to open its doors to new democracies and, in my view, it is in its vital interest to do so, it is extremely important, if not of capital importance, that it help to reconstruct and develop the civil society in these countries (...). The way in which society structures itself cannot, of course, be imposed from on high. But the climate and the conditions which are conducive to its development can be put in place. In this sense, aid for new democracies should be given in the wider context of sustainable development and reinforcement of the civil society at pan-European level.
>
> The more varied, differentiated and interlinked the various civil European structures, the more willing the new democracies will be to join them and the faster the principle of trust in the citizens and subsidiarity will apply in them, thereby reinforcing their stability. But that is not all: the foundations of the European Union as a supranational community will grow all the stronger. (Havel, 2000)

In other words, Havel argued that it was necessary to stimulate and consolidate support for shared values in the new member states to achieve greater trust in the EU as a whole. In 2018, we seem to find ourselves in a situation where the interpretation of the fundamental values that have long been considered obvious focal points in the EU—democracy, human rights and the rule of law—no longer seem self-evident. In the autumn of 2016, President of the European Commission Jean-Claude Juncker (2016) went so far as to say that the EU is in an existential crisis. In such a context, questions naturally arise about the common identity of the EU, the ideological and emotional cement that ultimately holds the Union together.

Identity, Core Values and Normative Power

The relationship between identity and trust may not be entirely straightforward, but according to socio-psychological research, a common identity encourages the growth of trust within the in-group or collective (Turner, 2000). Trust, whose synonyms include confidence, belief and faith, can be described in somewhat dry language as a dependent variable created in contacts between individuals or groups who believe they have something in common and feel a sense of affinity with each other. If such identity-based trust exists, individuals are more likely to engage in or take risks on behalf of shared projects or relatively abstract goals, even though the prize is anything but a sure thing. The connection can be intuitively understood: as individuals, we prefer to trust those whom we believe we have something in common with rather than those who seem utterly foreign or indifferent to us. Trust can also be extended upwards, to political leaders, for example, who enjoy legitimacy because they are thought to promote, safeguard and preserve central shared values and sentiments of affinity.

Why and whether a common EU identity should be pursued is endlessly debatable and the answer depends on one's general political beliefs. The European Commission has been engaged in an effort to evoke and reinforce some kind of common identity within the EU since the 1970s, but the work has often been criticised for excessive focus on superficial attributes, such as an EU flag, an anthem, or the symbols on notes and coins in a currency common to most member states (Bottici & Challand, 2013; Shore, 2013). For those who consider the long-term effectiveness and durability of the EU as positive things, it is clear that these characteristics are predicated upon a shared vision of some kind or at least a shared understanding of the values that the peoples and their political leaders are willing to stand up for and defend (Petersson & Hellström, 2003). If these conditions exist, the growth of trust within the Union will also be fostered.

In the 1990s, many analysts predicted that national identities were on their way out and the era of the nation state was coming to an end. Economic transactions, cultural expressions, online communications, pandemics and natural disasters were all forces that did not respect national borders but moved freely across them. At the same time, and as a reaction to the pressure across the national borders, local identities and communities were reinforced. The term 'glocalisation' referred to precisely the cross-pressure in which global and local identities became increasingly important at the expense of national identities. Common regional identities, such as those represented by the EU, however, were thought to be more in keeping with the times than the old national variety.

The national identities, however, proved resilient. This has been especially apparent in times of crisis, whether involving terrorist attacks, financial crises in the eurozone area or the migration crisis that put the borders of EU states under pressure in 2015 in connection with record-high arrivals of refugees and asylum seekers from the Middle East, Africa and Asia.

The tendency in times of turbulence to gather around the ingrained values that the nation states are believed to represent is a known phenomenon. This seems to be a way to maintain the personal sense of security as far as possible. The EU identity, however, is not as entrenched and is instead often perceived by many as nothing more than words on paper.

As of today, a common EU identity therefore seems a very long way away from replacing or supplanting the national identities within the member states. However, the problem remains that some shared intellectual goods need to be there to motivate the individual member states and their populations to remain in the Union and even make certain sacrifices to achieve common goals. Widely shared beliefs in the good that can be achieved together must exist to give the political leaders of the member states legitimacy in the eyes of the electorate, especially in times when the engines of economic growth are sputtering. Ultimately, it is a matter of trust: between the governments of the countries and the people they elected to represent. The question has gained renewed currency after the 'Brexit' referendum in June 2016, when a plurality voted in favour of leaving the EU. There is risk that other countries may do likewise if there are no clear and present incentives to remain. If there is no shared vision for what people want to achieve and the economic advantages are not immediately discernible, what reason is there to stay? When, as previously mentioned, Juncker in the autumn of 2016 expressed that the EU was in an existential crisis, he put into words the lack of a sense of affinity that seemed to dominate after a year of discord in relation to the migration crisis and 'Brexit'.

What, then, can persuade popular majorities to think being part of the Union is worthwhile? Benedict Anderson (1983) emphasised in his time that nationalism has an unusually strong motivating power that can induce otherwise rational individuals to sacrifice their lives in times of armed conflict and war for the abstract principle, that is, nationalism. In Anderson's words, it is a matter of an imagined community, but this perception is so strong that it becomes profoundly real in its consequences. The EU cannot generate any such emotionally mobilising force, nor would it be desirable. Former European Commission President Jacques Delors (1989) once sighed, in an oft-quoted statement, that you cannot fall in love with a single market. Another former President of the Commission, Romano Prodi (2000), pointed to Europe's Judeo-Christian roots and common cultural heritage in the broad sense, with roots in the ninth century of Charlemagne, as the foundation stones of a common identity in the

EU. The history, however, seems too remote and rather too controversial to seriously mobilise popular feeling in a positive and constructive way.

More recent history, however, can be unifying through the deterrent effects of twentieth-century disasters in Europe, with two world wars, Nazism and the Holocaust, but this remains a negative definition, a common identity defined based on the joint determination to never allow the horrors of the past to be repeated. If, however, one wants to build a community of identity in the EU based on a positive definition of what unites in the present, apart from the endeavour to prevent a repetition of old evils, the inevitable conclusion is that the natural foundation of the EU's continued development must be shared values in relation to current political and social reality. After all, there is no common ethnicity, religion or culture in a broad sense to build upon.

In the words of Roxana Barbulescu (2016), the EU is a political union of democracies which protects human rights and presents itself as a beacon of human rights on the global scene. That is a summary as good as any. Support for democracy, human rights and the rule of law has long been considered a self-evident normative basis for the activities of the EU. These norms are written into the previously mentioned Copenhagen criteria, established by the European Council in 1993. They have subsequently been said to constitute an absolute requirement for negotiations with new states on membership to even commence. The more precise formulation of the introductory gateway criterion—which states the conditions for opening membership talks—is that new candidate countries must have 'stable institutions guaranteeing democracy, the rule of law, human rights and respect for and protection of minorities' (European Commission, 2017).

If the interpretations of these maxims begin to waver, this criterion is not quite as imperative and commanding of respect. The impact is deadened when different views are represented within the EU regarding which interpretations are correct. Another dilemma is that even if meeting the Copenhagen criteria constitutes a prerequisite for beginning membership talks with the EU, existing member states that fail to fully comply with the criteria are at no risk of exclusion. Once a country has become a member, control practically ceases. While there are mechanisms to temporarily deprive erring members of certain rights, including voting rights in the European Council following the 'nuclear option' of Article 7 of the Treaty on European Union, these are blunt instruments and seldom used (see also Joakim Nergelius' chapter in this volume). Herein lies an undeniable weakness, not least on the moral level.

In the wake of Joseph Nye (2004), it has become popular to talk about 'soft power'. Without a doubt, it was the norm dimension based on what was expressed in the Copenhagen criteria that, along with a strong economy, constituted the basis of the EU's international influence and standing after the end of the Cold War. To use the expression coined by Ian Manners (2002), the EU had 'normative power'. According to him, there were five influential core norms and four minor norms propounded by the EU. All of these were ultimately based on the Copenhagen criteria.

Following Manners, the EU's normative power was, in the final instance, a matter of its opportunities to gain support for its interpretations of what the core norms mean and what can be considered normal and recommendable to do in a given situation, in both domestic and foreign relations. It was a matter of conviction and presumptions that cannot be compelled but which evolved through the power of good example. Convictions lead the way, not sanctions and coercion. How relevant is the notion of the EU's normative power today, more than halfway through the 2010s? Is the positive picture still justified?

Four Developmental Paths for the EU

In a fairly recent book (co-written with Hans-Åke Persson and Cecilie Stokholm Banke), I discuss four contending visions of Europe's future development (Persson, Petersson, & Stokholm Banke, 2015). These four visions were Europe as a promised land, as a bogeyman, as an anachronism and as a contested ideal.

The first scenario referred to the persistent appeal of Europe in the world, among the candidate countries in the Western Balkans or countries like Georgia that aspire to be candidate countries, and on the individual level among migrants who make their way to the EU from other parts of the world. Here, the vision of EU-Europe as a promised land has hardly faded in recent years. This is still painfully clear. According to the International Organization of Migration (IOM), more than 1.3 million of refugees and migrants crossed the Mediterranean Sea in 2015 and 2016 alone on their way to EU-Europe in search of a better life (IOM, 2015, 2016).

The diametrically opposed vision of the EU as bogeyman refers to the risk of repetitions in the EU of parts of Europe's sombre past, its dreadful twentieth century with two world wars and the Holocaust, as well as, lest we forget, Europe's dark colonial history. It was the Stygian experiences of the twentieth century that inspired far-sighted statesmen in Europe to join together in the early 1950s laying the foundations of today's EU. Their rationale was that a repeat of the disasters of the past must be prevented at any cost. This pioneering endeavour has certainly been successful for a long while and was symbolically recognised when the EU was awarded the Nobel Peace Prize in 2012 for its work with peace, reconciliation, democracy and human rights in Europe. But things are not perfect, by any means. Extrapolations of elements in the present are found in the bogeyman vision, where many people seem not the least bit wary of the errors of the past. On the contrary, there are deeply troubling tendencies. These include aspects such as an increase in 'Us vs Them' thinking within the individual member states, rising xenophobia, higher numbers of hate crimes and the growing influence of extreme right-wing nationalist movements. From having been a promised land, the EU or parts of it might be degenerating into a cold and inhospitable place where it is dangerous for those identified as foreigners to be.

The outlook that the EU should appear to be an anachronism is a prediction of stagnation. Its argument is that Europe's influence is past its prime. EU-Europe, in its ingrained self-confidence, is resting on former laurels. Based on several economic indicators, the EU is at risk of being outstripped by the so-called BRICS countries (Brazil, Russia, India, China and South Africa), for example, and is therefore increasingly relegated to playing second fiddle to these countries and the US. The long-lasting peace among the core countries of the EU since the end of World War II is taken for granted and no longer inspires as it once did. When the EU was hit by the consequences of the global financial crisis in 2007 and the eurozone crisis in 2008 and onwards, much of the economic basis for the Union's global influence collapsed. Even though growth has also withered in the BRICS countries, the EU was unable to respond to the economic challenge presented by these more dynamic parts of the world. In 2016, Brexit brought the problem of the EU as a possible anachronism to a head. One of the top countries in the EU is leaving: what's next?

The last scenario, finally, is the EU as contested ideal. This refers to what this chapter discusses more specifically: the risk that the core values of the EU will be undermined when dissonant voices join the European chorus about what are the central values, or even try to drown it out. There has been an increasingly strong tendency in recent years for countries both within and outside the EU to lay claim to speaking for Europe. Richard Sakwa (2014) has discussed this development in relation to the concept of Greater Europe, which thus encompasses considerably more than the EU. In this context, the EU is no longer even the obvious hub. The interpretation of the EU's ingrained fundamental values as expressed in the Copenhagen criteria are being challenged by outsider countries like Russia and Turkey. At the same time, increasingly vociferous challenges are coming from inside the EU itself. Which way development should go is no longer obvious. The likely consequences are that trust within the Union will diminish as the member states diverge on questions of values and the EU's standing outside its borders will decline. Its normative power will palpably weaken in relation to the rest of the world.

Whether we like it or not, the cohesion of the EU ultimately depends upon boundaries, both physical and psychological. All collective identities are based on what the in-group is and, perhaps above all, what it is not. The EU's influence as a normative power largely depends on its capacity to draw clear lines of demarcation between it and other parts of the world that do not embrace the principles expressed in the Copenhagen criteria. The core values of democracy shine brightest when set against the darkness of authoritarianism. Expressed somewhat more brutally, the EU identity, as an identity to be proud of in positive terms, is based on the fact that the EU is not Russia, with its authoritarian development and lack of respect for borders acknowledged under international law. It is also based on the fact that the EU is not Turkey, with its mass arrests, purges and threats to reinstate capital punishment in the wake of the failed military coup in 2016. The core values of the Copenhagen criteria, the goodness of the open society, also shine brightly in relation to the challenges of the Islamic State's terrorism and religious fanaticism. This is a pitched battle. And yet, the lustre of the normative power may be dulled if EU member states go too far in their efforts to respond to threats from the outside. It is vital to the common identity, and thus to trust, that the non-democratic traits we otherwise claim distinguish 'Them' do not tarnish 'Us'.

A Kidnapped West Redux: Or Turning Fish Soup Into an Aquarium?

Today, in the late 2010s, the challenges to the EU's core values from the inside are coming not least from Central Europe. As Iver B. Neumann (1999) noted, use of the term 'Central Europe' at the end of the Cold War was fraught with tension. Representations of Central Europe took on three major forms. The most common use of the term 'Central Europe' referred to three countries in the geographical centre of Europe: Czechoslovakia (which still existed), Hungary and Poland. These made up the 'Visegrad bloc'. The second use of the term 'Central Europe' was propagated by a number of states, from Estonia, Latvia and Lithuania in the north to Bulgaria and Romania and the countries of the former Yugoslavia in the south, which also claimed to fit within the political-geographical frame of reference indicated by the designation of Central Europe. Thirdly, the term 'Central Europe' was found in a state of tension with the term 'Mitteleuropa' where Germany, rather than the Visegrad bloc, was clearly the centre. Neumann's interpretation is that the first-mentioned usage gained the greatest currency, which had important effects. The discourse on a Central Europe comprising mainly the Czech Republic, Slovakia, Hungary and Poland was so influential that it seemed self-evident that these states should be prioritised for membership in the EU as well as the NATO military alliance. That they were considered to be at the head of the line was connected to the assumption that they had the shortest route to reshaping their states in line with the demands of democracy and the market economy.

The Czech author Milan Kundera's (1984) essay *A Kidnapped West* had tremendous impact among Western European politicians and the public at the time. He argued that Western Europe was represented by the EU, while Central Europe had been kidnapped by the Soviet Union. Culturally, however, it was freethinking and potentially dynamic, and thus essentially different from the stagnant and static Eastern Europe. Central Europe therefore was and remained something completely other than Russia and the Soviet Union. The argument became an important aspect of the self-representation of Central European leaders and was also embraced by influential political leaders in Western Europe.

Reincorporating Central Europe with the rest of Europe in the EU became a symbolically important endeavour. By making the term 'Central Europe' accepted in the vernacular, along with the interpretation that the region consisted of the Czech Republic, Slovakia, Poland and Hungary, the political leaders in the Visegrad bloc garnered sympathy for the idea that their countries constituted a vital part of the European project. They were participants in a larger European identity, which was in turn defined to a significant extent based upon the involvement of the Central European states. The great and important mission in connection with the Eastern enlargement of the EU in 2004 was therefore to finally make EU-Europe whole again, to give Central Europe full access to the European legacy and the European community to which it had for so long been denied entry. As Neumann (2015) reminds us, however, it was not necessarily so that

Central Europe must be interpreted as the centre of EU-Europe. Logically, Central Europe is instead the place where influences from the European 'West' and the European 'East' meet and clash. It was therefore an erroneous conclusion from the outset that the EU would remain the same in terms of values after the Eastern enlargement as it was before. Apropos the unification of Europe, a popular joke at the time of the end of the Cold War had it that while it is easy to turn an aquarium into a fish soup, it is much harder to turn a fish soup back into an aquarium. Developments have shown that his evocative description was not necessarily off the mark.

About ten years after the big enlargement, certain governments of Central Europe started to break the consensus on how the EU's core values should be interpreted. This may be seen as an irony of fate, since the EU put so much political prestige on the line to bring these states into the EU-European project in the first place. Perhaps the transformation to a working market economy was so arduous for the new democratic leaders that developing a new political culture was put on the back burner. If so, Havel's warning was indeed justified.

Illiberal Democracy

The term 'illiberal democracy' is usually ascribed to Fareed Zakaria (1997). He used the term to describe regimes that indeed held elections but gave short shrift to the rule of law and loosely interpreted what the country's constitution had to say about checks and balances between branches of government. Above all, the term suggested that the liberal element of democracy, as regards the rights of minorities and individual liberty, was ascribed less importance by the regimes in question.

The emergence of illiberal democracy in the EU is of relatively recent vintage, with Hungary on the forefront. The country's populist-influenced leader, Prime Minister Viktor Orbán, came to power after the national elections in 2010, at the head of a coalition government led by his national conservative party *Fidesz*. After the elections, this government could rely on a two-thirds majority in parliament, which made it possible to amend the constitution. A number of restrictive changes to judicial independence have since occurred. Freedom of the press has been curtailed in pace with increases in state political control over the media and the initiation of constitutional amendments. Laws have been enacted that make insulting or disparaging national symbols a crime punishable with imprisonment.

Orbán even goes so far as to advocate reinstatement of capital punishment in Hungary (The Guardian, 2015). To seriously broach this subject is symbolically as far as one can go if one is aiming to distance oneself from the EU's core values. When Turkish President Recep Tayyip Erdogan, after the failed military coup in 2016, indicated that the death penalty might be reinstated in Turkey because, as he put it, the people demanded it, leading politicians in the EU including the German Minister of Foreign Affairs, Sigmar Gabriel (Swedish Radio, 2017), emphasised that if this were to happen, the country's membership talks had reached the end of the road. Capital punishment was a Rubicon, a red line, which could not be crossed under any circumstances. Here again, there is an obvious difference between EU member states and candidate countries. As mentioned, opportunities to impose sanctions on existing members are heavily restricted.

As the negative reactions from outside Hungary pile up, the Orbán government seems to become only more intent upon being the bête noire of the EU. A referendum on refugee reception was held in Hungary in 2016. The main question asked was whether the voters would allow the EU to be able to mandate the obligatory resettlement of 'non-Hungarian citizens' in the country. The referendum was initiated by reason of the EU's proposed quota system for the allocation of refugee reception within the Union, a principle that the Hungarian government, together with the Slovakian, strongly opposed. A stunning 98 per cent of those who voted sided with the government's position in the polls, but the referendum was nevertheless declared invalid due to the voter turnout being below the required 50 per cent.

In his nationalist rhetoric, Prime Minister Orbán identifies enemies, foreign and domestic, that wish Hungary ill. It is the threats from these forces that, according to him, justify the authoritarian elements of his government's policies. His speeches during the migration crisis of 2015 and leading up to the referendum in 2016, where he links migration with terrorism, are glaring examples of this. Orbán is thus responsible for what is called in the literature securitisation of migration issues in political debate (Huysmans, 2000), where he seeks to legitimise the forceful pushback against migrants that he considers necessary to protect the country from threats inside and outside its borders. He advocates a zero vision in the migration area: Hungary should not accept any refugees, period, regardless of what is happening in the world. Those who do not agree with the Prime Minister's policy are not real Hungarians, according to the rhetoric.

The hard line is supported in popular opinion, which thus seems to favour a very restrictive stance on the refugee issue. Orbán also tries to strike a balance against the right-wing extremist party *Jobbik*, which usually goes further than his own party *Fidesz* in rhetoric and policy proposals.

If anything, Orbán seems proud of the challenge he is lobbing at the EU's normative, fundamental values. In a platform speech in the summer of 2014, he urged his audience to understand 'systems that are not western, are not liberal, are not liberal democracies, perhaps are not even democracies, and yet manage to make their nations successful' (Orbán, 2014). The gist of his argument was that Hungary is now exploring how the country can liberate itself from 'Western dogmas' and optimally organise a society that is competitive in the world arena. He suggested that countries like Russia, China, India, Turkey and Singapore are states worthy of serving as models for Hungary's political and economic development. This is a far cry from what happened at the end of the Cold War, when Hungarian leaders were the first in the Eastern Bloc to cut holes in the fence that demarcated the Iron Curtain and thus open the country in earnest to democratic values and other influences from the West.

It should perhaps be stressed that Orbán never actually defined what illiberal democracy entails in his platform speech. Illiberalism was presented only as the negation of liberalism, which Orbán argued incorporates 'corruption, sex and violence', but the Prime Minister did not delve more concretely into which liberal rights and freedoms should be curtailed. He did emphasise, however, that 'values of Christianity, freedom and human rights' would still be respected in an illiberal Hungary, although he did not put much emphasis on the EU's core values of democracy and the rule of law in this context. This might have been a harbinger of the future direction of Hungarian policy. In any case, the reference to Christian values is likely to have given Muslims in the country reason to feel stigmatised.

Hungary is no longer alone in appearing to be an illiberal democracy within the EU. The parliamentary elections in Poland in 2015 brought the national conservative party *Prawo i Sprawiedliwość* (PiS, Law and Justice) then headed by Prime Minister Beata Szydło, and endorsed by Party Chairman Jarosław Kaczyński, to power with the backing of an absolute majority in the Parliament. In many ways, Kaczyński seems to be the real leader of the Polish movement towards illiberal democracy. As early as 2011, he expressed his wish to create a 'Budapest in Warsaw' (The Financial Times, 2016).

After the change of government in 2015, a new media law that empowered the government to appoint about 20 senior positions in state-owned radio and television channels constricted freedom of the press and freedom of expression. One move in particular that garnered much outside attention was the attempt by the new culture minister to ban the production of a play by the Nobel laureate Elfriede Jelinek on the grounds that the opening scene was pornographic. State censorship, which had been lifted from Polish arts and culture with the liberation from the Eastern Bloc, seemed to be on the way back.

Most crucially, however, on the strength of the election results in 2015, the government was able, as in Hungary, to amend the constitution. It quickly pushed through a restriction of the powers of the constitutional court. Extraordinary judicial appointments were made in violation of existing regulations and the government decreed that decisions by the Constitutional Tribunal would henceforth require a two-thirds majority. As the Polish government moved in 2017 to initiate laws giving itself the power to dismiss Supreme Court judges and give veto power to government-appointed members of the National Council of the Judiciary, which selects judicial candidates, the European Commission reacted very strongly. It warned that the EU was on the brink, for the first time ever, of triggering the 'nuclear option' of Article 7 TEU, under which the Polish government could lose its voting rights in the EU institutions. Under the influence of strong domestic protest rallies and the negative international reactions, the Polish President, Andrzej Duda, decided however to block the two most controversial laws, and the threat was not carried out at the time (The Guardian, 2017).

Islands of the East in the West

Until Hungary and Poland became the standard bearers for illiberal democracy in the EU, the challenges to the EU's interpretive monopoly in the matter of what constitutes European values came from the outside, primarily from Russia. The idea of Russia's 'sovereign democracy' was launched soon after Vladimir Putin's first term as President began in the early 2000s, where the main message was that no outside state had any right to interfere in how Russia chose to interpret and apply the concept of democracy and what it entails (Chen, 2016; Makarychev, 2008). It was the great power's sovereign right to choose its interpretations and chart its own course, which need not at all harmonise with that of the US or the EU.

Ever since he came into power in the late 1990s, Putin has consistently managed to maintain his popularity among the Russian electorate (Petersson, 2017). The four times he has run for president so far, in 2000, 2004, 2012 and 2018, he was elected in the first round. His approval ratings are astoundingly high and have only rarely dropped below 65 per cent, a rating that his political colleagues in the West can only achieve in their dreams. Putin's heavy-handed emphasis on the idea of Russia as a predestined great power seems to appeal to Russian voters, along with his imposition and maintenance of law and order after the political chaos and economic weakness of the 1990s. The hosting of the 2014 Winter Olympics in Sochi became a symbolic manifestation of Russia's resurgence as a global power. Actions such as the annexation of Crimea that same year and the intervention in the civil conflicts in Ukraine and the war in Syria have also been highly popular among the voters (Hutcheson & Petersson, 2016). In connection with these events, Putin's approval curve shot up and stayed there. In the monthly surveys taken in the autumn of 2017 by Moscow-based Levada Center, 83 per cent of respondents still expressed their approval of the president's policies (Levada Center, 2017).

The popularity Putin enjoys among the populist right wing in the West is, on the face of it, highly surprising. This development is particularly disquieting when it is put in relation to the discussion on European core values. With his harsh rhetoric, his macho ideal and his authoritarian image and policy, Putin has become something of an idol among European right-wing populists (Klapsis, 2015). The leaders of the Hungarian *Jobbik* party have described him as a guarantor of European values, as opposed to a putatively degenerate EU. Politicians like Marine Le Pen in France and Nigel Farage in the UK have repeatedly expressed their admiration for his politics and style. On their website, the Greek ultranationalist Golden Dawn are looking forward to a Russian-Greek alliance between the two Orthodox states in the areas of trade, energy and national security (Golden Dawn, 2016).

Considering these somewhat unexpected expressions of sympathy, as the previously mentioned Neumann (2015) has so vividly put it, the political East may pop up anywhere on the European political map in the future, and even off the same. This very much includes the formerly acknowledged bastion of Western liberal democracy—the US. During the election campaign in 2016, the populist Donald Trump expressed his admiration in several speeches for his Russian counterpart Putin (and vice versa), and has since becoming US President indicated what seems to be a very muddled view of democracy. More than one year into its political lifespan, the political course of the Trump administration is volatile and erratic. Even if it is clear that the candidate preferred by Moscow emerged victorious from the US presidential election, it is still too early to tell the extent to which the political East has truly reached all the way to Washington, DC. Even so, the effects of the Trump administration on the political climate in Europe and the rest of the world may be as profound as they are unpredictable.

As if Europe's own problems were not enough. The antipathy towards refugees and asylum seekers is making itself felt across the entire European political map. Right-wing populist parties across the entire EU are castigating these groups, in alignment with the views represented by Orbán and Kaczyński in their illiberal democracies in the Visegrad bloc. Migrants are depicted by default as a threat to national security, a serious burden on social welfare systems and a general threat to putative national cultures and values. In several countries, such as Denmark and Austria, the established parties have moved closer to the perspectives and views of the populist factions in a bid to win over their voters and opinion support. This is yet another manifestation of the increasingly patchy backing of the EU's core values. It seems clear that the migration crisis has put trust within the EU and, especially, between EU residents and recently arrived migrants to a serious test.

A somewhat different challenge to the European core values is coming from the official EU candidate country Turkey. When President Erdogan responded to criticism of Turkey's inadequate respect for democracy, human rights and the rule of law in March 2016 (four months before the failed military coup in the country), he was quoted as saying, 'Democracy, freedom and the rule of law…for us, these words have absolutely no value any longer' (The Independent, 2016). After the failed coup, things got far worse. Tens of thousands of people were dismissed from their positions in public administration, the military, media and education. Fifteen private universities were closed, putatively due to connections to the oppositional *Gülen* movement. Turkey is ruled by emergency laws, mass arrests have taken place, copious reports of torture are being made and reinstatement of capital punishment is under discussion. In spite of such actions, the EU is so far maintaining its ambition to continue membership talks with Turkey, even though German Chancellor Angela Merkel in the early autumn of 2017 vowed to seek to end the talks (Reuters, 2017). Under the present circumstances, the EU clearly seems to put its core values at stake by continuing talks with Turkey.

Illiberalism, Canaries and Legitimacy

Using Hungary as an example, Jan-Werner Müller (2016) cautions against widespread and accepted use of the term 'illiberal democracy', which can help solidify and legitimise the power of authoritarian regimes. He argues that the concept can be misleading and that an unwarrantedly positive impression may be given that these regimes are primarily opposed to the materialism and selfish individualism of the market economy. This would obscure the fact that they are also attempting to limit protection of minorities, freedom of speech and assembly, as well as media pluralism, all of which are at the heart of democracy. The political orientation is not so much illiberal as it is undemocratic: things should be called what they really are.

It is bad enough that countries like Hungary and Poland seem to have made illiberal and undemocratic ideas their own. The line of thinking expressed by Abby Innes (2015) is even more alarming: developments in Hungary and Poland might be a memento mori for Europe at large. She argues that the pressure on democracy in Hungary can be compared to the canaries in the coal mines of yesteryear. When toxic gases began billowing through the mine shafts, the canaries were the first to die, thus giving an early warning to the miners, who could take themselves to safety. What Innes is suggesting is that Hungary, with the economic stresses it has endured during its transition to democracy, the market economy and sustainable social welfare systems, has in many ways, and in magnified form, been ahead of the rest of the EU when it comes to the urgency and means of getting out of a deep economic crisis. For Hungary, the need arose after the end of the Cold War, while the euro countries did not have their crisis to overcome until 2007-2008 and later. There is thus reason, according to Innes, to study the Hungarian warning signs carefully: democracy in Hungary may be the EU's canary. Populism, national conservatism and illiberal currents may easily arise in countries closer to the core of Europe, she argues, and the essence of democracy may be the first to die. Hardly subtle strategies to maintain the goodwill of voters may be tempting and easy ways for political elites to achieve the legitimacy they need to stay in power. Identifying scapegoats, such as refugees, is a classic recipe.

In the late nineteenth and early twentieth century, the famous German sociologist Max Weber (1978) determined that there are various ways for the political elites to acquire more long-term and enduring support, legitimacy, from the electorate. A common definition of legitimacy is the existence of widespread beliefs that the power of leaders is lawful, rightful and in accordance with the will of the people. Weber differentiated three ideal types: charismatic authority (based on the charisma and personal qualities of the leader), traditional authority (when power is vested in a person, group or family who have held power for so long that it seems as if there is no longer any alternative) and rational-legal authority (the mature, Western type, in which public trust is gained through conscientious observance of existing laws and rules). The dilemma that the illiberal leaders in the EU are actualising is that there seems to be a movement in various places in the member states away from rational-legal legitimacy and towards charismatic legitimacy. Instead of careful observation of the letter and the spirit of existing laws and constitutions, leaders influenced by populism are using charismatic addresses and oversimplified solutions—such as stopping all refugee immigration—to address complex social problems. As the charismatic style of leadership generally prefers black-and-white descriptions of reality in which an 'Us' is contrasted with a threatening 'Them', this is a trend that certainly does not encourage the development of trust within the EU.

Protect the Core Values and Secure Their Interpretation

The Eastern enlargement in 2004 included ten countries, eight of them in the former Eastern Europe. When it was implemented, it was considered a major advance for Western liberal order and democracy, although some problems were foreseen, primarily in relation to labour markets and social safety nets. The kidnapped Central Europe would now be fully liberated and Europe made whole again. But the enlargement led to tensions within the Union in a way that few people other than the prescient Václav Havel could predict. It included states whose political systems and civil societies were still scarred by their experiences of the Cold War and their prolonged affiliation with the Soviet-dominated Eastern Bloc. The integration of Central Europe thus did not entail a simple enlargement of the core of the EU: instead it seems to have involved a partial redefinition of the core.

In Hungary and Poland, new governments came to power in the 2010s, supported by discontented electoral majorities and with a somewhat divergent view of what constitutes the core values of the EU. The accepted interpretations of what the democracy, human rights and rule of law of the Copenhagen criteria are, and what they mean, were challenged. These governments seemed most inclined to listen to the Siren song of authoritarian forces in Russia and perhaps Turkey. As this is written, it seems by no means self-evident that the democratic and liberal model represented by the old EU will be competitive in the long run or that its normative, preferential rights of interpretation vis-à-vis the rest of the world can be maintained. The EU seems to be moving into a phase where the only instrument available to play is second fiddle. The Golden Age of the EU may already have passed; the Union may seem to be an anachronism, as 'Brexit' perhaps suggests.

The trials of the EU's fundamental values are thus emanating from authoritarian states outside its borders and from illiberal member states at its centre but not only from there. This has to do not only with a political East that is spreading here and there across the entire EU territory, it is rather an illiberal patchwork quilt being sewn under the influence of a protracted economic crisis. The growing support of the populist parties in public opinion in recent years is a serious concern and seems, if anything, to be a challenge to the core values of the EU. The pushing of simple solutions to complex problems is gaining widespread support in public opinion in the member states. The knee-jerk characterisation of refugees and other migrants as threats to national security, terrorists and general burdens on national resources and values is happening all over the EU. Perhaps the populist challenge is actually the toxic gas pouring out of the EU's political mine?

A unifying vision for the EU member states and their people is needed to continue moving forward together, regardless of the economic crises and Brexit. There must be consensus as to how the core values should be interpreted and implemented. The Copenhagen criteria should therefore be extended with an authoritative and shared interpretation of what its maxims entail. In this way, the criteria can be protected from attempts to set up competing or conflicting interpretations, whether these are purported to be of a sovereign or illiberal nature. Democracy, human rights and the rule of law must never be allowed to become beautiful words devoid of concrete content; the EU must remain a beacon. In turn, this means that concern for democracy, the rule of law and human rights must also imbue the relationships among people who reside in the Union's territory but are not her citizens.

Impactful sanctions against existing member states that breach the accepted interpretation of the core values must be considered in the future. What should be done in relation to candidate countries that claim the maxims are of no value at all is another problem that must be addressed. One is forced to conclude that continued membership talks with Turkey, which for all intents and purposes is breaching the EU's core values under the mantle of emergency legislation, are in the current circumstances a contravention of the Copenhagen criteria. The EU would certainly be enlarged, but it would most likely have to sell its soul along the way.

A common identity would foster trust between EU member states and their populations to be further developed and consolidated. Such an identity must, however, grow organically and support for the common values would be the most fertile soil. Unconditional unity around the interpretation of the Copenhagen criteria is essential to promoting a sustainable common identity and trust within the EU.

References

Anderson, B. (1983). *Imagined communities: Reflections on the origin and spread of nationalism*. London: Verso.

Barbulescu, R. (2016). Still a beacon of human rights? Considerations on the EU response to the refugee crisis in the Mediterranean. *Mediterranean Politics, 22*(2), 301–308.

Bottici, C., & Challand, B. (2013). *Imagining Europe: Myth, memory, and identity*. Cambridge: Cambridge University Press.

Chen, C. (2016). *The return of ideology: The search for regime identities in postcommunist Russia and China*. Ann Arbor: University of Michigan Press.

Delors, J. (1989). Address given by Jacques Delors to the European Parliament, 17 January 1989. Retrieved October 11, 2017, from https://www.cvce.eu/content/publication/2003/8/22/b9c06b95-db97-4774-a700-e8aea5172233/publishable_en.pdf

European Commission. (2017). Conditions for membership. Retrieved October 11, 2017, from https://ec.europa.eu/neighbourhood-enlargement/policy/conditions-membership_en

European Council Conclusions. (1993–2003). Retrieved October 25, 2017, from http://www.consilium.europa.eu/en/european-council/conclusions/1993-2003/

Financial Times. (2016). Poland's new government finds a model in Orban's Hungary. Retrieved October 24, 2017, from https://www.ft.com/content/0a3c7d44-b48e-11e5-8358-9a82b43f6b2f?mhq5j=e5

Golden Dawn. (2016). Golden Dawn welcomes the leader of Russia, Mr. Vladimir Putin, to Greece. Retrieved November 1, 2017, from http://www.xryshaygh.com/en/view/golden-dawn-welcomes-the-leader-of-russia-mr.-vladimir-putin-to-greece

The Guardian. (2015). Hungary PM: Bring back death penalty and build work camps for immigrants. Retrieved October 11, 2017, from https://www.theguardian.com/world/2015/apr/29/hungary-pm-death-penalty-work-camps-for-immigrants-viktor-orban

The Guardian. (2017). Poland hits back at EU 'blackmail' over judicial reforms. Retrieved October 11, 2017, from https://www.theguardian.com/world/2017/jul/26/poland-hits-back-eu-blackmail-judicial-reforms

Havel, V. (2000). Address by Mr Václav Havel, President of the Czech Republic. Retrieved October 11, 2017, from http://www.europarl.europa.eu/sides/getDoc.do?pubRef=-//EP//TEXT+CRE+20000216+ITEM-012+DOC+XML+V0//EN

Hutcheson, D., & Petersson, B. (2016). Shortcut to legitimacy: Popularity in Putin's Russia. *Europe-Asia Studies, 68*(7), 1107–1126.

Huysmans, J. (2000). The European Union and the securitization of migration. *Journal of Common Market Studies, 38*(5), 751–777.

The Independent. (2016). President Erdogan says freedom and democracy have 'no value' in Turkey amid arrests and military crackdown. Retrieved November 1, 2017, from http://www.independent.co.uk/news/world/europe/president-erdogan-says-freedom-and-democracy-have-no-value-in-turkey-amid-arrests-and-military-a6938266.html

Innes, A. (2015). Hungary's illiberal democracy. *Current History, 114*(770), 95–100.

International Organization for Migration. (2015). Retrieved October 24, 2017, from https://www.iom.int/news/irregular-migrant-refugee-arrivals-europe-top-one-million-2015-iom

International Organization for Migration. (2016). Retrieved October 24, 2017, from https://www.iom.int/news/mediterranean-migrant-arrivals-top-363348-2016-deaths-sea-5079

Juncker, J.-C. (2016). State of the Union Address 2016: Towards a better Europe—A Europe that protects, empowers and defends, Strasbourg, 14 September 2016. Retrieved October 11, 2017, from http://europa.eu/rapid/press-release_SPEECH-16-3043_en.htm

Klapsis, A. (2015). *An unholy alliance: The European far right and Putin's Russia*. Brussels: Wilfried Martens Centre for European Studies.

Kundera, M. (1984). A kidnapped West or culture bows out. *Granta*, no. 11. Retrieved October 24, 2017, from https://granta.com/a-kidnapped-west-or-culture-bows-out/

Levada Center. (2017). Putin's approval rating. Retrieved November 1, 2017, from http://www.levada.ru/en/ratings/

Makarychev, A. S. (2008). Russia's search for international identity through the sovereign democracy concept. *The International Spectator, 43*(2), 49–62.

Manners, I. (2002). Normative power Europe: A contradiction in terms? *Journal of Common Market Studies, 40*(2), 235–258.

Müller, J.-W. (2016). The problem with 'illiberal democracy'. *Social Europe*. Retrieved October 11, 2017, from https://www.socialeurope.eu/the-problem-with-illiberal-democracy

Neumann, I. B. (1999). Central Europe 1950–2000. *Slavica Lundensia, 19*, 15–28.

Neumann, I. B. (2015). Authoritarian East. *Global Affairs, 1*(1), 93–94.

Nye, J. K. (2004). *Soft power: The means to success in world politics*. New York: Public Affairs.

Orbán, V. (2014). Full text of Viktor Orbán's speech at Băile Tuşnad (Tusnádfürdő) of 26 July 2014. Retrieved October 11, 2017, from https://budapestbeacon.com/full-text-of-viktor-orbans-speech-at-baile-tusnad-tusnadfurdo-of-26-july-2014/

Persson, H.-Å., Petersson, B., & Stokholm Banke, C. (Eds.). (2015). *Playing second fiddle: Contending visions of Europe's future development*. Malmö: Universus Academic Press.

Petersson, B. (2017). Putin and the Russian Mythscape: Dilemmas of charismatic legitimacy. *Demokratizatsiya, 25*(3), 235–254.

Petersson, B., & Hellström, A. (2003). The return of the kings: Temporality in the construction of EU identity. *European Societies, 5*(3), 235–252.

Prodi, R. (2000). *Europe as I see it*. Cambridge: Polity.

Reuters. (2017). In shift, Merkel backs end to EU-Turkey membership talks. Retrieved November 1, 2017, from https://www.reuters.com/article/us-germany-turkey-merkel/in-shift-merkel-backs-end-to-eu-turkey-membership-talks-idUSKCN1BE15B

Sakwa, R. (2014). *Frontline Ukraine: Crisis in the borderlands*. London: IB Tauris.

Shore, C. (2013). *Building Europe: The cultural politics of European integration*. London: Routledge.

Swedish Radio. (2017). Turkiet på väg mot dödsstraff. Retrieved November 1, 2017, from http://sverigesradio.se/sida/artikel.aspx?programid=83&artikel=6676882

Turner, M. E. (Ed.). (2000). *Groups at work: Theory and research*. Hove, UK: Psychology Press.

Weber, M. (1978). In G. Roth & C. Wittich (Eds.), *Economy and society: An outline of interpretive sociology*. Berkeley, CA: University of California Press.

Zakaria, F. (1997). The rise of illiberal democracy. *Foreign Affairs, 76*(6), 22–43.

Citizens' Trust in the EU as a Political System

Linda Berg

When the British citizens voted for the UK to leave the European Union on 23 June 2016, there were astonished reactions across Europe. Even though the campaign had been criticized for a lack of objectivity on both sides, the outcome can be seen as one of many indications that citizens' trust in the EU as a political system has weakened in the light of recent economic and political crises, as well as concern over immigration (Hobolt, 2016). Moreover, 'Brexit' can be seen as merely the latest of several major crises for the EU in recent years. The long-term economic crisis and an inability to deal with the extensive refugee flows across the Mediterranean are other examples of when the EU and its member states have been criticized for its incapacity to reach joint solutions. The European integration project has thus been said to be facing difficult, almost existential challenges (Tosun, Wetzel, & Zapryanova, 2015).

In the wake of these crises, there have been many examples of popular dissatisfaction and protest. There is pertinent civic criticism of what is perceived to be an inadequate ability to cope with growing social, economic and cultural divisions in Europe (Hobolt & Tilley, 2014; Hobolt & de Vries, 2016; Serricchio, Tsakatika, & Quaglia, 2013). At the same time,

L. Berg (✉)
University of Gothenburg, Gothenburg, Sweden

A. Bakardjieva Engelbrekt et al. (eds.), *Trust in the European Union in Challenging Times*, https://doi.org/10.1007/978-3-319-73857-4_4

EU member states have very different views on how to handle global and European challenges, leading to a lack of support for joint actions and difficult European leadership (Aggestam & Johansson, 2017). Moreover, many EU member states continue to have persistent economic difficulties. Consequences of public sector retrenchments have led to major challenges, protests and distrust among the most affected citizens. In addition to mass demonstrations, we have also seen increased opinion support and election successes for political parties challenging the existing elite, often with a strong EU-sceptic agenda (Hobolt & Tilley, 2016).

In the light of dissatisfaction and insecurity, politics have been radicalized. Tensions and contradictions between different groups have increased and the tone of conversation tends to be heated. The sense of cohesion between countries, and groups within countries, is questioned and raised as arguments in discussions about the value of the membership in the EU. In other words, the popular trust in the EU is questioned, especially by those most negatively affected by the economic and other crises and the EU's perceived inability to handle them (Hobolt & de Vries, 2016). Nevertheless, it should of course also be noted that this trend of decreasing political trust is not unique to the EU. There is a long-term trend of a generally reduced trust in political institutions and actors, globally and nationally, in most countries (Dalton, 2013).

This chapter focuses on the citizens' perspective and investigates how citizens' trust in the EU as a political system and its institutions has changed over time, as well as how trust vary between different member states and social groups. The chapter is based on theory and previous research on European integration, political legitimacy and trust, using European and Swedish survey studies for the empirical analyses of explanations to differences in perceptions about the EU.

Citizens' Trust, Identification and the European Integration Process

Trust is an important but elusive concept within social science research, as it can be defined and interpreted in different ways (Warren, 1999). In this chapter, the focus is on citizens' own perceptions. Somewhat simplified, we can distinguish between two main forms of citizens' trust: inter-personal trust and trust in the political system. Inter-personal trust is also referred to as social or generalized trust and can be described as a *horizontal* relationship between different individuals in a society, who do not know each other but still display trust in other persons. Inter-personal trust is perceived to be at the core of a well-functioning society as it is expected to reduce costs of transaction and allows people to spend more time and energy on productive cooperation (see also Andreas Bergh's chapter in this volume). Contrastingly, trust in the political system, also referred to as political trust, can be seen as a *vertical* relationship between citizens and the institutions of the political system (Zmerli & van der Meer, 2017). This chapter focuses on the vertical version of citizens' trust, and more specifically the trust citizens may—or may not—have in the European integration and the political institutions of the EU.

Despite the theoretical distinction between these two types of trust, it is important to consider their interconnectedness. Studies show that people who tend to trust other people in general also tend to display trust in the political system and its institutions. In connection to the EU, early integration theorists like Karl W. Deutsch and Ernst Haas have argued in a similar manner that increased cooperation and contact between persons in different European countries would over time increase the sense of community, a European identity, which in turn would contribute to increase the trust and support for the European integration project as such (see e.g. Deutsch, 1966). David Easton (1965) put it this way 'Underlying the functioning of all systems, there must be some cohesive cement—a sense of feeling of community amongst the members. Unless such sentiment emerges, the political system itself may never take shape or if it does, it may not survive' (Easton, 1965, p. 176).

Citizens' political trust can be based on rational as well as emotional aspects, and these can interact in variable ways. The basic principle is that all form of political governance has two aims: to deliver political goods (outcome) and to function as an expression of social community. In relation to this, Lisbeth Hooghe and Gary Marks have launched what they call a post-functional theory of European integration (Hooghe & Marks, 2009). They argue that identity is a key aspect in order to understand multilevel governance in general, and particularly European integration. Moreover, people do care about who governs, but the problem is that the political level which is the most effective to make decisions rarely correspond to the territorial divisions people identify with. This mismatch of efficacy and political structure can lead to political conflicts, which in turn can be triggered feelings of identity and attachment. Strong identifications can both increase and decrease support for European integration. What matters the most is whether or not identifications are exclusive, and whether or not these sentiments are fuelled by EU-sceptical political parties. The importance of identity is expected to matter the most when debated EU issues not only relate to economy but also connect to political values. National identities are shaped by national pressure and socialization, which European integration process lacks. European integration can therefore be seen as an experiment in identity formation, without the historically most important force to shape identifications.

Who Trusts the EU as a Political System?

Broadly defined, explanations of variations in attitudes to the EU can be divided into two main groups: explanations based on self-interest (utility) and explanations focusing on cultural factors, mainly identity. These two main groups are usually referred back to the ground-breaking research by David Easton (Easton, 1965, 1975) about political system support. Easton clarified the difference between what he called *specific* and *diffuse* support. The former is based on self-interest and expects citizens' support for the political authorities to be related to the authorities' efficacy, the political outcome. The latter is a form of diffuse, emotional political system support, which can be seen as a 'reservoir of goodwill' that contributes to citizens' continuous support, even during (at least shorter) periods of dissatisfaction with policy or political leadership.

Easton moreover distinguished between what he called the different 'objects' of the political system. He argued that in order to fully understand political system support (and trust), we need to understand that it is a multidimensional phenomenon, and that the support can be directed towards three different objects: the political society, the political regime and the political authorities.

Following Easton, many other researchers (Dalton, 2004; Norris, 1999) have elaborated Easton's model and differentiate between five different 'objects', or 'components', which can also be argued to represent more or less of diffused or specific support, subsequently from the first (highest) to the fifth (lowest):

1. *The Political community* is mainly related to support for the political system as such and is perceived as the most diffuse form of support;
2. *The Political regime—principles* focuses on the citizens' principle support for democracy and democratic values;

3. *The Political regime—effectiveness* concerns the citizens' evaluations of how well the democratic political system functions in practice;
4. *The Political regime—institutions* focuses on the more specific support for the institutions of the political system, e.g. government and parliament;
5. *The Political actors* component is the most specific, mainly involving support for individual authorities, parties and politicians.

Applying this division to the question of this chapter, citizens' trust in the EU, the first component relates to overall attitudes to the EU as such, or the attitude to one's country's membership of the EU. The second component deals with the principal support for democracy, whereas the third focuses on evaluations of the functioning of democracy in the EU specifically. The fourth component captures the direct trust in the various institutions of the EU, whereas the trust in the individual members of European Parliament can be seen as examples of the fifth component. The idea is that all of these components can vary independently of one another, and that attitudes placed further down in the scale are expected to be more volatile, whereas the upper form of support is expected to be more stable over time. However, Easton argued that there is also a relationship and a potential 'spillover' from one object to another. The previously mentioned idea of a reservoir of goodwill illustrates such a relation between the various objects. On the other hand, Easton was also clear about the fact that long-term problems of support for the lower objects could undermine the support for the political system at large. It is in other words important to study both higher and lower level objects, or components, of political system support.

In correspondence to other research analysing the vertical form of trust using survey data, the main concept used in this chapter is political trust. Trust is also closer to how the questions are formulated in the survey studies used for the empirical analyses. Two main components are analysed here: the more specific form of trust in the political institutions of the EU and the wider, and more diffuse, issue of overall attitude to the EU (or one's country's membership).

Focusing on these two components facilitates the comparison and discussion of differences between, on the one hand, a form of political trust placed 'further down' in the scale of political system support, expected to be more volatile, and, on the other hand, a more diffuse form of trust concerning general attitudes to the EU as a political system. A comparison between them provides a better ground to assess the seriousness of citizens' trust in the EU. The following section provides an overview of citizen attitudes to the EU over time, as well as how the trust in EU institutions has developed over time. Variations across countries follow, including a discussion about the theoretical explanations of variations across countries. The chapter continues with an overview of explanations of variation in attitudes at the individual level, that is, between different groups within the same country and end with a concluding discussion including some recommendations.

Citizens' Trust in the EU Over Time

There is a large variation in public opinion about the EU, not least depending on how questions in surveys are posed. Some questions focus on general attitudes or perceptions about whether one's country's membership is a good or bad thing; other questions are more detailed inquiries about specific EU institutions or policies. Questions like these are regularly asked in large-scale European survey studies. The longest yearly time series can be found in the Eurobarometer data. The standard Eurobarometer surveys are normally carried out as face-to-face interviews with about 1000 citizens in each EU member state. Apart from a variation of questions about current affairs, there are yearly questions about trust for EU institutions and general EU attitudes, as well as a large number of background questions. The interviews are made by national institutions on behalf of the European Commission. The combined datasets are later made available for scientific research.

When citizens of EU member states are asked whether they perceive their country's membership of the EU to be a good thing, a bad thing or neither, the trend in opinion over time is quite stable. Since the 1980s, the tendency has been for a majority of people to answer that they perceive their country's membership to be 'a good thing'. Usually, the share of positive responses have been around 45–55 per cent, whereas the share of respondents answering 'a bad thing' has been around 15–20 per cent, and the share of those answering 'neither good nor bad' around 25–30 per cent. At the time of the economic and euro crisis, there is a drop among the share of positive attitudes and somewhat of an increase among those with a negative view (or neither), but these changes are fairly limited. It is usually not more than a few percentage points, and the positive views remain in majority. In other words, regarding a more general perception of overall membership in the EU, the changes over time are relatively small, and especially when displayed as averages across all EU member states.

A somewhat more visible change during the years of crisis can be found when analysing the question of whether the EU 'conjure up for you a very positive, fairly positive, neutral, fairly negative or very negative image'. Figure 1 shows that since the early 2000s, the largest share (among 40 per cent) has answered that they have a fairly positive view of the EU, but this share is declining to below 30 per cent during several years around the peak of the economic and euro crisis. Since 2010, the share of respondents with a neutral view of the EU is the largest, with around 40 per cent. Moreover, the fairly negative group has increased from around 10 per cent during the 2000s to around 20 per cent during the 2010s.

Even if we can see a decline in the positive image of the EU since the beginning of the economic and euro crisis, this trend is not necessarily too serious. Controversially, it can be argued to be seen as a sign of health that

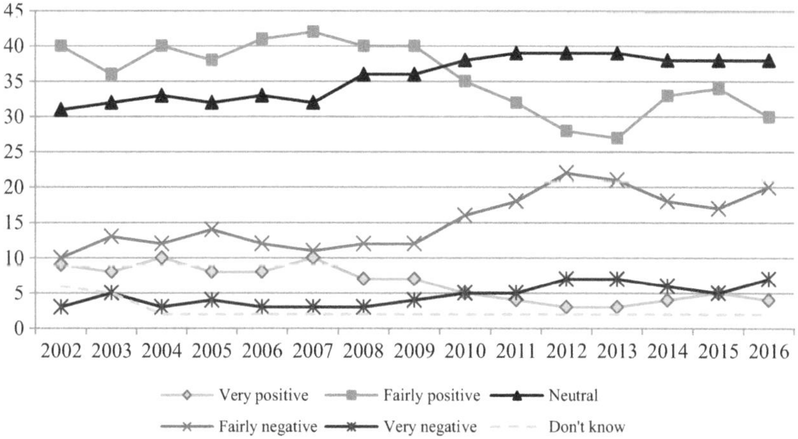

Fig. 1 Positive, negative or neutral image of the EU 2002–2016 (per cent, weighted average all EU). Source: The Eurobarometer. The question posed is 'In general, does the EU conjure up for you a very positive, fairly positive, neutral, fairly negative or very negative image?' The response options are mentioned in the questions, plus the 'don't know' option. The percentages are based on those who have answered the survey question, weighted according to population size in the EU member states

most respondents have a neutral image of the EU as such, as the focus of debate rather should be to discuss and hold varying perceptions about what policies that should be promoted. This is a very reasonable argument. However, to be satisfied by such reasoning and come to the conclusion that there is no need to further investigate the citizens' attitudes to the EU would come at a risk.

Most of all, there is a risk of missing the much more pertinent issue of the declining trust in the decision-making institutions of the EU. Since 2010, the trust in the three most important EU institutions—the European Commission, the Council of the European Union (the Council of Ministers) and the European Parliament—has decreased significantly. Only around 35 per cent of respondents claim to have trust in the Commission and the Council. The trust in the European Parliament has had a somewhat higher level of trust ever since the Eurobarometer started asking about it, but even so, the trust has decreased from around 55 per cent during most parts of the 2000s to around 40 per cent in the last years. As can be seen in Fig. 2, the share of people answering that they tend not to trust the European Parliament has instead increased noticeably, and

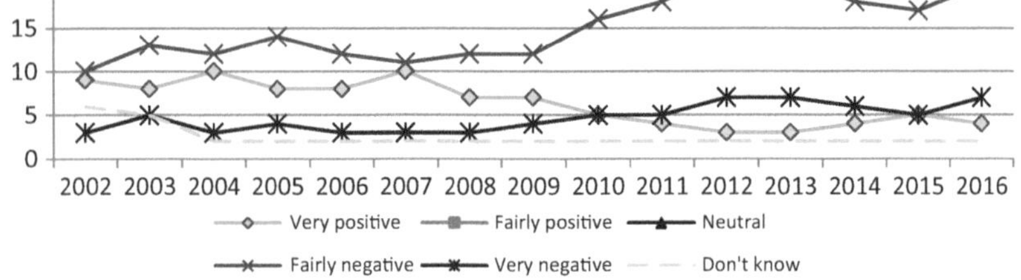

Fig. 2 Trust in the European Parliament 1993–2016 (per cent, weighted average all EU). Source: The Eurobarometer. The same question is posed for several EU institutions and asks for each of them whether or not the respondent tend to trust or not tend to trust it. The three response options are visible in the figure. The percentages are based on those who have answered the survey question, weighted according to population size in the EU member states

now hovers close to the 50 per cent mark. Although the levels of trust have been somewhat lower for the Commission and the Council during the same time, the tendency and pattern is very similar.

Combining the insights from these different ways of measuring citizen's attitudes, the overall image is that most citizens remain positive about their countries' membership; that the previous overall fairly positive image of the EU has begun to be a bit eroded since the beginning of the crisis; and that the trust in the EU institutions has declined severely. It is potentially even more serious that the European Parliament has lost so much of public trust, around 15 percentage points, since it is the EU institution often referred to as the voice of the public. Being the only directly elected EU institution, with a clearly expanded decision-making power the last years, makes the signs of decreasing citizen trust particularly ominous.

A Closer Look at the Citizen Trust Over Time in One Country: The Case of Sweden

A closer look of the development of citizen attitudes over time in one country can increase our understanding of the problems in terms of citizens' trust that the EU faces. Sweden is a particularly interesting country in this regard, as the country became a member of the EU in 1995, following a referendum about the membership the year before, where the 'yes side' won by a small margin, leaving the country hugely divided for many years and often referred to as one of the most hesitant EU member states (second to the UK). In contrast to the UK, however, the attitudes in Sweden do display a different pattern over time. There are also some similarities, and some differences, compared to the previously shown averages of the EU as a whole.

In Fig. 3, the Swedish opinion on EU membership over time is shown. The data used comes from the Swedish SOM Institute (Society, Opinion and Media), which have measured attitudes to Swedish membership of the EU every year since 1991. Throughout the 1990s, the opponents of membership were constantly larger than the supporters, apart from at the referendum in 1994. It was not until the early 2000s, following the first Swedish EU presidency in 2001, that support for the EU membership started to increase. Since then, the share of supporters has been continuously larger than the opponents, albeit the clear opinion shifts at times.

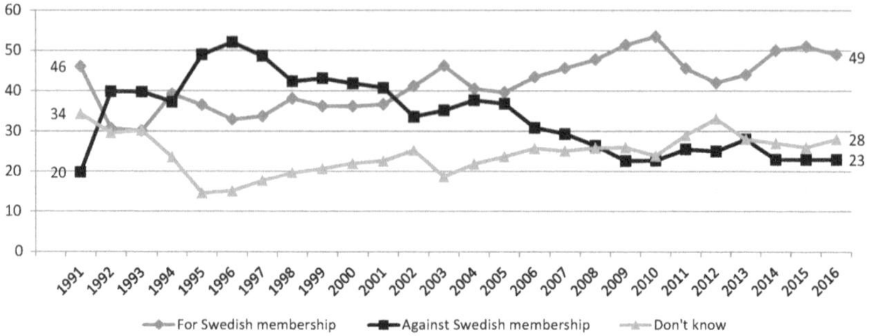

Fig. 3 For or against Swedish membership of the EU 1991–2016 (per cent). Source: The National SOM study 1991–2016. The question posed is 'What is your opinion of the Swedish membership of the EU?' The response alternatives are 'Generally for Swedish membership of the EU; Generally opposed Swedish membership of the EU; Have no specific opinion'. The percentages are based on those who have answered the survey question

In 2009 and 2010, the Swedish support for EU membership was at its all-time high, exceeding 50 per cent. However, this support decreased drastically the following years, as the consequences of the economic and euro crisis became more noticeable also in Sweden (and in the media coverage). The downward trend ended in 2013, followed by an increase of the support again. The last years the opinion has been stable, with a support for membership around 50 per cent, that is, similar levels of support as before the peak of the crisis. Interestingly, there is no sign of a clear decrease of support even after the so-called refugee crisis in 2015 or the 'Brexit' referendum in 2016.

Similarly, to the development of attitudes to the EU over time in the entire EU, Fig. 3 does not indicate any severe decrease in political system trust in Sweden. Although the share of people supporting EU membership decreased somewhat during some years in the beginning of this decade, the percentages are now back to similar levels as before the peak of the euro crisis. However, when we turn to the issue of trust in EU institutions, the pattern is different, similarly to the public average of the entire EU.

Since 2010, Swedes' trust in the European Commission and the European Parliament has been relatively low. Overall, around 15–20 per cent have answered that they trust these institutions very much or to some degree. Another pattern is that the level of trust is almost always identical for these two institutions, which differs from the EU-wide opinion in which the parliament usually gets somewhat higher levels of trust. As can be seen in Fig. 4, in the Swedish data there is also no increase of trust in the last years, in comparison to the increase in support for EU membership as such. In fact, the share of respondents that tends to trust the EU institutions very much or to some degree has decreased somewhat again in 2015 and 2016. The image of a somewhat erosion of trust is even more apparent when we at the same time (in Fig. 4) can see that the satisfaction with democracy in the EU has decreased again since 2015. However, looking at the long-term trend, the levels of satisfaction and trust are still higher than that at the turn of the century.

It is also worth to remember that survey questions are posed in different ways and with different response options. Even a comparison of the question of trust in the EU institutions is difficult as in the Eurobarometer only offers two response alternatives (tend or tend not to trust), whereas

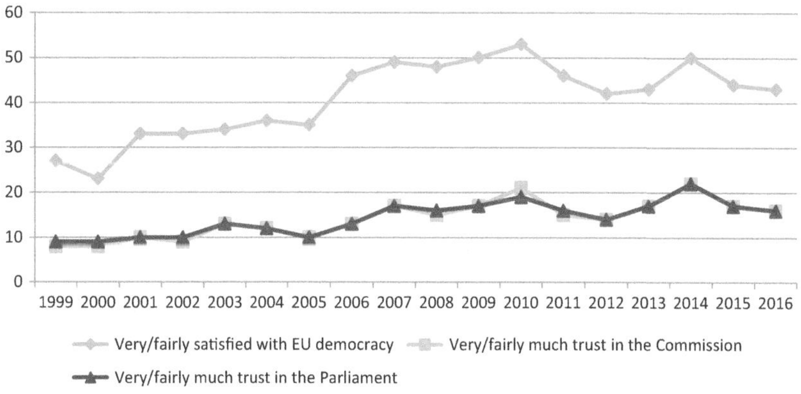

Fig. 4 Swedes' trust in EU institutions and satisfaction with democracy in the EU, 1999–2015 (per cent). Source: The National SOM study 1999–2016. The questions posed are 'How satisfied are you with the way democracy works in the EU?'; 'How much trust do you have for the way work is done in: the EU Commission; the European Parliament'. The response options are 'very/fairly satisfied; neither; not very/not at all satisfied' and 'very/fairly much trust; neither; fairly/very little trust'. The percentages are based on those who have answered the survey question

the response alternatives are more fine graded in the Swedish SOM-data, including a middle option (neither trusting nor not trusting) which tends to be the most common response, around 40–45 per cent.

Even if there are signs of decreased political trust in Sweden, especially in the form of trust in the EU institutions, the changes are not too dramatic. Nevertheless, if this is still a pattern in Sweden, it can be expected to be much more pronounced in countries where the effects of the economic and euro crisis were much more severe. The EU averages of public opinion can hide a large variation across countries, which is covered in the next section.

Trust in the EU in Different Member States

The trend over time is an important part of the discussion of citizens' trust in its own right. However, the averages across all EU member states do hide a lot of inter-country variation (as well as intra-country variation across different individuals and groups). This section starts with an overview of theoretical explanations of variations in (aggregated) levels of trust across countries, sometimes referred to as macro factors. These explanations usually concern differences in countries' economic situation, democratic stability, levels of corruption, functioning political authorities and political culture (Dalton, 2004; McLaren, 2017; Mishler & Rose, 2001).

Two broad main categories of explanations can be distinguished also at the macro level: factors relating to self-interest and factors relating to culture and identity. Applied to the issue of trust in the EU as a political system, we can thus examine explanations such as to what extent a country benefits from the membership in the EU (directly as well as to what extent the citizens perceive it to be beneficial), how long the country has been a member state and to what extent there is a European identity among the citizens.

Figure 5 displays the difference between those respondents with a positive image minus those with a negative image of the EU (the so-called opinion balance) in each country. Similar to Fig. 1 regarding the opinion trend over time, the main pattern in Fig. 5 also indicates a predominantly positive image of the EU in most countries. Nevertheless, the variation across countries is large, and the predominantly negative image can be found in countries where the economic and refugee crises have been most evident, such as Cyprus and Greece. More dominating negative image can

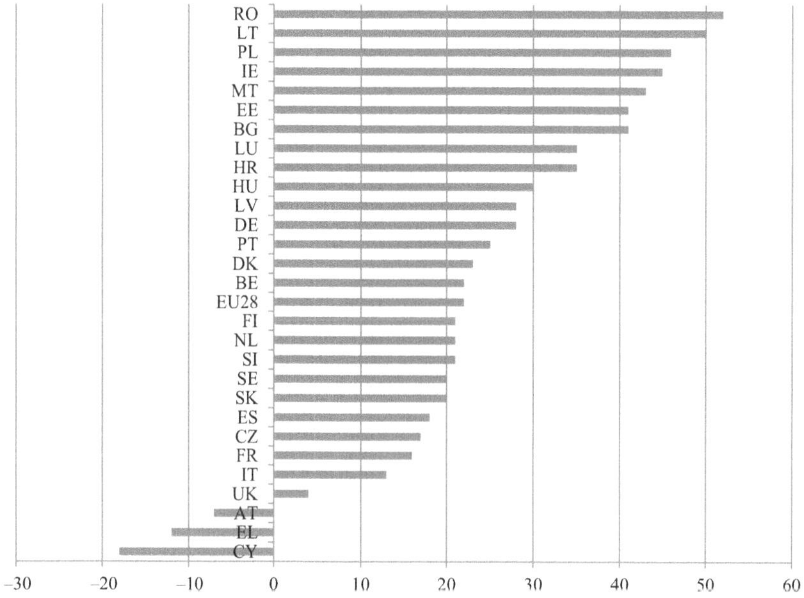

Fig. 5 Positive, negative or neutral image of the EU 2015 (opinion balance). Source: The Eurobarometer 2015. The question posed is 'In general, does the EU conjure up for you a very positive, fairly positive, neutral, fairly negative or very negative image?' The opinion balance is calculated by subtracting the share of respondents answering that they have a rather or very negative image from those answering that they have a fairly or very positive image

also be found in Austria, and in the UK, the 2015 opinion balance only had a few percentage points overweight to a positive image.

The largest shares of positive images can be found in a mix of EU member states. These positive images can, on the one hand, be found among large shares of the population in economically comparatively wealthy countries, such as Luxembourg and the Nordic countries, but, on the other hand, also in newer and more economically challenged member states such as Romania. To some extent this can be understood in terms of self-interest and rational factors in support for European integration (Hobolt & de Vries, 2016), but, for example, in Luxembourg, there is also a well-known prevailing European identification among the citizens, which also contributes to a higher share of positive attitudes to European integration (Kuhn, 2015). The overall impression regarding the cross-country variation thus corresponds to the pattern of the development over time previously shown; regarding the more diffuse support for the highest 'object', in the form of positive or negative image of the EU, the public opinion does not present too much of concern. However, as is seen in Fig. 6, the pattern again changes when we shift the attention to a more specific 'object' of political trust, that is, the European Parliament.

Trust in the European Parliament is much more varied across the member states of the EU. The opinion balance (i.e. the share of citizens answering they tend to trust the European Parliament subtracted by those answering that they do not tend to trust it) shows an almost half-split across the countries. Figure 6 illustrates several of the factors highlighted in previous research to be important in order to explain variation across

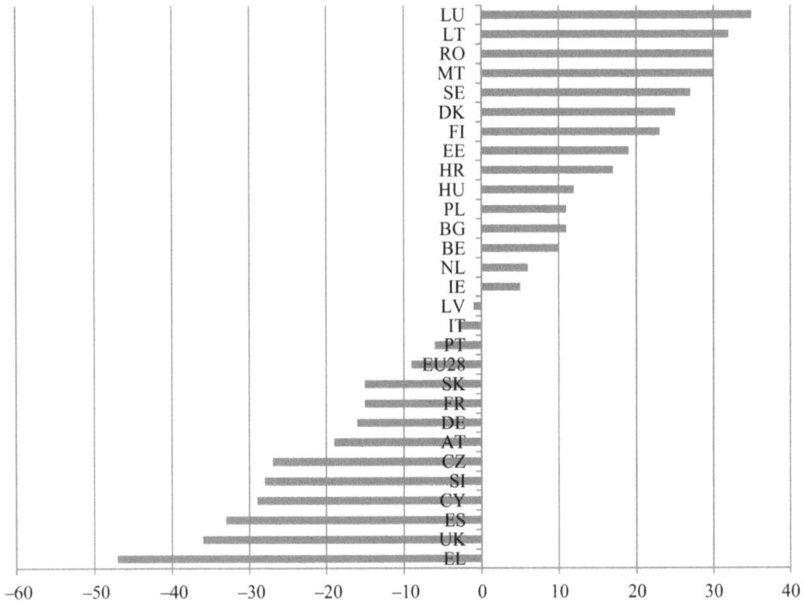

Fig. 6 Trust in the European Parliament 2015 (opinion balance). Source: The Eurobarometer. The same question is posed for several EU institutions and asks for each of them whether or not the respondent tend to trust or not tend to trust it. The opinion balance is calculated by subtracting the share of respondents answering that they tend not to trust from those answering that they tend to trust the European Parliament

countries. Starting at the top of the figure, we find among the countries with a positive opinion balance a number of stable countries with comparatively good economy and well-functioning political institutions, such as the Nordic countries. The top position is held by Luxembourg, which in addition to these factors also is one of the original founding member states and a very high share of citizens who feel as Europeans, a factor also known to affect trust in political institutions (Berg, 2007). But there are also a number of countries with a positive opinion balance which divert from this pattern, including Romania, Croatia and Hungary. This may seem counter-intuitive at first glance, but studies show that the comparison to the trust in national political institutions may end up favourably for the trust in European institutions. In countries where democratization is fairly recent and where problems with democracy, governance and corruption prevail, the EU institutions may be perceived as better governed and more well-functioning. Moreover, there is another factor that should be mentioned. The question of rational self-interest is not only in relation to overall economic development but also in relation to net gains of EU membership. According to this argument, citizens in countries that get more money back, mainly in the form of structural funds, from their EU membership compared to what they contribute, may be expected to have a generally more positive view on the EU in general as well as specific EU institutions.

In the lower half of Fig. 6, we find the countries where the opinion balance is negative, meaning that there is a higher share of citizens that tend to not trust the European Parliament than those who tend to trust it. In the very bottom we find on the one hand countries that have suffered extensively from the economic and financial crisis and the ensuing euro crisis, and the subsequent public retrenchments. Not too surprisingly, Greece is in the very bottom but also Spain and Cyprus show markedly large negative opinion balances. Dissatisfaction with national public service has been shown to have a clear negative effect on EU trust (Kumlin, 2009). The UK negative opinion balance can shed light on some of the other explanatory factors, that is, a lack of European identity and an overall scepticism to supra-state decision-making. In light of these figures, the outcome in the 'Brexit' referendum in June 2016 seems somewhat less surprising.

More problematic from a legitimacy perspective is that the opinion balance is negative in several of the oldest EU member states. Even in large core countries, such as Germany and France, we find more citizens responding that they tend not to trust the European Parliament than those who tend to trust it. This is a clear warning signal regarding the public trust in the EU decision-making institution which traditionally tends to have most trust among the EU institutions. It is furthermore problematic that this decreasing trust is so discernible considering the increased political powers the European Parliament has gained following the entry into force of the Lisbon Treaty in 2009.

Who Trusts the EU? Variations in Attitudes Across Individuals

In addition to the large variation in EU trust across countries, there is of course also a large variation across different individuals and groups within each country. The explanations of such variations among individuals are sometimes referred to as micro-level factors. Yet again the basic division in two main groups of explanations of trust and attitudes to the EU is useful. Also at the individual level, we can distinguish between explanations that mainly concern self-interest or economic rationality on the one hand and cultural factors relating to socialization and identification on the other hand (Berg, 2007; Mishler & Rose, 2001). In addition, cue taking and the importance of the national political context have also been shown to impact the individual-level variation in attitudes towards the EU (Hobolt & de Vries, 2016).

From a utilitarian, rational and self-interest perspective, those citizens who may have the most to gain from a membership in the EU can be expected to hold the most positive attitudes. These are factors relating to such aspects as high level of education, high income, youth, health, full employment associated with high-status persons living in bigger cities, whose working life benefits from European integration. Some scholars even argue that attitudes towards mass immigration and resistance to European integration have shifted the traditional focus of political debate, to be reinterpreted in terms of a new political cleavage, relating to the 'winners' and 'losers' of globalization (Kriesi et al., 2006).

Closely related are ideas that persons with a so-called high degree of political mobilization should find it easier to grasp such a highly complex political structure as the EU, and thus having fewer reasons to fear it. Several studies have confirmed that socioeconomic factors do matter for attitudes towards the EU, regardless of country, but it is far from the whole explanations and the importance of such factors tend to vary over time. One example of such a shift over time is that during the early days of

Swedish EU membership, men and older citizens tended to hold the most positive views, whereas, today, it is mainly the younger generation who tend to be most positive and the gender difference is no longer statistically significant (Berg & Bové, 2016). These changes over time illustrate another explanation, namely socialization. The EU membership may be perceived more natural to persons who have no memory of living in a country not being a member state. On the other hand, the younger generation can on average be thought to also perceive the EU membership from a self-interest point of view, regarding the potential of living, working or studying abroad in the near future.

Some other patterns associated with a utilitarian perspective have been more stable over time. It is more common for highly educated, white-collar workers living in big cities to be more positive towards the EU. But as Hooghe and Marks (2005) point out, even if rational self-interest arguments do play a role, it is not the full picture. The national debate regarding the EU is also very important. Many voters take cues from the political elite, political party, which they normally like or even identify with. The way the EU issues are politicized matter for the public's attitudes, and when the issues debated concern other aspects than economy, the chances are that other aspects, such as identity, will affect the EU attitude (Hooghe & Marks, 2005).

Among the more cultural aspects, it is thought to matter whether people have grown up (or if their parents have grown up) in other European countries. If so, they are expected to hold more positive views of the EU due to a socialization perspective. There are also some indications that people who have lived and worked in other EU states tend to be more positive to the European integration (Kuhn, 2015). This is usually related to the issue of individuals' identification with Europe. The question of a European identity is debated and can be understood and defined in different ways. Even when focusing only on the feelings individuals have, there are different views on how such feelings can and should be understood. From a more primordial view on identity, the national identification will always be strongest, or maybe even perceived as the only 'real' territorial identification. Contrastingly, from a constructivist view on identity as created, or an 'imagined' community, there is nothing strange about the potential of people identifying with several different territorial levels. Just as one person may identify with Munich, Bayern and Germany, another may identify with Scania, Sweden and Europe (Berg, 2007). In some parts of Europe, it is not even necessary that the state level is included among the levels of identification. As the recent events in Catalonia illustrate, there are definitely some people who identify with Barcelona, Catalonia and Europe—but not Spain. Most studies of identification and EU attitudes show that persons who identify only with their state—an exclusive national identification—tend to be the most negative towards the EU and European integration. People with a strong European identification on the other hand tend to have more positive attitudes to the EU, even in analyses controlling for rational, self-interest factors (Hooghe & Marks, 2004).

Who Trusts EU Institutions?

The overview of individual-level explanatory factors above has so far focused on variations in citizens' general EU attitudes and their countries' membership of the union. Using Easton's terminology, the focus has been the community 'object' of the trust in the EU as a political system. In this section, the emphasis is rather on the more specific trust in the EU institutions, which adds a few extra aspects. Given the fact that the 'object' of political trust—the political authorities—is placed further down and considered a more specific type of trust, there is an added expectation of specific factors to also be of higher importance. This is however not to say that diffuse aspects, such as European identity, are unimportant. As has been mentioned above, Easton argued that diffuse aspects of political trust could function as a reservoir of goodwill to sustain the overall system support through shorter periods of crises and citizen dissatisfaction (Easton, 1975).

Similar to studies on general attitudes towards the EU, a number of scholarly works have shown that persons who identify with Europe are more likely to also express trust in EU institutions to a higher degree than others, even under control for other explanatory factors (see below). The importance of a European identification tends to decrease but remains significant (Berg, 2007). However, in later years, the impact of European identification has been weaker, which potentially could be interpreted as a lack of strength of the idea of European identification as a reservoir of goodwill now, compared to the mid-2000s. Some other studies have especially focused on those individuals who identify equally strongly with all levels, from local levels (town or village) to Europe. In a study based on data from 2004, this group stood out as having the strongest level of trust in political institutions at all levels. It was even stronger than the trust in political institutions at one level (e.g. state) that individuals had who only identified with this level (e.g. an exclusive national identification). This relationship appeared in cross-section European data as well as national data (in Sweden). However, in 2015, those correlations are to a large degree lost when other factors are added to the analyses. This is again a signal of the importance to take the changing citizen attitudes towards the European Parliament seriously. The potential to lean back and rely on an expected reservoir of goodwill based on European identification is not really feasible anymore.

Turning to the difference in explanatory factors between general EU attitude and trust in EU institutions, one aspect is the expected importance of socioeconomic factors. One example concerns gender. While men in general have tended to be somewhat more positive to European integration at large, women tend to have a higher degree of trust in political institutions than men. Otherwise, most socioeconomic factors tend to have a somewhat lesser explanatory factor. While highly educated persons are mostly more pro-EU than those with a lower degree of education, this is not the case concerning institutional trust. Some scholars argue that this is due to the increased ability to understand and analyse decisions and policy outputs from EU institutions, and therefore also a higher likelihood to be critical.

While the general EU attitude may be supported by an idea of long-term gains, the trust in EU institutions is much closer connected to short-term evaluations of policy output. This brings us to the third form of explanatory factors, that is, the importance of the perceived economic and political development in one's own country, and to what extent that might spill over on to the trust in the EU institutions. This is often found in the so-called Blaming Europe approach (Hobolt & Tilley, 2014; Kumlin, 2009). The empirical analyses typically include survey items asking respondents about their perceptions of the national economy. These types of perceptions tend to have a fairly strong explanatory power regarding national political institutions (Mishler & Rose, 2001), but some scholars argue that such negative national evaluations of the economy also hit the trust for the EU institutions. This has also been more visible during stronger focus on the economic crises of the EU (Dotti Sani & Magistro, 2016).

In a fourth category of explanations, national politics is highlighted. Empirically, this usually entails adding questions about citizen evaluations of national government performance, as well as personal ideological preference. Ideological left-right preferences tend to affect incumbent evaluations. Citizens are more likely to make positive evaluations of incumbent governments they are ideologically close to. National party preferences also matter in another way. Voters tend to take cues from their party representatives regarding policy issues they feel less informed about (Armingeon & Ceka, 2013; Hooghe & Marks, 2005). Hence, the existence of political parties that actively politicize dissatisfaction with the EU institutions also increase the likelihood of partisans expressing similar views.

If we are to take seriously the theoretical expectation that actual politics matter for political trust, we must also investigate political outcome, for example, by analysing the expected impact of European decision-making within a number of policy areas (Hobolt & Tilley, 2013). This can be seen as a fifth factor. We already know that there is a large variation in perceptions of the impact of EU membership, depending on which policy issues are at stake. Some examples of this include that Swedish citizens tend to have fairly positive views regarding the impact of the EU membership on issues such as the conditions for enterprises, or research and innovation, whereas the views are much more negative regarding issues relating to crime, immigration and national self-determination. These forms of evaluations of different policy areas also tend to have a large and significant explanatory power in statistical analyses. People who think that EU membership has had a positive impact on most policy areas are, quite naturally, more likely to also express a higher degree of trust in the EU institutions. Reversely, dissatisfaction with the EU's influence in several policy areas tends to correlate with much lower degrees of trust in the political institutions of the EU (Berg & Bové, 2016; Bové, 2015).

The Citizens' Trust in the EU Decreases Most Where the Crises Have Been Most Salient

This chapter focuses on the vertical form of trust, that is, the trust citizens may have (or not) for the political system. Two aspects have been highlighted: first a more general attitude towards the EU, as well as the attitude towards one's countries membership, and secondly trust in the EU institutions, especially the European Parliament. The choice of these two aspects is based on the well-known political system support model by Easton (1965, 1975) and his argument about the importance of distinguishing between the different objects, or components, of political support. The first aspect corresponds to Easton's support for 'the political community' and the second to support for 'the political authorities'. Whereas the former is expected to be more closely connected to diffuse, affective emotions, the latter is expected to be more closely connected to specific, rational attitudes.

The analyses of survey data over time and across EU member states in this chapter show firstly that long-term political trust concerning the general EU attitude (as well as for one's countries EU membership) is declining. It is however a fairly slow decrease. It is, since 2010, most common for respondents (just under 40 per cent) to have a neutral image of the EU, in contrast to the previously most common 'fairly positive' image, which is now second. The share of respondents with a 'fairly negative' image is around 20 per cent. There are in other words no drastic shifts over time, not even during the height of the economic and financial crisis and euro crises, and the negative views are not dominating.

Nonetheless, there is a much more pronounced decline in the specific trust in the European Parliament and other EU institutions. This is especially noticeable from 2011 and onwards, when the majority of respondents (45–50 per cent) in EU28 have answered that they tend not to trust the European Parliament. Even in a country like Sweden, which has been comparatively less affected by the crises, it is apparent that the trust in the European Parliament decreased significantly from 2010. Regarding the more diffuse form of political system support, the Swedish public opinion has been in favour of the EU membership since 2001, with a dip around 2012, but a return to around 50 per cent the last three years. There is, however, no similar bounce back in trust in the EU institutions during the last years.

Aggregated data over time naturally subdues a lot of country variations. A closer look at variations across the EU member states reinforces the overall image. Regarding the issue of a general attitude of the EU, more people tend to be positive than negative in most countries, with the exception of Greece, Cyprus and Austria. But the country variation is much larger concerning the issue of trust in the European Parliament. Countries where more citizens tend to trust the Parliament can usually be described as being comparatively politically and economically stable, or contrastingly, as countries where the citizens' trust in the national political institutions tends to be even lower. The trust in the European Parliament can thus be expected to be larger if the citizens consider the Parliament as a higher political level of an overall well-functioning political system—or where it can be seen as the less problematic level in countries where the national political system is seen as flawed.

Variations in attitudes across individuals can to a large extent be understood in relation to the two main groups of explanations discussed in the chapter; rationality (self-interest) and cultural factors such as identity. The former often relates to who benefits or not from European integration, which also connects to the issue of 'winners' and 'losers' of globalization more broadly. Young, healthy and well-educated people living in cities are more likely to hold positive attitudes. Territorial identifications matter too. Especially the correlation between having a strong, excluding national identification and a negative image of the EU (or disliking one's country's membership of the EU) has increased lately.

Regarding the more specific trust in the EU institutions, there are also other aspects that matter, such as the importance of political cues from the national elite, and the relevance of perceptions of national and EU performance. One noteworthy change over time concerns the influence of identification with Europe on trust for the EU institutions. While a relationship still exists in analyses on newer survey data, it is noticeable that it is weak, and that the ability to counterweight other attitudes and dissatisfaction is limited. In the light of the slowly decreasing diffuse support for the EU as a political community, this highlights the importance of Easton's thinking. He stated that the diffuse form of political system support could function as a 'reservoir of goodwill' during shorter periods of turmoil and crises, but that after a while this diffuse form of system support could also be affected, which would reduce this function. A loss of this more diffuse support is also more difficult to restore.

Can Citizens' Trust in the EU Increase?

Despite that the citizens' trust in the EU as a political system is decreasing, it is important to remember that the development is not unambiguous. There is a large variation across countries and individuals depending on what form of trust we focus on, what objects (or components) of the total political system support. In addition, declining trust is part of a global trend, also affecting national communities, regimes and authorities.

Nevertheless, some aspects merit further attention. National political parties and actors have an important role to play in order to respond to and direct dissatisfaction in different directions. It is not unusual to see national political actors frame an issue as 'dictated by Brussels' to avoid criticism for unpopular decisions or claim national credit for popular results of common EU decisions. In a complex multilevel governance structure, it can be beneficial in the short term to avoid criticism in this way, but it is a perilous strategy that can backfire, as in the case of 'Brexit', and gradually contribute to erode the overall political system support. For political decision-makers who do after all consider the EU to be overall beneficial, it is important to not allow simplified images to dominate but rather to trust that most citizens are both able and willing to better understand how political decisions are made, and why. Honesty about the often difficult balance between effectiveness and influence, and proper arguments as to why certain decisions were made, as well as why the European cooperation is considered beneficial, would be a more long-term sustainable strategy.

The question of the citizens' trust in the EU as a political system is about so much more than merely one organization and a few institutions. The austerity measures imposed on countries heavily affected by the economic and financial crisis and the euro crises have illuminated how deeply interconnected the European economies are, and that especially in the eurozone there are limitations for national policy decisions. This in turn also affects the trust for the national political institutions. Trust in national parliaments decreased dramatically during the height of the crisis, and citizens have noticed that actors such as the EU, but also the IMF, put restraints on what political decisions are possible. And the support for democracy has also decreased.

In this chapter, it has been noted that the so-called reservoir of goodwill seems to no longer be enough to support trust in the EU in general. The years of crises have started to erode the identification with Europe, and the overall image of the EU, in countries such as Italy and Spain, which used to be on top in survey studies of these issues. Recommendations for EU in addressing these problems concern the immanent importance of listening and understanding citizens' concerns, knowledge and preferences. More nuanced knowledge of what issues and what solutions are preferred by the citizens is needed, as well as information on the EU directed to the general public and schools. We also need to better understand how public opinion swings occur, who is driving these forces and with what techniques and purpose, especially in an EU context. Some scholars argue that people can have conflicting attitudes regarding the EU at the same time. Others emphasize the multidimensionality aspect that it is one thing to analyse citizens' attitudes towards the EU as it looks today and quite another thing to analyse whether citizens prefer the EU to develop in a certain direction in the future. Many who are overall positive to the EU are at the same time negative to further European integration. They basically accept status quo, but nothing more. This is another aspect to consider for future EU reforms. The timing is probably not right to move forward with deepened—or widening—integration. Handling the consequences of 'Brexit' as well as possible for all parties involved and focusing on preserving the remaining EU27 will probably be an ambitious enough agenda for the coming years.

References

Aggestam, L., & Johansson, M. (2017). The leadership paradox in EU foreign policy. *JCMS: Journal of Common Market Studies*. https://doi.org/10.1111/jcms.12558 (Published online 26 April 2017).

Armingeon, K., & Ceka, B. (2013). The loss of trust in the European Union during the great recession since 2007: The role of heuristics from the national political system. *European Union Politics, 15*(1), 82–107.

Berg, L. (2007). *Multi-level Europeans. The influence of territorial attachments on political trust and welfare attitudes.* Gothenburg: University of Gothenburg.

Berg, L., & Bové, K. (2016). *Svenskarnas attityder till EU har stabiliserats. Analys av SOM-institutets undersökning 2015. 2016:9epa.* Stockholm: Swedish Institute for European Policy Studies.

Bové, K. (2015). *Does time make more converts than reason? An analysis of what drives public opinion towards the European Union in Sweden* (MA thesis in European Studies). Gothenburg: Department of Political Science. Retrieved from https://gupea.ub.gu.se/handle/2077/44617

Dalton, J. R. (2004). *Democratic challenges, democratic choices. The erosion of political support in advanced industrial democracies.* New York: Oxford University Press.

Dalton, J. R. (2013). *Citizen politics. Public opinion and political parties in advanced industrial democracies.* London: Sage Publications.

Deutsch, K. W. (1966). Integration and arms control in the European political environment: A summary report. *American Political Science Review, 60*(2), 354–365.

Dotti Sani, G. M., & Magistro, B. (2016). Increasingly unequal? The economic crisis, social inequalities and trust in the European Parliament in 20 European countries. *European Journal of Political Research, 55*(2), 246–264.

Easton, D. (1965). *A systems analysis of political life.* Chicago: The University of Chicago Press.

Easton, D. (1975). A re-assessment of the concept of political support. *British Journal of Political Science, 5*(4), 435–457.

Hobolt, S. B. (2016). The Brexit vote: A divided nation, a divided continent. *Journal of European Public Policy, 23*(9), 1259–1277.
Hobolt, S. B., & Tilley, J. (2013). Who's in charge? How voters attribute responsibility in the European Union. *Comparative Political Studies, 47*(6), 795–819.
Hobolt, S. B., & Tilley, J. (2014). *Blaming Europe? Responsibility without accountability in the European Union*. Oxford: Oxford University Press.
Hobolt, S. B., & Tilley, J. (2016). Fleeing the centre: The rise of challenger parties in the aftermath of the euro crisis. *West European Politics, 39*(5), 971–991.
Hobolt, S. B., & de Vries, C. E. (2016). Public support for European integration. *Annual Review of Political Science, 19*(1), 413–432.
Hooghe, L., & Marks, G. (2004). Does identity or economic rationality drive public opinion on European integration? *PS: Political Science & Politics, 37*(3), 415–420.
Hooghe, L., & Marks, G. (2005). Calculation, community, and cues: Public opinion on European integration. *European Union Politics, 6*(4), 419–443.
Hooghe, L., & Marks, G. (2009). A postfunctionalist theory of European integration: From permissive consensus to constraining dissensus. *British Journal of Political Science, 39*(1), 1–23.
Kriesi, H., Grande, E., Lachat, R., Dolezal, M., Bornschier, S., & Frey, T. (2006). Globalization and the transformation of the national political space: Six European countries compared. *European Journal of Political Research, 45*(6), 921–956.
Kuhn, T. (2015). *Experiencing European integration. Transnational lives and European identity*. Oxford: Oxford University Press.
Kumlin, S. (2009). Blaming Europe? Exploring the variable impact of national public service dissatisfaction on EU trust. *Journal of European Social Policy, 19*(5), 408–420.
McLaren, L. (2017). Immigration, national identity and political trust in European democracies. *Journal of Ethnic and Migration Studies, 43*(3), 379–399.
Mishler, W., & Rose, R. (2001). What are the origins of political trust? Testing institutional and cultural theories in post-communist societies. *Comparative Political Studies, 34*(1), 30–62.
Norris, P. (Ed.). (1999). *Critical citizens. Global support for democratic government*. Oxford: Oxford University Press.
Serricchio, F., Tsakatika, M., & Quaglia, L. (2013). Euroscepticism and the global financial crisis. *JCMS: Journal of Common Market Studies, 51*(1), 51–64.
Tosun, J., Wetzel, A., & Zapryanova, G. (Eds.). (2015). *Coping with crisis: Europe's challenges and strategies*. London: Routledge.
Warren, M. E. (Ed.). (1999). *Democracy and trust*. Cambridge: Cambridge University Press.
Zmerli, S., & van der Meer, T. W. G. (Eds.). (2017). *Handbook on political trust*. Cheltenham: Edward Elgar.

Is Migration Threatening Social Trust in Europe?

Andreas Bergh

A salient challenge for Europe is to make the most of the possibilities and to minimize the problems created by migration between countries. This applies to both migration within the EU and migration between the EU and other countries. According to estimates from the World Bank, slightly more than 3 percent of the world's population is residing in a country that is not their country of birth. The share is expected to increase to 5 percent over the next generation. Considering that the world's population is growing rapidly, these are large numbers. In a European context, the enlargements of the EU in 2004 and 2007 meant that many citizens from Poland have migrated to Ireland and the UK, and many from Bulgaria and Romania have migrated to Italy and Spain. More recently, refugee migration from Syria mainly to Lebanon, Jordan and Turkey, and also to EU member states, has put migration even higher on the agenda.

It bears noting that migration is often a highly effective way for people to improve their own lives. Clemens (2011) famously suggested that constraints on migration from poor to richer countries may be the greatest single distortion in the global economy. Hamilton and Whalley (1984) used data from 1977 to argue that the annual gains from free labor

A. Bergh (✉)
Lund University, Lund, Sweden

A. Bakardjieva Engelbrekt et al. (eds.), *Trust in the European Union in Challenging Times*, https://doi.org/10.1007/978-3-319-73857-4_5

mobility might significantly exceed global GNP. More recent estimates have revised the gains from free movement of labor substantially upwards (Docquier, Rapoport, & Salomone, 2012; Moses & Letnes, 2004). It is also clear, however, that migration can lead to frictions and social conflicts, possibly more so when people move to a place where complex social structures and institutions are already in place. This is especially true when people migrate to countries with fairly generous welfare arrangements (Storesletten, 2003).

This chapter discusses one specific challenge associated with migration: the relationship between migration and social trust. As will be shown, social trust is a key factor for both economic development and welfare state sustainability. It is thus important to ask if there are reasons to assume that migration and social trust are difficult to combine. The crucial importance of social trust comes from the fact that a society where people trust each other will work better in several ways. Large migration flows and ethnic diversity could potentially adversely affect social trust. Knowledge about the association between trust and migration is especially important considering the fact that migration flows often begin in countries with dysfunctional social institutions such as countries with high levels of corruption and end in countries with higher institutional quality. In addition to the example of Syria, a case in point for Europe recently is migration from Greece, which is often triggered by discontent with high levels of corruption (New Diaspore, 2016).

If social trust turns out to be highly fragile with respect to migration and diversity, the policy implications are difficult and need to be discussed thoroughly. If, on the other hand, social trust is relatively robust, migration may be one of the most efficient ways of helping those who are unfortunate enough to be born in countries with inferior institutions and low standards of living. This chapter summarizes research on the relationship between migration and social trust. First, social trust and its consequences are explained and discussed. Then, three ways in which social trust could be affected by migration are described. Finally, an attempt is made to address the question on how to strengthen social trust in contexts with high migration flows.

What Is Social Trust?

Social (or generalized) trust is the individual attitude that most people can be trusted. More specifically, it is the prior belief that other people will act honestly and trustworthy in situations where they also have the option to benefit themselves by not behaving trustworthy. People with high social trust are more prone to believing that anonymous others will act honestly and trustworthy, whereas people with lower trust are more prone to thinking that you cannot be too careful when dealing with other people.

The importance of trust can be analyzed in a game-theoretic setting. In the well-known trust game (Berg, Dickhaut, & McCabe, 1995), the first player (called the trustor) can make an investment that increases the payoff of the second player (called the trustee). The trustee can reciprocate by sending at least something back to the trustor. Because the investment is multiplied when it reaches the trustee, the total payoff will be higher. The investment would be maximized if and only if the trustor invests the full endowment. The catch is that a selfish trustee will not reciprocate and should thus not be trusted.

As noted by Arrow (1972), trust is a crucial element in most economic transactions. The seller of a good or a service must trust that the buyer will pay the price agreed upon, and the buyer must trust the seller regarding the nature of the good or the service. When buyers and sellers are already familiar with each other, the necessary mutual trust can more easily be achieved. The attitude that 'most people' can be trusted simplifies transactions also among people who do not know each other and perhaps have never even met. It is in that specific sense that social trust is fundamentally different from particularized trust, that is, trust in specific persons or organizations.

The simplest and also the most common way to measure social trust is to ask people to what extent they agree with the proposition that 'most people can be trusted'. The question can be asked as a yes/no question, but respondents can also be asked to answer on a numerical scale, where the extremes are the propositions 'most people can be trusted' and 'you can't be too careful when dealing with other people' (or similar statements). Questions regarding 'other people' or 'most people' may seem vague and difficult to answer. In fact, these questions are typically perceived to be easy to answer, and they are also easy to translate to different languages. Most importantly, the way an individual answers the question about whether 'most people' can be trusted has been shown to correlate with behavior in precisely the type of situations where trust theoretically should matter, that is, so-called social dilemmas, both experimentally and in real life (Acedo & Gomila, 2013; Sønderskov, 2011; Thöni, Tyran, & Wengström, 2012).

Figure 1 illustrates the share of the population with high social trust in 19 European countries according to *European social survey* in 2014 com-

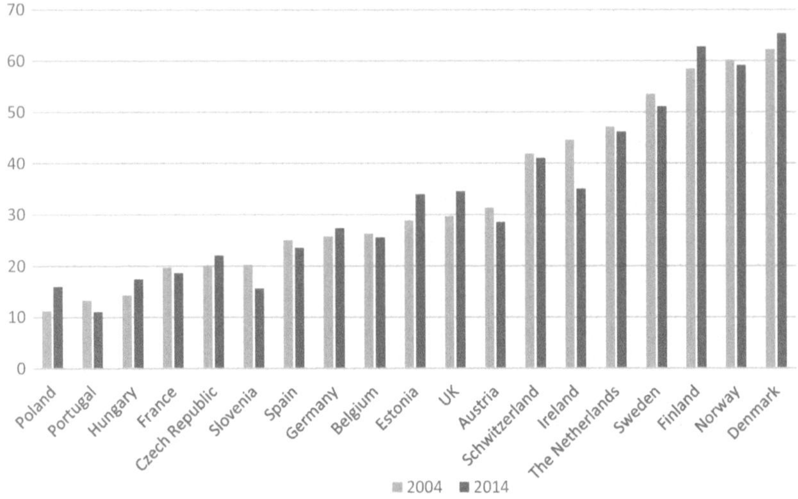

Fig. 1 Trust in selected European countries. Source: European Social Survey (2004) and (2014). The numbers in the figure represent the percentage of respondents with high social trust

pared to 2004. Two facts are worth noting here. First, that social trust seems to be highly stable over time. Second, that there are large differences between different countries. Among the few noteworthy changes, we see a decrease in social trust in Ireland and small increases in Estonia and Poland. The pattern—small changes over time, large differences between countries—is the same in other surveys and holds also for other time periods.

Using Eurostat's Urban Audit, Fig. 2 illustrates social trust in 14 European cities, by summing those who fully or partly agree that most people can be trusted. Trust is very high in Helsinki, Copenhagen and Stockholm. The fact that Sweden's third biggest city, Malmö, is somewhat lower highlights the fact that there are often important differences within countries. Istanbul and Athens are among the cities where trust is lowest according to data from Eurostat.

As can be seen in both Figs. 1 and 2, the differences in social trust within Europe are large. The same is true within the EU, where the difference between the highest and the lowest average trust levels are almost as the difference between the highest and lowest levels of trust globally. The

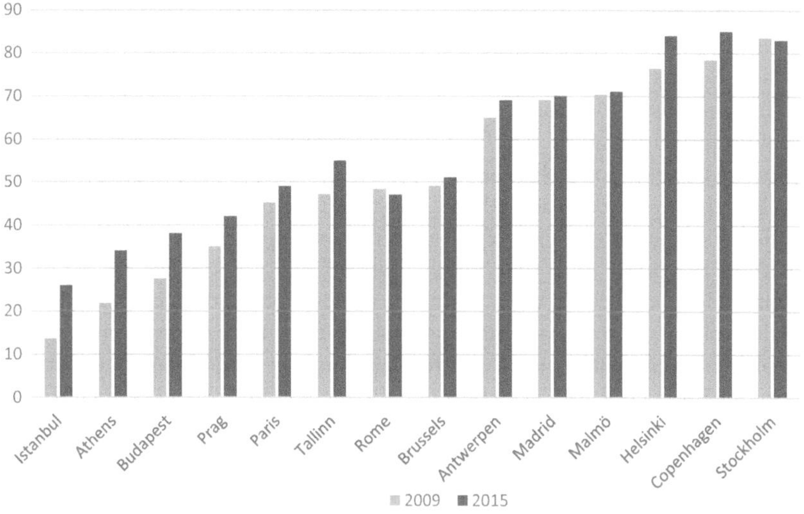

Fig. 2 Share with high trust in selected European cities. Source: Eurostat Urban Audit (2009) and (2015). The numbers in the figure represent the percentage of respondents with high social trust

EU includes Denmark which is probably the country with the highest trust level among all countries in the world, and the countries with the lowest average trust in the EU have only slightly higher average trust levels than Belize and Cambodia, which are both typically found at the bottom in global surveys. Increasing migration within the EU thus means migration between countries with very different levels of social trust.

Why Is Trust Important?

It is not known for sure how people interpret the trust question about 'other people'. One possibility is that when we answer questions about other people, we implicitly reveal something about ourselves. There are also indications that the social trust question is interpreted as referring to people with whom the respondent does not identify, that is, the so-called outgroup (Delhey, Newton, & Welzel, 2011). Bjørnskov (2010) notes that in the long run, trust and trustworthiness cannot logically differ systematically at the macro level unless individuals fully ignore their experience with other people. The implication is that when social trust is constantly high, it is an indication of high average trustworthiness. That interpretation is also supported by experimental evidence (Sapienza, Toldra-Simats, & Zingales, 2013).

A hands-on indication that the standard social trust question captures something important is the 'lost wallet' experiment. When the Reader's Digest Magazine lost 192 wallets in 16 cities across the world, the share of wallets that were returned to the owner is positively correlated with the social trust measured in surveys. In all, it is perhaps not surprising that the share of the population that agrees that most people can be trusted on a country level correlates with a number of desirable outcomes. Social trust is also related to state capacity, in the sense that it is easier to initiate and implement political projects and reforms such as social insurance institutions and universal welfare when social trust is high. The combination of trust and trustworthiness also means that systems such as these are less likely to be exposed to fraud or misuse. Empirically, the positive correlation between historical trust levels and welfare state size is strong, also when controlling for other factors that explain welfare state size (Bergh & Bjørnskov, 2011; Bjørnskov & Svendsen, 2013).

Trust has also been shown to be positively correlated with macroeconomic stability (Sangnier, 2013), and trust plays an important part in explaining economic reforms: trust facilitates liberalizing reforms and makes deliberalizing them more difficult (Berggren & Bjørnskov, 2017). For central bank independence reforms, the need for reform is greater, the lower social trust is, and the ability to undertake reform is greater, the higher social trust is (Berggren, Daunfeldt, & Hellström, 2016). It has also been shown that interest rates and credit ratings are more sensitive to inflation and growth problems in low-trust countries compared to high-trust countries (Bergh & Bjørnskov, 2018).

Countries with higher social trust are also characterized by lower levels of regulation (Aghion, Algan, Cahuc, & Shleifer, 2010). A plausible interpretation of that finding is that trust toward people in general means a higher trust in business owners to make decisions without interfering laws and regulations. Perhaps most importantly, there is also a causal association between country-level trust and economic growth (Algan & Cahuc, 2013). To summarize, social trust is a crucial factor for understanding economic development and why some countries are able to combine high taxes with a strong economic development.

Countries with high average social trust also tend to have high institutional quality (Bjørnskov, 2007). This means that they are characterized by rule of law, low corruption, independent courts and a relatively efficient public bureaucracy. It is difficult, however, to establish if these associations reflect a causality from trust to institutions, from institutions to trust or from something else to both trust and institutions (Berggren & Jordahl, 2006). In any case, the strength of the cross-country correlation means that countries with low average social trust are almost exclusively countries with high levels of corruption and inferior institutions, regardless of which way causality runs.

At the individual level, there are also benefits from having high social trust. On average, it is beneficial to put trust in others. People with higher trust in others are more successful economically and also rate their health as being better (Ljunge, 2014a). Partially, this is likely to be a psychological effect, but there is also a very real economic effect: in many cases, beneficial economic outcomes require putting trust in others—which is a risky decision. By abstaining from many interactions, the low-trusting person will minimize losses and also miss many opportunities. When people on average are more likely to be trustworthy, the trusting will in most cases be rewarded. There is a catch, however: having too much trust in low-trust environments may result in other people taking advantage of you. The right amount of trust thus seems to be high, but one should be careful not to be naïve (Butler, Giuliano, & Guiso, 2016).

Trust and Migration: Three Reasons to Worry

Why would high levels of social trust be affected by migration? There are three ways in which migration may affect trust, that all have been subjected to research, albeit to different degrees:

1. Migrants from countries with low average trust levels who move to high-trust countries may bring lower trust to the new country, thereby lowering the average level of social trust in the new country;
2. Migrants from high-trust countries to low-trust countries with inferior institutions may lower their trust as a result of experiences in the new country;
3. Migration (of all kinds) may lead to higher ethnic diversity, which may adversely impact social trust.

Ultimately, it is an empirical question whether there indeed exists a trade-off between trust and migration. If low average trust levels in some countries is a result of these countries having inferior institutions, it is possible (and perhaps even plausible) that migrating to a country with better institutions means that the individual belief about other people changes for the better. Knowing that a functioning, non-corrupt legal system is in place might prompt people to infer that illegal, dishonest and cheating behavior is being punished and therefore that most people can be trusted. The same reasoning would however apply in the reverse, that is, that migrants from high-trust countries to countries with inferior institutions will not bring their high-trust levels with them.

When it comes to the effect that ethnic heterogeneity has on social trust, there are competing claims. According to the contact hypothesis, more contacts between different groups will decrease social frictions and promote mutual understanding. According to the conflict hypothesis, the effect is the opposite: more contacts between groups with different nationalities or ethnicities strengthen the feelings of solidarity within each group but increase distrust and competition between them. The effect of ethnic heterogeneity on social trust has been studied intensively empirically.

Migration from Countries with Low Trust

What happens when a person migrates from a low-trust country to a high-trust country? Theoretically, several factors are likely to be relevant. To a certain degree, social trust is a part of a person's personality and thus something that is constant over different contexts. On the other hand, trust is also likely to be influenced by experiences of other peoples' behavior, as well as by expectations about the behavior of others. In that sense, it is rational to be not so trusting in a country where distrust is the prevailing norm and more trusting in a country where trust and trustworthiness prevail. If institutions matter, as described above, one would also expect the same person to have higher trust in an environment with higher institutional quality.

A number of studies have examined social trust among migrants from low-trust countries to high-trust countries, for example, by studying migration from Turkey to Denmark. Ideally, trust would be observed both in the country of origin and in the destination country, but such data have not been analyzed. By comparing, for example, Turks residing in Turkey to Turks who have migrated to Denmark, and by making the comparisons

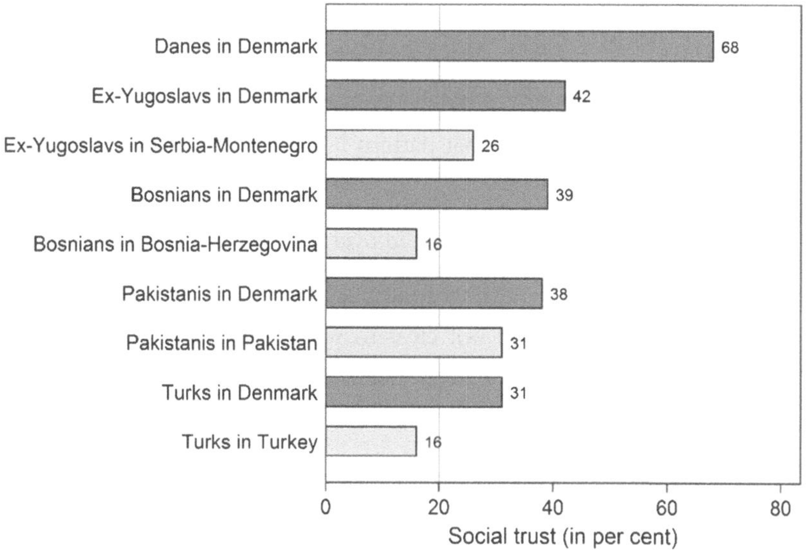

Fig. 3 Trust among different migrant groups in Denmark compared to home country trust and native Danes. Source: Nannestad, Tinggaard Svendsen, Thisted Dinesen and Mannemar Sønderskov (2014) and World Values Survey.[1]

between people with similar characteristics, it has been shown that Turks who have migrated to Denmark are more trusting than those who remain in Turkey. As indicated in Fig. 3, the same pattern holds also for other countries of origin with lower trust than Denmark.

Because trust varies with factors such as age, education and income, the comparisons illustrated in Fig. 3 are made between Turks in Denmark and Turks in Turkey that are as similar as possible when it comes to these individual characteristics. Doing so minimizes the risk that differences in trust are a result of selection bias that will exist if Turks who decide to migrate to Denmark tend to be more highly trusting than those who stay in Turkey. It is still possible, however, that the comparison is influenced by selection of some personal trait that is not observed and captured by the data. For example, it has been shown that people with higher trust tend to have better health. That means it is possible that the higher trust among Turks in Denmark compared to Turks in Turkey is not a result of Danish institutions but rather a result driven by Turks with good health being more common among those who migrate (either in general or to Denmark).

It is also worth noting that while trust among Turks in Denmark is higher than among Turks in Turkey, it is still only roughly half of the trust among Danes in Denmark. That pattern holds for all immigrant groups studied. There are also no signs in the study by Nannestad and colleagues (2014) that trust increases with the time spent in Denmark. Other studies have found that social trust is inherited over generations, and especially so from the mother's side (Ljunge, 2014b). In all, while immigrants from low-trust countries typically have higher trust than those who remain in the home country, it is still not clear to what extent that is a result of migrants being more trusting or a result of migration to countries with better institutions.

Migration from Countries with High Trust

Several studies have analyzed trust in the context of migration from low-trust countries to high-trust countries. Much less has been done regarding the opposite direction of migration flows, that is, when people migrate from a high-trust country to a low-trust country. When people migrate from the Nordic countries, most destination countries will be countries with lower trust and inferior institutions.

Trust among migrants from a high-trust country was first analyzed by Dinesen (2016) using answers from a special survey conducted by the Swedish Society, Opinion and Media (SOM) institute directed toward Swedish expatriates in 2014. The data clearly show that Swedish expatriates are a highly trusting subsample of the already highly trusting Swedish population. Using the same survey data, Bergh and Öhrvall (2016) showed that these differences remain when controlling for several individual characteristics such as age, sex, education and political orientation. Even more interesting is that one factor explains the entire difference in trust between Swedes in Sweden and migrants from Sweden, namely self-rated health. Swedish expatriates perceive their health to be better than the average Swedish person, and that difference explains why trust is higher among Swedish expatriates compared to the Swedish population.

What has happened to social trust among Swedish expatriates who have lived a long time in countries with inferior institutions? Bergh and Öhrvall (2016) show that the answer depends on the age at which the person arrived in the new country. Among those who were older than 30 years when they arrived, trust is independent of length of stay even in the most corrupt countries. On the other hand, expatriates who were 30 or less when they arrived to highly corrupt countries and to countries with inferior rule of law are likely to adjust their trust levels downwards. This finding thus confirms the hypothesis that institutions affect trust.

The finding that age at emigration matters supports the so-called impressionable years hypothesis in psychological research (Krosnick & Alwin, 1989). As can be seen in Fig. 4, the adjustment of social trust seems to take place during the first ten years, and there are no signs of further decrease. In fact, because the trust levels in this group is very high among those who have recently arrived in their new country, the level that appears to be stable among those who have spent ten or more years in their new country is very close to the level of trust among Swedes in Sweden (which has been roughly constant for several decades).

In countries where corruption is low, there is no correlation between trust and time spent in the new country—regardless of age at arrival. In short, the findings support the idea that institutions and experiences matter for trust, but institutions seem to be detrimental for trust only when people are in their impressionable years. It is also worth emphasizing that while many of the effects are statistically significant at traditional levels, the decrease in trust is not huge. Young Swedish expatriates are initially highly trusting (around 8 on the 0–10 scale), but those who have lived longer than five years in the most corrupt countries have average trust, somewhere between six and seven, with no signs of a further decrease. These results also fit well with the fact that US citizens with Swedish ancestry are still today more likely to agree that most people can be trusted.

Migration, Ethnic Heterogeneity and Trust

In addition to how trust among migrants themselves may change as a result of migrating to another country, increasing migration may lead to increasing ethnic heterogeneity, which may in itself affect social trust, also among those who were born in the destination country. The relationship between ethnic heterogeneity and social trust has been studied intensively by sociologists, political scientists and economists (for a recent survey, see Dinesen & Sønderskov, 2018). Several studies in the US suggest that states with more ethnic heterogeneity also have lower trust. Studies done in Europe show more varying results, and a recent Swedish study indicated a negative effect from ethnic heterogeneity on trust toward the local community but not for trust toward people in general (Lundstedt & Nissling, 2016).

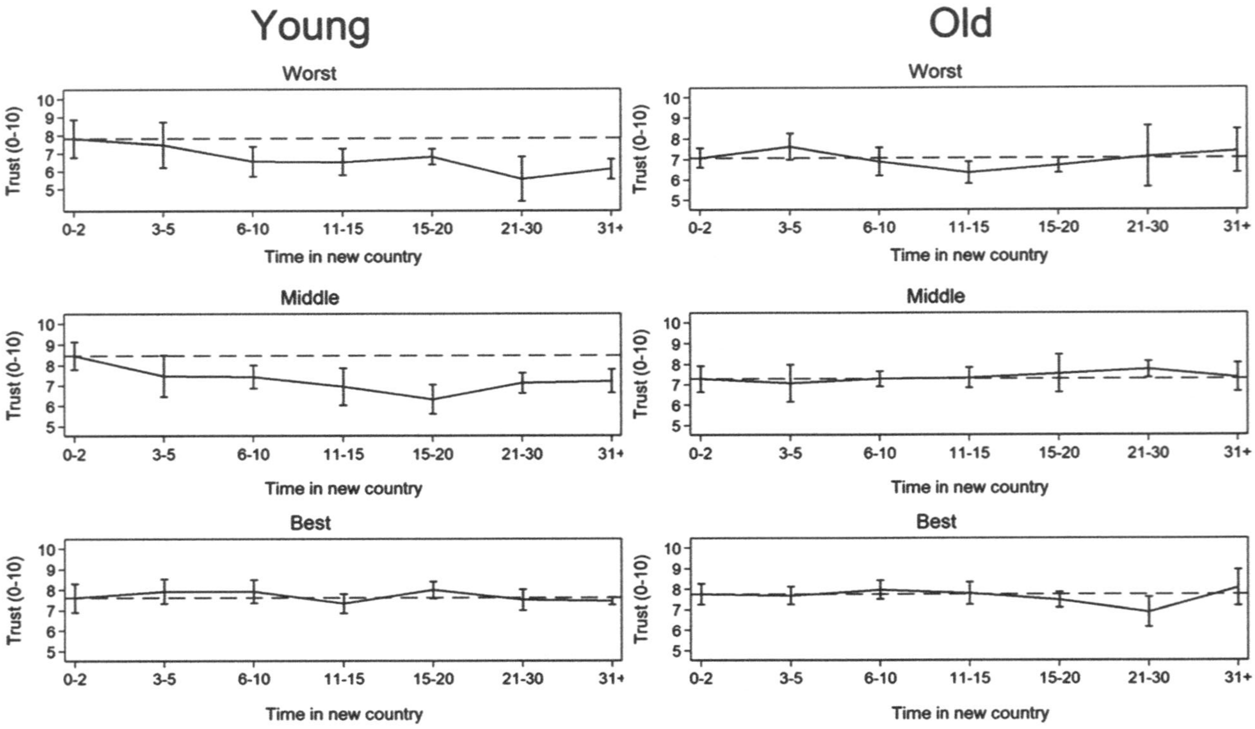

Fig. 4 The effect on trust of length of stay in countries with different degrees of perceived corruption depending on age at arrival (cut-offs ≤30, >30). Source: Bergh and Öhrvall (2016). The graphs show trust controlling for individual characteristics including self-rated health

The cross-country association between social trust and ethnic heterogeneity is negative, but the size of the effect is small and statistical significance is low. In comparison, when it comes to significance, size and robustness to controlling for other factors that matter for trust, ethnic heterogeneity is much less important for trust than, for example, country-level income inequality (Bjørnskov, 2008; Jordahl, 2008). There are also studies that suggest that individuals who regularly talk with their neighbors are less influenced by the racial and ethnic character of their surroundings than people who lack such social interaction (Stolle, Soroka, & Johnston, 2008).

In a detailed Danish study, Dinesen and Sønderskov (2015) identified effects of ethnic heterogeneity on social trust levels of native Danes. They argue that people use the local cues available to them when evaluating the overall trustworthiness of others. One such cue is the ethnic background of others in one's social environment. By examining the relationship between ethnic diversity and social trust in small geographical areas down to a radius of 80 meters of the place of residence, they find a negative effect of ethnic diversity in small areas, what they call micro-contexts. The relationship becomes insignificant in more aggregate contexts and ceases to exist in the most aggregate context they examine, which is a circle with a radius of 2500 meters (roughly a third of the size of Manhattan).

Studies have also examined if the relationship is moderated by other factors. For example, one might expect the trust of people with higher education to be less sensitive to ethnic diversity. The effect of local diversity, however, seems to be independent of not only education but also length of residence in neighborhood, gender, income and unemployment (see e.g. Putnam, 2007). It is worth noting that while the effect found by Dinesen and Sønderskov is very robust, it is also relatively small. A one standard deviation increase in ethnic diversity leads to a predicted reduction in trust of 0.06 points on the scale running between 0 and 10. The size is similar to the partial effect of around one year of education. However, the findings by Dinesen and Sønderskov have interesting implications that merit further attention, both by researchers and in the political debate. First of all, they suggest that studies that do not find an effect of ethnic diversity on trust may have focused on too high levels of aggregation. Second, the results suggest that if segregation means that few natives in high-trust countries will live in micro-contexts with high ethnic diversity, it might mitigate adverse effects on social trust that would otherwise arise.

A Psychological Perspective on Trust

Is it surprising that social trust seems to be a sticky personal trait? One possible answer to that question is hinted at by research in psychology. Economists and political scientists often see trust attitude in a rational choice context, where the decision to put trust in others can be understood by thinking about the consequences of doing so: that is, if others are expected to be trustworthy, trusting them is the rational thing to do and will ultimately benefit the trusting person. Another possibility is that people choose to be trusting as a way to be nice toward other people. In that case, trust is not driven by selfish concerns but still consequentialist, in that the trusting person expects the consequences of putting trust in someone to be beneficial for him or her.

Recent research in psychology suggests that trust cannot be understood by looking at the expected consequences of trust. It has been shown that when people act trustingly, they do not do so because they expect trusting behavior to have certain consequences (Dunning, Fetchenhauer, & Schlösser, 2012; Schlösser, Fetchenhauer, & Dunning, 2016). They do so because trusting acts feel right for them in the moment. It has also been shown that people are more prone to taking risks when it involves trusting another person compared to taking risks in general. While these results are highly interesting, they also make it more difficult to design policies that promote trust: if trust is best explained by feelings, there are not many choices available for policy makers that matter.

Promoting Trust in the EU by Strengthening the Rule of Law

Research on trust and migration is advancing rapidly and new studies continue to add a lot to our knowledge about these topics. A few results and patterns, however, seem to be robust and appear in several studies of high quality. For example, it is sometimes said that trust takes a life-time to build but can be destroyed in a few seconds. When it comes to social trust, however, this is probably not true. There are studies that identify factors that have adverse effects on trust, but rather than destroying trust, the effects are typically relatively small. For social trust, research rather suggests that it is difficult to build, but once you have it, it is relatively robust.

It is important to keep in mind that social trust is conceptually different from trust in specific institutions such as the political system in the EU (see the chapter by Linda Berg in this volume). If trust in political institutions spills over on trust toward people in general, it is important that the EU system is characterized by high levels of institutional quality. The direction of causality between different types of trust is, however, difficult to identify. People who tend to have high trust in other people also tend to be more trusting toward political institutions. But that does not mean that institutional trust explains social trust, though that mechanism is plausible. It is also plausible, however, that trust toward people in general affects trust in political institutions. A third possibility, finally, is that both types of trust are driven by feelings as suggested by psychological research. If that is the case, it is probably wrong to speak of trust in one dimension as being the cause of trust in another dimension. Instead, trust in different dimensions are actually parts of everyone's personality.

Turning to the issue of whether trust and migration is compatible or not, the stickiness of trust is a mixed blessing. When people move from a high-trust country to a low-trust country, there is no or only a small drop in trust levels. For migration in the opposite direction, there is some but incomplete adjustment upwards. A possible, perhaps overly optimistic interpretation of previous research is that migration may cause a ratchet effect for global trust levels: when people from high-trust countries move to countries with lower trust, the migrants tend to remain highly trusting, especially if they are older than 30 at the age of emigration. On the other hand, the findings in Dinesen (2012) and Nannestad and colleagues (2014) suggest that the trust among migrants from low-trust countries will increase when they migrate to high-trust countries. These results combined suggest the possibility of a ratchet effect such that global migration will tend to increase average trust among all countries. The ratchet hypothesis is admittedly speculative but merits further investigation, especially by looking closer at social trust among second-generation immigrants in both high- and low-trust countries.

When it comes to the effect of ethnic diversity on social trust, several studies find a negative effect. Again, the size of the effects found is not very large and it also probably occurs only in a very local context. Finally, it is worth stressing that two results appear to be both robust and useful for policy implications: (i) corruption and inferior rule of law are both detrimental for social trust and (ii) income inequality and social trust is strongly negatively associated. These two patterns may very well be connected. Countries with low corruption also tend to have lower income inequality. As discussed by Bergh and Bjørnskov (2014), we should probably not expect that all policies that increase redistribution also simultaneously increase trust. Educational reforms may have such desirable consequences if they contribute to a more equal distribution of human capital and thus promote a more egalitarian distribution of income before taxes and transfers.

The current trend toward higher within-country inequality is most likely a warning sign, especially if paired with corruption and deteriorating institutional quality. If there are problems associated with institutional quality and increasing inequality in Europe, there is a risk that social trust among young Europeans will be negatively affected even though the trust among most adults remains constant. If that is the case, the effect on social trust will be visible only after some time has passed. By the time we see falling trust levels in the survey data, it may be more difficult to do much about it. Promoting trust by strengthening the rule of law in most EU member states is perhaps not seen as the most acute challenge that Europe is facing in relation to last years' economic and migration crises, but it may well be one of the most important ones.

Notes

1. Comment: Social trust refers to the share who agrees that most people can be trusted, according to survey results presented in Nannestad et al. (2014). The estimate regarding Danes in Denmark is an average over estimates from different waves of the European Values Study and a number of similar surveys, taken from Berggren and Bjørnskov (2011). The comparison is made controlling for differences in age, sex, education and religiosity.

References

Acedo, C., & Gomila, A. (2013). Trust and cooperation: A new experimental approach. *Annals of the New York Academy of Sciences, 1299*(1), 77–83.

Aghion, P., Algan, Y., Cahuc, P., & Shleifer, A. (2010). Regulation and distrust. *Quarterly Journal of Economics, 125*(3), 1015–1049.

Algan, Y., & Cahuc, P. (2013). Trust and growth. *Annual Review of Economics, 5*(1), 521–549.

Arrow, K. J. (1972). Gifts and exchanges. *Philosophy & Public Affairs, 1*(4), 343–362.

Berg, J., Dickhaut, J., & McCabe, K. (1995). Trust, reciprocity, and social history. *Games and Economic Behavior, 10*(1), 122–142.

Berggren, N., & Bjørnskov, C. (2017). The market-promoting and market-preserving role of social trust in reforms of policies and institutions. *Southern Economic Journal, 84*(1), 3–25.
Berggren, N., & Jordahl, H. (2006). Free to trust: Economic freedom and social capital. *Kyklos, 59*(2), 141–169.
Berggren, N., Daunfeldt, S. O., & Hellström, J. (2016). Does social trust speed up reforms? The case of central-bank independence. *Journal of Institutional Economics, 12*(2), 395–415.
Bergh, A., & Bjørnskov, C. (2011). Historical trust levels predict current welfare state design. *Kyklos, 64*(1), 1–19.
Bergh, A., & Bjørnskov, C. (2014). Trust, welfare states and income equality: Sorting out the causality. *European Journal of Political Economy, 35*, 183–199.
Bergh, A., & Bjørnskov, C. (2018, forthcoming). Trust us to repay: Social trust, long-term interest rates, and sovereign credit ratings. *Journal of Money, Credit and Banking*.
Bergh, A., & Öhrvall, R. (2016). The moldable young: How institutions impact social trust. *IFN Working Paper*, no. 1132.
Bjørnskov, C. (2007). Determinants of generalized trust: A cross-country comparison. *Public Choice, 130*(1–2), 1–21.
Bjørnskov, C. (2008). Social trust and fractionalization: A possible reinterpretation. *European Sociological Review, 24*(3), 271–283.
Bjørnskov, C. (2010). How does social trust lead to better governance? An attempt to separate electoral and bureaucratic mechanisms. *Public Choice, 144*, 323–346.
Bjørnskov, C., & Svendsen, G. T. (2013). Does social trust determine the size of the welfare state? Evidence using historical identification. *Public Choice, 157*(1–2), 269–286.
Butler, J. V., Giuliano, P., & Guiso, L. (2016). The right amount of trust. *Journal of the European Economic Association, 14*(October), 1155–1180.
Clemens, M. A. (2011). Economics and emigration: Trillion-dollar bills on the sidewalk? *Journal of Economic Perspectives, 25*(3), 83–106.
Delhey, J., Newton, K., & Welzel, C. (2011). How general is trust in 'most people'? Solving the radius of trust problem. *American Sociological Review, 76*(5), 786–807.
Dinesen, P. T. (2012). Does generalized (dis)trust travel? Examining the impact of cultural heritage and destination-country environment on trust of immigrants. *Political Psychology, 33*(4), 495–511.
Dinesen, P. T. (2016). Tager de tilliden med? Udenlandssvenskeres sociale tillid. In M. Solevid (Ed.), *Svenska utlandsröster*. Gothenburg: SOM Institute, University of Gothenburg.
Dinesen, P. T., & Sønderskov, K. M. (2015). Ethnic diversity and social trust: Evidence from the micro-context. *American Sociological Review, 80*(3), 550–573.

Dinesen, P. T., & Sønderskov, K. M. (2018). Ethnic diversity and social trust: A critical review of the literature and suggestions for a research agenda. In E. M. Uslaner (Ed.), *The Oxford handbook on social and political trust*. Oxford: Oxford University Press.

Docquier, F., Rapoport, H., & Salomone, S. (2012). Remittances, migrants' education and immigration policy: Theory and evidence from bilateral data. *Regional Science and Urban Economics, 42*(5), 817–828.

Dunning, D., Fetchenhauer, D., & Schlösser, T. M. (2012). Trust as a social and emotional act: Noneconomic considerations in trust behavior. *Journal of Economic Psychology, 33*(3), 686–694.

Hamilton, B., & Whalley, J. (1984). Efficiency and distributional implications of global restrictions on labour mobility: Calculations and policy implications. *Journal of Development Economics, 14*(1), 61–75.

Jordahl, H. (2008). Economic inequality. In G. T. Svendsen & G. L. H. Svendsen (Eds.), *Handbook of social capital*. Cheltenham: Edward Elgar.

Krosnick, J. A., & Alwin, D. F. (1989). Aging and susceptibility to attitude change. *Journal of Personality and Social Psychology, 57*(3), 416–425.

Ljunge, M. (2014a). Social capital and health: Evidence that ancestral trust promotes health among children of immigrants. *Economics and Human Biology, 15*, 165–186.

Ljunge, M. (2014b). Trust issues: Evidence on the intergenerational trust transmission among children of immigrants. *Journal of Economic Behavior and Organization, 106*(2012), 175–196.

Lundstedt, J., & Nissling, S. (2016). Lägre tillit med ökad etnisk mångfald? *Ekonomisk Debatt, 44*(8), 31–41.

Moses, J. W., & Letnes, B. (2004). The economic costs to international labor restrictions: Revisiting the empirical discussion. *World Development, 32*(10), 1609–1626.

Nannestad, P., Tinggaard Svendsen, G., Thisted Dinesen, P., & Mannemar Sønderskov, K. (2014). Do institutions or culture determine the level of social trust? The natural experiment of migration from non-western to western countries. *Journal of Ethnic & Migration Studies, 40*(4), 544–565.

New Diaspore. (2016). Young talented Greeks working abroad—2016. Retrieved November 1, 2017, from http://www.newdiaspora.com/icap-brain-drain-2016/

Putnam, R. D. (2007). E Pluribus Unum: Diversity and community in the twenty-first century. *Scandinavian Political Studies, 30*(2), 137–174.

Sangnier, M. (2013). Does trust favor macroeconomic stability? *Journal of Comparative Economics, 41*, 653–668.

Sapienza, P., Toldra-Simats, A., & Zingales, L. (2013). Understanding trust. *The Economic Journal, 123*(573), 1313–1332.

Schlösser, T., Fetchenhauer, D., & Dunning, D. (2016). Trust against all odds? Emotional dynamics in trust behavior. *Decision, 3*(3), 216–230.
Sønderskov, K. M. (2011). Explaining large-N cooperation: Generalized social trust and the social exchange heuristic. *Rationality and Society, 23*(1), 51–74.
Stolle, D., Soroka, S., & Johnston, R. (2008). When does diversity erode trust? Neighborhood diversity, interpersonal trust and the mediating effect of social interactions. *Political Studies, 56*(1), 57–75.
Storesletten, K. (2003). Fiscal implications of immigration: A net present value calculation. *Scandinavian Journal of Economics, 105*(3), 487–506.
Thöni, C., Tyran, J. R., & Wengström, E. (2012). Micro foundations of social capital. *Journal of Public Economics, 96*(7–8), 635–643.

Trust in the Euro and the EU's Banking Union After the Financial Crisis

Clas Wihlborg and Sarkis J. Khoury

Popular referenda have become the Achilles heel of the European integration process in the twenty-first century. Before the 'Brexit' vote in 2016, French and Dutch voters voted against the EU's proposal for a new constitution in 2005. The Irish voted against the Lisbon Treaty (a watered-down version of the constitutional proposal) in 2009, although they supported the Treaty in a second referendum. The voters in Denmark voted against participation in the European Monetary Union (EMU) in 2000 and the Swedish voters followed the Danish example in 2003. But the 'Brexit' vote is the heaviest blow so far to the majority of the citizens' political representatives in the UK and elsewhere in the EU, including the European Commission, as they generally support the idea of 'ever deeper integration' as envisioned by the founders of the EU. The results of these referenda can be interpreted as lack of trust or confidence among citizens in many EU member states that the European integration process will deliver general benefits on the national level. This lack of confidence in the

C. Wihlborg (✉)
Chapman University, Orange, CA, USA

S. J. Khoury
University of California at Riverside, Riverside, CA, USA

A. Bakardjieva Engelbrekt et al. (eds.), *Trust in the European Union in Challenging Times*, https://doi.org/10.1007/978-3-319-73857-4_6

integration process revealed itself first in Western and Northern Europe, but after the debt crisis in the euro zone erupted in 2010, the support for the process has diminished in Southern and, not least, Eastern Europe as well. The wave of immigrants into Europe in 2015 and 2016 weakened support further in the latter group of member states, in particular (see Linda Berg's and Andreas Bergh's chapters in this volume).

There are many aspects to the European integration process. The focus in this chapter lies on the harmonization of laws and regulation with respect to banking and of the institutional framework for monetary policy. Other aspects of financial and policy integration in the EU are discussed as well, albeit not as thoroughly. 'Trust' and 'confidence' vis-à-vis the integration process are used interchangeably throughout the chapter. In other words, trust within a country is interpreted as citizens' confidence that the integration process will deliver net benefits on the national level in some form. Peoples' trust or confidence in institutions cannot easily, however, be measured on a scale. In this chapter, it is assumed that citizens' confidence in the European integration process in a particular EU policy area increases with stronger beliefs or perceptions that the reform process contributes to economic welfare and with an increasing proportion of citizens with such perceptions. This is not to deny that political attitudes to various EU institutions and reforms may be based on a number of non-economic factors such as nationalism, and highly visible effects may have a disproportionately strong impact on trust at the expense of more subtle effects that cannot be directly observed. There is also a possibility that attitudes may be skewed in favor of short-run effects at the expense of longer-term costs and benefits. However, in the longer term, it is reasonable to assume that perceptions are grounded in reality. Confidence in harmonization of law, regulation and other institutions within the EU therefore requires that most citizens of each EU member state experience economic benefits from this harmonization.

The main question addressed in this chapter is whether a more flexible integration process with a greater role for institutional competition among EU member states could increase the economic benefits and/or reduce the economic costs associated with harmonization of monetary policy and harmonization of laws and regulation of financial institutions, with an emphasis on banks. If so, the trust and confidence in the integration process should also be strengthened. A more flexible integration process implies that subgroups of member states within the EU can harmonize institutions at different speeds and in different dimensions. In other words, institutional harmonization would occur with different speeds over long periods. The end point of harmonization need not be complete similarity, but differences may remain reflecting preferences revealed through political processes in the individual member states. Flexible integration implies a 'multi-speed Europe' for the foreseeable future. Leading representatives of the EU have long refused to accept this type of integration process although it has to some extent become a reality in many areas. The EMU and the euro zone are the most obvious examples of a degree of flexibility in the harmonization of institutions since EU members can opt out of the currency union.[1]

The chapter runs as follows. In the next section, the economic criteria for countries to benefit from irrevocably fixed exchange rates among them are reviewed as prerequisites for benefits from, and thereby for trust in, a monetary union. The EU and EMU approach to the financial and debt crisis after 2007 are discussed thereafter as evidence of lacking prerequisites for several EU counties' participation in the euro zone. One EU response to the crises was to propose the formation of a banking union to strengthen the economic foundations for the EMU. The following section focuses on changes in transaction costs resulting from harmonization imposed on all EU member states while the section thereafter discusses harmonization over time through a process of institutional competition. Next, the EU's approach to banking law and regulation before the crises is reviewed. Costs and benefits of the harmonization within the proposed and partially implemented banking union are then discussed in the seventh section. Finally, the concluding addresses reforms that may enhance trust in both the monetary and the banking union in the EU. In particular, we discuss whether increased flexibility along with stronger institutional competition has the potential to strengthen trust in the EMU and the regulatory framework for banking. We argue that there are potential benefits from increased flexibility but, to derive them, increased flexibility must be combined with a degree of harmonization in specific areas to avoid a 'race to the bottom' in the quality of regulation of banking.

Foundations for Trust in the European Monetary Union

The economic benefits of monetary integration and harmonization were conceptualized in the Delors report titled *One Union, One Money*, published by the European Commission (1990). It built on the Werner report of 1970 and elaborated on the economic arguments in favor of a monetary union. Microeconomic benefits in the form of reduced transactions and information costs, as well as reduced exchange rate risk, were emphasized. Furthermore, the Delors report emphasized that free capital flows make any exchange rate regime along the spectrum between irrevocably fixed rates in a monetary union and freely floating rates unstable and crisis-prone. Credibility of fixed rates would be obtained only in a monetary union where exit would not be an option.

It is well known that monetary harmonization has costs as well as benefits. Wyplosz (2006) points out that the potential disadvantages of a monetary union were passed over rather lightly in the Delors report. He takes the view that the omission of important elements of the Optimum Currency Area (OCA) theory in the Commission's argumentation for a common currency 'is the Monetary Union's original sin'. The OCA theory spells out criteria for a country's choice of exchange rate regime. This literature was rich already in the late 1970s (see e.g. Tower & Willett, 1976) and it was revisited frequently in the early 1990s around the time when the Maastricht Treaty was negotiated (see e.g. Wihlborg & Willett, 1991).

The most well-known and widely accepted criterion for a currency area is labor market flexibility in the form of either mobility within the area or flexibility of relative real wages across industries as well as countries. A second criterion is fiscal policy cooperation enabling transfers in case member states are in different phases of the business cycle. The general thrust of these criteria for fixed exchange rates between regions is that when asymmetric shocks hit the two regions and relative cost and price levels cannot be affected by exchange rate changes, alternative mechanisms for adjustment must exist to make full employment possible. There is general agreement that the EMU is indeed not an OCA in terms of labor market flexibility and fiscal policy. However, several economists have pointed out that the costs of the EMU in terms of macroeconomic adjustment would be mitigated and even eliminated to the extent OCA criteria for fixed exchange rates are endogenous. This would mean that labor market institutions adjust to achieve the required flexibility once exchange rates are irrevocably and credibly fixed in a monetary union (Frankel & Rose, 1998). Similarly, fiscal policy authorities would adjust to the circumstances of a monetary union.

Evidence on endogenous institutional development enhancing wage flexibility and mobility in labor markets, in particular, has been reviewed and discussed by De Grauwe and Mongelli (2005) and Willett, Permpoon and Wihlborg (2010). They concluded that the labor market criteria for a currency union had not been achieved endogenously even a decade after the formation of the EMU. The inability of Greece, Portugal, Spain and Italy to adjust their relative cost levels within the EMU without facing very high levels of unemployment offers a stark illustration of the macroeconomic adjustment costs associated with rigidities in labor and product markets within a currency union. The fiscal policy criterion for an OCA stating that fiscal transfers should be possible within a currency union has encountered resistance within the EMU since government tax and revenue policies have been recognized as national concerns. The incentives of national governments to run fiscal deficits when interest rates converged among members of the EMU were recognized at an early stage in the EMU. The EU's Growth and Stability Pact with limitations on fiscal deficits (i.e. 3 percent of GDP annually) was motivated by these concerns.

Fiscal policy coordination would recognize that differences in economic conditions require differences in fiscal stance and transfers among different parts of a currency area. Large-scale transfers within the EU are constrained by EU treaties except in the areas of agricultural policy and some types of funding for structural adjustment. Lacking fiscal coordination, the limited harmonization implied by the Growth and Stability Pact was supposed to prevent EU member states from running up deficits that would threaten the ability of the European Central Bank (ECB) to attain its inflation target. However, the ineffectiveness of the Pact has been widely recognized with Germany and France violating its rules already before the financial and debt crises.

The need for fiscal integration implied by the Growth and Stability Pact has been widely debated. One argument is that sufficient incentives to constrain deficit and debt creation could be created by increased interest rates on bonds issued by EU member states lacking fiscal discipline. The counter-argument is that the fiscal policy-making process does not respond strongly to changes in the interest rate on national debt. The interest differentials between euro-denominated bonds issued by different EU governments in the euro zone were negligible or small before the global financial crisis erupted in 2008. Even then, interest rate differentials did not increase dramatically during the period leading up to the Greek debt crisis in early 2010. It seems that market actors believed in the existence of an implicit insurance of sovereign debts before 2010 in spite of a no-bail-out clause in EU treaties.

The perceived insurance of sovereign debt risk in combination with lack of fiscal policy coordination within the framework of a weak Growth and Stability Pact had the consequence that EU member states with weak mechanisms for fiscal discipline were able to run deficits and to increase their debt to GDP ratios without having to face market penalties until the debt crisis was a fact. Already at the time when the EMU was formed, there was widespread skepticism about the long-term prospects of the currency union among economists, in particular, labor markets in the EU countries were considered rigid in comparison to labor markets in the US, and no mechanism for fiscal transfers among member states had been set up. The Maastricht criteria for membership in the EMU were not enforced. In particular, the criterion that the national debt to GDP ratio must not exceed 60 percent was violated by Belgium and Italy, in particular, but several other EU member states were very close to this ratio. Other criteria with respect to each member country's interest rate and inflation differential relative to an average among member states had been achieved as a result of convergence during the 1990s. The decline in inflation rates in several countries was achieved at a cost in terms of unemployment, however.

The discussion so far refers to the original OCA criteria. During the 1970s, inflation became an important policy objective and one aspect of exchange rate regime choice.[2] Countries with low credibility with respect to anti-inflation policy could avoid the costs of a prolonged effort to gain credibility by joining the monetary union where the ECB was tasked to monitor price stability as its only objective. The ECB was given strong independence to prevent short-term policy preferences in euro zone members from influencing its policies. Several members of the EMU had long been unable to achieve such a low inflation rate with their own currencies without sacrificing employment. For these countries in the southern parts of euro zone, in particular, membership in the EMU implied a kind of insurance that domestic inflationary pressures would not translate into high inflation expectations. Thus, it would become feasible for these countries to reduce inflation rapidly without high costs in the form of unemployment.

In spite of the high trust in the ECB's anti-inflation policy and the low inflation expectations across the euro zone, the danger facing individual member states was that they would not be able to keep their general cost levels in production from increasing at a higher rate than the average inflation rate. Such increases in a country's cost levels relative to other members in the euro zone would lead to declining competitiveness in the form of a real exchange rate appreciation. Wihlborg, Willett and Zhang (2010) show that the real exchange rates of Greece, Portugal, Spain and Italy appreciated almost continuously from the time they adopted the euro until 2009. The only period of inflation convergence occurred during the years before the EMU was formed in 1999. Thus, it seems as if the cheap route to monetary policy credibility through EMU membership may actually have reduced the urgency to implement structural reforms in several countries. The current sovereign debt crisis in Greece, Portugal, Spain and Italy may be partly blamed on the lack of institutional reform in these countries affecting wage and price flexibility and the mobility of people between regions and industries in spite of ten years with the euro. The relative situation for southern euro zone countries may have been worsened by successful reforms in the northern euro zone in, for example, Germany and the Netherlands.

Debt Crisis and Crisis Management in the EMU

Falling GDP in most EU member states during the financial crisis in 2008 and 2009, expansionary fiscal policies, bank bailouts and large current account deficits associated with lack of competitiveness combined to make debt to GDP ratios unsustainable in Greece to begin with, followed by Ireland and Portugal, and then Spain and Italy. In Ireland, the enormous costs of bank bailouts contributed to an explosive rise in the debt to GDP ratio. Interest rates on ten-year sovereign bonds rose in 2010 to a level as high as 15 percent for Greece, 11 percent for Ireland and 7–8 percent for Portugal (Cabo-Valverde, Benink, Berglund, & Wihlborg, 2015). The EU's approach to the Greek debt crisis was initially to impose fiscal austerity as a condition for bilateral loans from other EU countries to manage short-term payment problems. These loans proved to be insufficient even for Greece alone, but the situation worsened when the debt crisis spread to Ireland and Portugal. Loan defaults and renegotiations of loan conditions were considered unacceptable by EU decision makers, as was exit from the monetary union.

After the spread of the crisis to Ireland and Portugal, the European Financial Stability Mechanism (EFSM) was created but its capacity was insufficient when Italy and Spain were drawn into the crisis. The European Financial Stability Facility (EFSF) was agreed by the Council of the EU in 2010 and was set up with capacity to lend EUR 440 billion to crisis countries. The International Monetary Fund (IMF) participated in rescue operations as well, but national interest rates remained stubbornly high, indicating a lack of trust in the ability to avoid debt default in one or more of the crisis countries. By mid-2011, the interest rate on Greek ten-year bonds remained at 15 percent while the rates for Ireland and Portugal were 12 percent. The rate on Spanish and Italian debt was between 5 and 6 percent while the more or less risk-free German bond rate was 2 percent.

The focus of the EU's crisis management in 2011 was still based on the perception that the path out of the debt crisis was fiscal austerity supported by loans to avert payment problems on debt and aid to countries where the banking system required support. EU ministers also debated and agreed on a new fiscal pact involving increased supervision of and control over the fiscal stance of EU member states. In 2011, the European Stability Mechanism (ESM) was formed with the objective to strengthen the capacity and the coordination of crisis management. In December 2011, a fiscal pact was announced wherein some budget responsibility would be centralized to the EU level. EU countries that violated budget agreements would be automatically penalized. But these efforts to mitigate the debt crisis had little impact on the interest rate levels in the southern euro zone countries, indicating that market actors had little trust in the EU's approach to the crisis. In January 2012, the Italian ten-year bond rate reached 7 percent.

The ECB contributed during 2011 and early 2012 to alleviate the crisis in euro zone members by buying government bonds and accepting these bonds as collateral for loans to banks. In March 2012, the president of the ECB, Mario Draghi, announced that the ECB had done enough, and that it would be up to individual governments to take responsibility for the costs of crisis management. In May 2012, the Spanish government announced that its banks were in need of support amounting to between 30 and 130 billion euro. The Spanish government would need aid to avoid a banking crisis. Only when Draghi, in July 2012, made a 180-degree turn, and stated that the ECB would do 'whatever it takes' to buy sovereign debt and save the euro zone in its current configuration, did interest rate levels start to come down substantially.

The stress on the banking systems in the crisis countries in the euro zone also led to calls for a banking union as an additional criterion for an Optimum Currency Area. The common monetary policy was predicated on the even transmission of monetary policy to different parts of the EMU, but the transmission mechanism had been fragmented by the crises in the banking systems of several euro zone countries. This fragmentation was the result of the strong linkage between sovereign and banking system risk. The high costs of bailing out distressed banks contribute to sovereign risk, and sovereign risk weakens banks with a high proportion of domestic government bonds in their portfolios. The fiscal situation in many EMU countries was too weak for the national governments to rescue weak banks without worsening the debt crisis. The EU's response to this situation was to propose the formation of a banking union with strongly harmonized regulation, centralized supervision and centralized crisis management. Thus, monetary harmonization had spilled over into demands for harmonization of the banking systems and their regulation.

An agreement with respect to the formation of a banking union was reached in 2014. The responsibility for supervision and bank crisis management would be centralized. To reduce the potential common costs of crisis management, the plans for the banking union included greater participation of the private sector in the rescue and recapitalization of failing banks. These issues are discussed in more detail below. All the reforms and policy measures described above had the objective to strengthen trust in the euro zone as a permanent entity that could be expanded to include new members but not be broken up by having existing members leave. There is little doubt that the single most effective measure to strengthen trust in this regard was Draghi's statement that the ECB would do whatever it takes to prevent a breakup of the euro zone. The benefits of the fiscal pact and the banking union can possibly be realized only in the long term.

Even if trust in the EMU as a permanent currency union was strengthened by the actions of the ECB, it is not clear that confidence in the benefits of the EMU for all its members was strengthened. On the contrary, the fundamental problems caused by rigidities in labor and product markets, and lack of convergence of cost levels remained a serious drag on the economic recovery in the crisis countries within the euro zone. One important lesson from the years of crisis management within the euro zone is that the ECB can alleviate liquidity problems for countries and banks, but it does not have the power to address fundamental issues of solvency, which for euro zone countries involve issues of competitiveness and productivity. Attempts by the ECB to support counties within the euro zone with solvency problems led it to take a partially fiscal role outside the scope of its original mandate and, thereby, accepting risk on behalf of taxpayers across the whole euro zone. It can be argued that these policies were necessary for the survival of the EMU in a situation when political processes in the individual member states were unable to deal with the underlying causes of the crisis in the southern euro zone. However, the long-term effects on trust in the benefits of the EMU for all its members are still uncertain since the required fundamental reforms in the crisis countries have still not been implemented.

Harmonization, Transactions Costs and Obstacles to Mobility

The cornerstone of the EU from an economic point of view is the Internal Market based on the 'four freedoms' for goods, labor, capital and services. Initially, the Internal Market aimed at reducing or eliminating discriminatory barriers to trade. These barriers may be explicit such as tariffs or they may be more subtle, taking the form of, for example, particularly costly testing requirements for imported goods, delays in licensing procedures for foreign financial institutions and domestic bias in public procurement. Formal discriminatory barriers within the EU have been almost completely removed in the markets for goods. Capital is also generally mobile although there are sector-specific exceptions (see below). Some backtracking has occurred, for example, by the designation of eleven industries in France as 'strategic' and off limits to foreign acquisitions. Substantial barriers remain in the Internal Markets relating to labor and services. An agreement on a new Services Directive was reached in 2006 after years of negotiations. The agreement is considered a failure by those aiming for completely open markets within the EU while others consider it an important step toward free trade in services like media, postal services, water, gas, electricity, health and insurance.

It was soon discovered that differences in standards, regulation, legislation and business practices across EU countries generate barriers to trade as well. Such barriers tend to increase the costs of trading with another EU country relative to trading domestically. This kind of trade barrier is not discriminatory if all economic actors are treated equally within each country. Instead, it is a source of difference in information and transactions costs for firms and individuals between trading on a domestic and European level. Language and cultural differences might also be sources of such barriers as well. 'Institutional harmonization' within the EU has the objective of reducing barriers in the form of differences in standards, regulation and law. Common rules with respect to, for example, product liability, health standards, financial regulation, corporate law, bankruptcy law and labor law would clearly reduce transactions costs in intra-EU trade. The trade creating effects of internal harmonization has made it attractive on the EU agenda for increasing integration. However, there are potentially substantial costs associated with internal harmonization if it is imposed across all EU member states. These costs are often neglected in the debate.

Taking the case of language harmonization as an illustration, it is obvious that there are both costs and benefits from requiring all economic transactions to be prepared and concluded in, say, French. Certainly, working in the same language across the EU might entail great benefits, but there would also be substantial costs for those who must learn the common language, and who may never learn the nuances of it. Furthermore, the agreed-upon language need not be the least cost language to learn and use if the political process leading to the language decision is biased in favor of a specific country. Much work goes on within the EU on harmonization of rules and regulation in the areas of environment and health, financial services, corporate law, accounting, and so on. Benefits of harmonization in a particular area are obvious in cross-border transactions, but there are costs as a result of differences between EU-mandated rules and the most efficient rules for a country, given its legal and regulatory system, legal history, conventions and business practices. Furthermore, there is no guarantee that the political process leads to the most efficient harmonized rule or regulation. Some EU member states will certainly be able to enjoy benefits of institutional harmonization if an EU directive mandates rules that are similar to these members' old rules. In other member states, the harmonized rules are instead likely to be associated with substantial costs.

Sykes (2000) points out that differences in, for example, preferences and income between national jurisdictions imply that their optimal regulatory policies are likely to differ as well. He also point out that optimal regulatory policies are often unknown. The complexity of social systems implies that in a number of areas we simply do not know how institutions should be designed optimally. This means that costs and benefits of harmonization across jurisdictions with different initial legal and regulatory conditions are not easily observed or understood (see Eva Storskrubb's and Ester Herlin-Kernell's chapters in this volume on harmonization in civil and criminal law within the EU). If a number of experts would be asked how they would want to legislate in order to develop the optimal financial and corporate governance system, each expert would probably come up with a different solution even if they were referring to the same country. For example, corporate governance systems and mechanisms, that differ substantially across the EU, are the result of a set of laws in the areas of company law, investor and creditor protection law, financial sector regulation and, not least, conventions that have developed over decades in different cultural and legal environments (Schmidt & Spindler, 2002).

When costs and benefits of harmonization and approaches to harmonization in the EU and elsewhere are discussed, both differences in preferences and the complexity of social systems must be taken into account. The case for mandatory harmonization of particular laws and regulatory approaches seems to be based on the presumption that a 'best practice' can be identified and applied in all EU member states. In the financial sector capital, requirements for banks offer an interesting illustration of the issues, since the Basel Committee has long been striving to harmonize these requirements worldwide. The EU implements the international agreements through EU directives. One stated objective of capital requirements is to create a 'level playing field' for banks with different home countries. However, the risk associated with a certain type of loan differs across countries with different competitive conditions, accounting rules, deposit insurance schemes, bankruptcy law and corporate governance. Unless all these aspects of the banking environment are harmonized, equal capital requirements for similar types of loans establish a de facto '*un-level* playing field'.

Prerequisites for Effective Institutional Competition in the EU

Harmonization or a substantial degree of harmonization within the EU can be achieved in many areas through other means than EU directives that must be implemented similarly and EU regulations that apply as written across all EU member states (see Göran von Sydow's chapter in this volume). While complete harmonization is one extreme, the reliance on 'institutional competition' among countries setting their own laws, regulations and standards represents another. Institutional competition implies that laws or regulation developed successfully in one country can be adopted fully or partially in another country in order to improve its economic performance. The conditions for such competition can be weak or strong. It requires that the political process is responsive to the economic interests of citizens. Also, the removal of discriminatory trade barriers in markets for goods, services, capital and labor strengthen institutional competition since domestic firms and individuals become exposed to competition from abroad.

Free trade in goods and services is sufficient to create a degree of institutional competition with respect to law and regulation affecting supply conditions in each country since comparative advantages in the production of various products and services are affected by law and regulation in each country. Regulatory differences would remain among countries to the extent preferences with respect to regulation affecting supply conditions differ. Examples of such regulation are labor safety standards and regulation of emission of pollutants. The country with high tolerance for pollution would obtain a comparative advantage in products generating pollution in production. Free trade in goods and services cannot be implemented without mutual recognition of regulation and other factors affecting differences in supply conditions. However, free trade does not require mutual recognition of regulation with respect to product characteristics affecting demand. Countries would be able to implement laws and regulation affecting demand conditions as they see fit. The international trade regime under the World Trade Organization (WTO) was originally based on the presumption that countries would remain sovereign with respect to non-discriminatory regulation affecting both supply conditions and characteristics of products and services. This trade regime, also called free trade with 'territoriality-based national treatment' by Trachtman (2000), limits institutional competition and the need for mutual recognition to regulation and law affecting supply conditions in different countries.

In the situation described above, harmonization of regulation and law affecting supply conditions has costs to the extent harmonizing countries have different preferences with respect to regulation. Harmonization of characteristics of products and services also has costs if preferences differ with respect to the quality of products and services. If we assume that free trade is combined with mutual recognition in quality characteristics of products and services, then free trade would occur in all products and services as long as they satisfy regulation and standards in at least one of the countries practicing mutual recognition. Trachtman (2000) calls this regime 'rootless jurisdiction' and he notes that mutual recognition, as well as harmonization, in this case would be associated with a loss of sovereignty for the countries with respect to regulation affecting product characteristics. However, informed individuals would be able to choose among products or services from countries with different regulation with respect to quality.

Free trade with mutual recognition in this sense would introduce institutional competition with respect to regulation affecting consumers. The outcome of this institutional competition with respect to characteristics of goods and services could lead to 'race to the bottom', 'race to the top' or to differentiated regulation with exporters in different countries supplying differentiated products and services to different consumer groups in importing countries. The last alternative may be considered an acceptable and even efficient outcome with respect to product characteristics for which social values do not differ from private values. 'Race to the bottom' would occur under mutual recognition for quality characteristics of products and services, which are valued higher socially than privately. Examples of such qualities could be cigarettes generating relatively low medical costs, low alcohol content in wine and low transfat products. 'Race to the top' would occur if the social valuation of (costly) qualities of products and services is lower than the private valuation. For example, if the regulators enforce some requirement on product safety but consumers generally value product safety higher than the regulator, exporters in a country with strict regulation would gain a competitive advantage. The aviation industry may be an example since airlines from countries known to be strict with respect to safety standards may gain a competitive advantage because the private value of safety standards is likely to be very high. Below, we discuss if banking is to be considered as being a 'race to the top' sector.

A comparison of costs and benefits of institutional competition with mutual recognition relative to costs and benefits of harmonization favors the latter when harmonization reduces transactions costs in international trade substantially, when there are strong economies of scale in production and when conditions exist for a 'race to the bottom'. Institutional competition with mutual recognition is favored when preferences with respect to regulation differ substantially, when economies of scale are relatively unimportant, when conditions for a 'race to the top' exist and when there is uncertainty about the optimal design of regulation. If private and social preferences are similar, costs of harmonization would be relatively high when preferences differ substantially across countries, and there is uncertainty about the design of regulation.

One of the most studied cases of institutional competition is the area of corporate law in the US where each state has its own legislation. Romano describes how corporate law has developed and become increasingly harmonized while remaining dynamic. She considers US states as 'laboratories' and argues that 'the law-making pattern we observe indicates a dynamic process in which legal innovations originate from several sources, creating a period of legal experimentation that tends to identify a principal statutory formulation that is thereafter adopted by a majority of states. It is difficult to imagine that such dynamism could be generated by the centralized lawmaking that exists at the national level' (Romano, 2006, p. 210). The main benefit of institutional competition in this case arises as a result of uncertainty about the privately and socially most efficient corporate law, as also noted by Sykes (2000).

Vaubel (2009) argues that an information asymmetry between governments and voters favors competition among governments, basically because providers of public goods are more effectively controlled by institutional competition than by their poorly informed voters (Vaubel, 2009). Similarly, Kerber (2000) argues that inter-jurisdictional competition may be a superior way of supplying public goods and services. Kerber also points out that only a competitive system of jurisdictions can be compatible with both decentralization and mobility, and that inter-jurisdictional competition is largely ignored within the EU in contradiction to the EU Treaty, wherein decentralization (subsidiarity) and mobility are prominent principles (ibid.). Both Sykes (2000) and Trachtman (2000) note that the choice in any particular area of law and regulation is not necessarily between complete harmonization through EU Directives that must be implemented identically in all member states and pure institutional competition with mutual recognition.

Trachtman (2000) compares three jurisdictional structures with different degrees of institutional competition. One, denoted 'rootless jurisdiction', is characterized by far-reaching mutual recognition. The second jurisdictional structure is 'territoriality-based national treatment'. As noted above, this structure constitutes the basic rule governing international trade outside the EU today. Within the EU, this structure describes the allocation of jurisdictional responsibility for law and regulation in areas wherein member states retain sovereignty. The third jurisdictional structure is called 'managed recognition with essential harmonization'. Trachtman notes that the EU applies this structure in many areas as a constraint on institutional competition. 'Essential harmonization' should reduce the likelihood of 'race to the bottom' (see below).

Costs and benefits of institutional competition relative to harmonization of institutions must be evaluated on a case-by-case basis taking the scope of free trade and mutual recognition into account. Free trade in services combined with full mutual recognition of regulation of service providers in their home country would create institutional competition with respect to such regulation. Home country regulation of the behavior and qualifications of the service providers would be recognized by the host country. 'Race to the top' would occur in this case if the private valuation of the qualifications of the services exceeds the social valuation. 'Race to the bottom' would occur if the social valuation of these services incorporates the concern that investors must be protected against their own lack of concern. Free trade with national treatment would imply that domestic and foreign service providers operating in a host country are subject to this country's regulation. In the insurance industry, free trade in insurance services with national treatment implies only that there is no discrimination between insurance companies in different jurisdictions while mutual recognition would imply that insurance services accepted by authorities in one jurisdiction can be offered in other jurisdictions. Corporate governance mechanisms are closely linked to rules and regulation within the financial sector. Harmonization of one aspect of the complex maze of explicit and implicit rules that define corporate governance can have very different effects in different countries with substantial differences in legislation, conventions and business practices. Corporate governance is also an area where 'best practice' is almost impossible to determine. Hertig and McCahery (2003) have suggested that institutional competition in the EU in complex legal areas could be enhanced by the implementation across the EU of one nonmandatory legislative solution (e.g. EU company law) that is made available in each country in competition with existing national law.

Harmonization and Institutional Competition in Banking Before the Debt Crisis

On the face of it, banking regulation seems to satisfy many of the criteria for effectiveness of institutional competition, which have been identified above. First, there is little agreement on what is the most effective regulatory structure in banking taking into account both efficiency and stability objectives. Second, the great differences within the EU with respect to corporate governance, bankruptcy law and business practices are likely to cause differences in efficient banking regulation and supervision. Third, banking is an area where regulatory capture of national regulators and rent-seeking of banks can distort the regulation and supervision in favor of national banks.[3] Fourth, the financial sector in general seems particularly suitable for institutional competition generating 'race to the top' since consumers of financial services put a high value on trust in advice and the ability of managers of their wealth to live up to commitments.

The EU adopted early on the principle of mutual recognition in the regulation of a wide range of financial services including banking. The EU Banking Directive was one part of the 1992 program to create the Internal Market with free mobility of products, services, labor and capital. The EU Directive provided the right for any EU bank to set up branches across the EU under a single license issued by the home country. These branches would all be subject to home country regulation and supervision for safety and soundness. Deposit insurance for branches would also be the responsibility of the home country. There was less attention to crisis management with the implication that the allocation of the costs of managing a crisis in a cross-border bank became a potential source of conflict. The Banking Directive in combination with free mobility of capital established conditions for institutional competition with respect to safety and soundness regulation and supervision in the EU for banks operating across the EU under a single license.

In spite of the opportunity to establish branches across the EU, only a small part of cross-border banking within the EU has taken place in branches. Instead, most cross-border banking in the EU has developed through subsidiaries under the formal jurisdiction of host country regulators and supervisors. One reason for the preference for subsidiaries could be that subsidiary organizations generally enjoy greater financial synergies than branch organizations.[4] This is particularly important if bankruptcy costs are high and the likelihood of bailout in a crisis situation is also high. At the same time, subsidiary organizations have not had a disadvantage with respect to operational synergies because they have been able to integrate operations and functions across subsidiaries in spite of the legal separation.[5] Another and possible more important explanation for cross-border banking in subsidiary organizations is that both home and host country supervisors objected to large cross-border operations in branches. Host country authorities have not accepted the idea of having large retail banks in their jurisdictions under foreign control and home-county authorities have been uncomfortable with deposit insurance responsibility for depositors in foreign branches. In other words, supervisors have not accepted the principle of mutual recognition in spite of its formulation in the EU's Banking Directive. Although the Directive states that banks have the right to set up cross-border branches, they are unlikely to do so without the approval of supervisors in both home and host countries in the EU.

The lack of acceptance of the principle of mutual recognition among European bank supervisors weakened institutional competition in supervision and safety and soundness regulation. Supervisors were able to favor domestic banks as 'national champions' without having to fear that depositors would flee the domestic banks. The likelihood of bailouts in case the domestic banks became insolvent contributed further to lack of institutional competition with respect to the quality of regulation with respect to risk-taking. The banking system that developed during the 1990s and the first years of the 2000s was characterized by increasing concentration on the national level and cross-border operations in strongly integrated subsidiaries that could not be separated in times of crises. For this reason, bankruptcy costs for large banks became very high. The transparency of the regulatory jurisdiction over banks' assets in a crisis, in particular, suffered. To make the situation worse, only few countries had established legal frameworks for resolving banks in distress (Wihlborg, 2012). Crisis management and resolution became a complex procedure involving authorities in home and host countries with conflicting interests. All these factors strengthened the perception that many banks were both 'too big to fail' and 'too complex to fail'. The only available option for managing crisis in an important bank was to bail out the bank's creditors by issuing guarantees for their claims. Competition among banks to become particularly skilled at risk management thus became severely undermined.

In spite of the early acceptance of mutual recognition as a principle and, therefore, of institutional competition, the regulatory framework within the EU failed to produce a safe and sound banking system in Europe. We argue that the failure of mutual recognition and institutional competition was caused by the strong implicit protection of banks' creditors. Misdirected private sector competition in banking had the effect of turning institutional competition into a possible 'race to the bottom' instead of 'race to the top'. Current reforms and proposals in the EU to harmonize regulation and supervision can be viewed as responses to this failure of mutual recognition.

The Development of the Banking Union Within the EU

A high degree of explicit and implicit protection of banks' depositors and other creditors has the consequence that banks do not compete for funding by promoting their skills in risk evaluation and management. Depositors and other creditors 'undervalue' trust in the banks when they choose which bank to deposit and invest in. In particular, relatively large, systemically important banks seem to enjoy relatively high implicit creditor protection, providing them with a competitive advantage in terms of funding costs. An IMF report presents estimates of the value of the implicit subsidy relatively large banks enjoy (IMF, 2014).[6] There is also an academic literature providing evidence that banks respond to explicit and implicit protection of creditors by increasing their default risk (see e.g. Prabha & Wihlborg, 2014).

Since 2008, the European Commission has proposed a large number of new rules to better regulate, supervise and govern the financial sector. Most of these rules are now in force or being finalized (European Commission, 2014). An important objective is to achieve that 'tax payers will not foot the bill when banks make mistakes'. Another is to 'break the vicious circle between banks and national finances' in the euro zone. The EU banking union should allow for centralized application of EU-wide rules for banks in the euro area (and in any non-euro member states that would want to join). Therefore, the supervision should not be prone to protection of national interests. The new regulatory framework establishes common rules for banks in all 28 EU member states, set out in a 'single rulebook'. The Capital Requirements Directive and Regulation (Memo 13/690) aims at preventing banking crises in the first place. If banks fail, the Directive on Bank Recovery and Resolution (BRRD) (Memo 14/297) sets up a common framework to manage the process of winding down the banks with a minimum of systemic consequences. All EU savers are guaranteed that deposits up to euro 100,000 euro are protected (Directive on Deposit Guarantee Scheme (DGS) Memo/14/296).

The banking union for the euro zone goes further and includes a Single Supervisory Mechanism (SSM), a Single Resolution Mechanism (SRM) and a Single Deposit Insurance. The first two pillars have been implemented while the common deposit insurance system for the euro zone remains under debate as of early 2018. As of November 2014, the ECB became the supervisor for 120 significant banks in the euro zone, together holding about 82 percent of the bank assets in the euro zone. The SSM sets out the framework for supervision that should ensure that all banks abide by the 'single rulebook' (Memo/13/780). Daniele Nouy, the Chair of the Supervisory Board of the SSM, stated in 2014 that 'the goals are to perform supervision with a truly European view, to ensure the effectiveness of the Supervisory Board, to foster convergence of supervisory practices and to integrate local supervisory practices to the benefit of all SSM members' (Nouy, 2014). A Supervisory Manual covering issues such as 'methodology for the Supervisory Review and Evaluation Process (SREP), off-site and on-site reviews, risk assessments, and model validations' should ensure that 'the same supervisory standards will be applied across Banking Union'.

This description of the EU banking union along with the quotes from an important Chief Supervisor shows clearly that the ambition with respect to harmonization of regulation of banks is very high. This regulatory framework leaves little room for institutional competition among regulators and it seems intended to ensure that banks in all EU member states follow the same rulebook enforced by the Single Supervisor. The SRM (Memo/14/295) entered into force on 1 January 2015. It establishes a Single Resolution Board (SRB) and a Single Resolution Fund (SRF) to manage and fund the resolution process even for cross-border banks. Rules for 'bail-ins' of bank creditors and resolution functions apply from 1 January 2016. The common deposit insurance has the objective of creating competitive neutrality between banks across the euro area. The difficulty of coming to an agreement on this aspect of the banking union is that some euro members are unwilling to provide a fiscal backstop to banks in countries with weak banking systems and large non-performing loans. Even if banks pay insurance premiums to build up a deposit insurance fund for the whole euro zone, European taxpayers must ultimately stand behind the deposit insurance.

There are costs and benefits of the envisioned banking union of the EU. The main cost is likely to be associated with the common rulebook for banks and the application of the same 'European' supervisory model and methodology. It seems unlikely that the common rulebook and the supervision can accommodate the great variety in corporate governance, insolvency law, enforcement and business culture across EU member states. Contracts for various types of credit differ substantially explicitly and implicitly. Thus, identical looking contracts are likely to be associated with very different risk levels.[7] A second cost is associated with the dynamics of lending and supervisory practices. Increased centralization reduces the ability to innovate and learn. Best practices in different countries are supposed to be incorporated in the common rulebook and supervisory mechanism but, once practices are the same, experimentation and innovation are likely to decline relative to a pluralistic system.

There are important benefits as well associated with the common supervisory mechanism. In particular, the 'regulatory capture' of each national regulator by the major banks in its jurisdiction is bound to decline or be eliminated. There is little doubt that such regulatory capture is an important problem that weakens supervision of risk-taking and strengthens the tendency of national regulators and governments to bail out 'national champions'. Over time, the regulatory capture could move up to the EMU level instead so that the largest banks in the euro zone, rather than the largest national banks, would have the strongest leverage in their dealings with the supervisor. It is hard to predict the speed of the consolidation process in the banking sector in the euro zone, which is likely to occur when there are incentives to create 'too big to fail' banks with great political clout within the EU banking union.

The implementation of the SRM is the most important piece in the banking union. If it becomes sufficiently strong and eliminates 'too big to fail' banks and other sources of implicit protection of banks' creditors, the banking industry is most likely in for enormous adjustment and restructuring under stronger market discipline. Banks will restructure based on true economies of scale and scope and not based on implicit subsidies. It will also reduce the need for detailed supervision of risk-taking and, thereby, reduce the regulatory burden that is likely to accompany the common rulebook. The SRM took effect in January 2016. It incorporates bail-in rules that expose banks' non-insured creditors to losses of failing banks. Banks' bondholders must take losses in the form of 'haircuts' before authorities can add capital from other sources. Since the prospect of losses for creditors can be a source of runs on a bank and contagion to other banks, the SRM includes measures to mitigate potential contagion effects of bank failures. Experiences with bail-ins under the resolution procedures are still lacking. We may have to wait and see an important European bank resolved by a resolution board before the effectiveness of the procedures can be fully evaluated. There is some evidence that the costs of debt for UK banks increased after the Special Resolution Regime was implemented in 2009 (Brierley, 2016). The largest Danish bank, *Danske Bank*, complained that their costs of funding increased after Denmark's implementation of bank resolution procedures in 2010.[8] Furthermore, ratings agencies like Fitch have started to take into account reduced likelihood of state support in their government support ratings.

There are still doubts that market discipline on large and complex international banks has increased to such an extent that their funding cost advantage has declined. One reason is that the systemic risk exception from placing a bank under a resolution board can be attractive for politically sensitive authorities (European Shadow Financial Regulatory Committee, 2014). Another reason is that the large complex banks often operate with subsidiaries in several countries. There is uncertainty about contractual recognition of cross-border claims in resolution proceedings and conflicts between countries may arise with respect to burden sharing. The Italian authorities' approach to the crisis in the *Banco Monte del Paschi* in 2016 has also undermined the confidence in the SRM. The government managed to protect a large share of the bank's bondholders through a recapitalization scheme in spite of the EU's prohibition of state support (European Shadow Financial Regulatory Committee, 2017). This case illustrates the difficulty of imposing a harmonized set of rules for dealing with problem banks in countries with very different levels of non-performing loans and very different traditions with respect to relations between banks and their customers.

One potential area of tension within the EU banking union arises as a result of national responsibility for fiscal affairs and supranational responsibility for supervision and crisis management. As noted above, European taxpayers are ultimately the stakeholders in efficient supervision. Thus, incentives of supervisors and crisis managers should be aligned with interests of these taxpayers. There is no European fiscal authority, however. A resolution authority requires access to fiscal resources as a source of funding and is ultimately accountable to taxpayers. Thus, a far-reaching banking union is inconsistent with national responsibility for fiscal policy unless the losses of failing banks can be shifted to their creditors. The buildup of resolution and deposit insurance funds should reduce the reliance on national taxpayers, but the ultimate responsibility for funding must lie with them. If the fiscal burden associated with resolution of banks can be allocated among EU member states, then the banking union has the advantage of having very large fiscal resources behind it. This would also contribute to the credibility of delinking banking risk and sovereign risk within the euro zone.

We conclude this section by noting that confidence that the banking union will achieve its objectives of breaking the link between sovereign risk and bank risk, reducing the fragmentation of the monetary transmission mechanism, within the euro zone, as well as in the regulatory framework for the EU as a whole, requires confidence in all three pillars of the framework: (i) effective supervision, (ii) bank crisis management and (iii) common deposit insurance. There is little doubt that the expanded role of the ECB in both supervision and crisis management has contributed to increased confidence in the banking union and the viability of the euro zone as a currency area. This expanded role that includes fiscal responsibility may turn out to be controversial since the ECB is a purely technocratic institution without democratic accountability. The common deposit insurance cannot be implemented without agreement of the allocation of fiscal costs of bank failures. Several EU countries are unwilling to take on the fiscal burden associated with a common fiscal backstop in the EU to deal with banking crises. The key pillar is the bank resolution mechanism that, if credible, will strengthen market discipline on banks' risk-taking, and reduce the need for both stronger supervision and the fiscal burden of bank failures. Confidence that the resolution mechanism will be strong enough to come to grips with the 'too big to fail' problem is still lacking. Institutional competition has potential advantages in banking as well as other financial services, but the strong protection of banks' creditors has created conditions for 'race to the bottom'. It has taken a harmonized approach to banking regulation after several years of crisis in the euro zone to generate momentum toward reform of bank resolution mechanisms with the objective of reducing the implicit protection of banks' creditors. Thus, it has taken a harmonized approach to generate reforms that, if successful, may eliminate 'race to the bottom' and, thereby, generate favorable conditions for institutional competition.

Can Trust in Monetary and Banking Unions Be Strengthened with Greater Flexibility in Harmonization?

Six years after the beginning of the so-called debt crisis in the southern parts of the EMU, confidence in the long-term survival of the euro zone in its current configuration is still lacking. The ECB's actions have no doubt strengthened confidence in the ability of Greece and the other crisis countries to remain within the currency union. At the same time, these countries would benefit from abandoning the euro if they do not implement fundamental labor and product market reforms, as well as other reforms that could strengthen these countries' ability to adjust to economic shocks. The political systems in these countries seem to prevent necessary reforms, however. As a result, they suffer the costs of remaining within the euro zone in terms of low growth rates and high unemployment levels.

Flexibility of monetary harmonization, which would allow countries to switch exchange rate systems according to circumstances, is contradictory to the idea of the EMU as an irrevocable currency regime. The question is whether a one-time reconfiguration of the euro zone would damage the long-term credibility of the euro zone as a permanent currency union for the remaining members and future additions. It can be argued that a currency union wherein all members truly satisfy the criteria for irrevocably fixed exchange rates and benefit from adopting the common currency could gain more trust. At the time the EMU was formed, the ambition within the EU was to maximize the number of members that would adopt the euro. There was little regard for the longer-term ability of each country to satisfy the well-accepted criteria for an irrevocably fixed exchange rate. Alternatively, it was believed that each country, once a member of the EMU, would implement the necessary institutional reforms that would make them thrive within the currency union. However, the rigidities of the political processes in several countries were underestimated.

The EU has over time recognized that flexibility is needed in the process of monetary harmonization. EU member states that do not consider adopting the euro are able to keep their own currencies and central banks without penalty. Sweden and Denmark are cases in point here. At the same time, several countries have been denied EMU membership or their memberships have been delayed on the grounds that they do not satisfy the Maastricht criteria. The case of Lithuania, which was denied membership in 2006, is a case in point. Membership can also be denied on the grounds that EU member states do not have mechanisms and institutions in place to sustain competitiveness within the EMU. Thus, in the monetary policy sphere, there is, de facto, multi-speed integration although the flexibility of the integration process is one-directional.

The creation of the EU banking union for the euro zone, if fully implemented, may strengthen the trust in the euro since it would shift the fiscal burden of banking crises from individual countries to taxpayers across the whole euro zone. Several EMU members are unwilling to accept this burden sharing, which weakens trust in both the euro and the banking union.

If the bank resolution procedures, that allocate some of the burden of bank failures to banks' creditors, become credible for large as well as small banks, the fiscal burden of bank failures would be reduced. Thus, the credibility of bank resolution procedures are most likely critical for member countries to accept fiscal burden sharing and, therefore, critical for trust in the banking union as well as the euro zone.

Perhaps ironically, the credibility of the bank resolution procedures, with substantial participation of banks' creditors in losses of both small and large banks, would reduce or even eliminate the need for fiscal burden sharing, and harmonized regulation and supervision. Instead, institutional competition could enhance the efficiency of the banking sector as well as of regulation and supervision because 'race to the top' would be possible with credible resolution procedures. A prerequisite is that the resolution procedures are sufficiently harmonized for mutual recognition to be a reality.[9] The benefits of institutional competition could then outweigh any benefits from harmonized practices of financial regulators and supervisors. The benefits of harmonized rules are primarily derived from reduced transactions costs in cross-border activity while costs may arise as a result of differences between the 'best practice' in the institutional environment of a country and the practice required by the EU. These costs can be avoided with flexible integration and institutional competition. Another longer-term benefit of institutional competition is that it provides incentives for a search for 'best practices'. Such a search is hindered by standardized and relatively static regulation and law. On the other hand, the benefits of institutional competition cannot be obtained unless conditions for 'race to the top' are satisfied.

We conclude with a note on 'Brexit'. In spite of the costs and complications that 'Brexit' entail, there is a potential benefit for the financial sector if the EU and the UK can agree on conditions that will strengthen institutional competition for financial regulation. This requires that financial services firms in the two jurisdictions will be able to supply services in both the EU and the UK with a single license as many firms do now. As long as the UK is a member of the EU, the single license requires far-reaching harmonization in financial regulation. Institutional competition could therefore potentially be strengthened post-Brexit if mutual recognition of financial regulation between the EU and the UK can be achieved with less stringent requirements for harmonization.

Notes

1. As of January 2018, the euro zone consists of Austria, Belgium, Cyprus, Estonia, Finland, France, Germany, Greece, Ireland, Italy, Latvia, Lithuania, Luxembourg, Malta, the Netherlands, Portugal, Slovakia, Slovenia and Spain. Other EU member states (except for Denmark and the UK) are formally obliged to join once they meet the criteria but, de facto, no EU member state can be forced to adopt the euro. Andorra, Monaco, San Marino and the Vatican have formal agreements with the EU to use the euro as their official currency and issue their own coins. Kosovo and Montenegro have adopted the euro unilaterally, but these countries do not officially form part of the euro zone and do not have representation in the ECB.
2. The theory of monetary policy began to incorporate the game theoretic concepts of time-inconsistency, monetary policy rules and credibility (see e.g. Kydland & Prescott, 1977; Barro & Gordon, 1983).
3. Sykes (2000) noted that institutional competition among regulators can reduce the scope for regulatory capture. Barth et al. (2012) provide evidence from the 2007–2009 financial crisis, supporting the view that regulatory capture is an important problem in the banking sector.
4. Luciano and Wihlborg (2018) show that a subsidiary organization can economize on bankruptcy costs since individual subsidiaries are able to enter bankruptcy.
5. Sweeney, Goldberg and Wihlborg (2007) analyze the case of the pan-Nordic bank Nordea. This bank is the result of the merger of four major banks in four Nordic countries. It operated subsidiaries in the four countries while having the strategic objective of integrating functions across the subsidiaries strongly. In 2004, the bank developed plans to reorganize as a branch organization, but the plan fell through as a result of objections from supervisors as well as for internal reasons. The plan was recently revived in 2017 with plans to create a bank with Finland as home country.
6. The IMF Global Financial Stability Report estimates that the funding subsidies for large banks in 2013 amounted to 15 basis points in the US, 20–60 basis points in Japan and the UK, and 60–90 basis points in the euro zone (IMF, 2014).
7. The great differences in non-performing loans in member states' banking systems are indicators of the differences in law and regulation that affect the credit risks banks are facing (European Shadow Financial Regulatory Committee, 2017).
8. For example, on 20 February 2012, the spread on interbank loans to the *Danske Bank* relative to Euribor was 7.05 basis points according to Wihlborg (2012).

9. The Bank Recovery and Resolution Directive (BRRD) for all EU members specifies requirements for procedures for closing and resolving insolvent banks at the national level. These procedures took effect on 1 January 2016. But their credibility has the same weakness as the SRM for the euro zone (Wihlborg, 2017).

References

Barro, R. J., & Gordon, D. B. (1983). A positive theory of monetary policy in a natural rate model. *Journal of Political Economy, 91*(4), 589–610.

Barth, J. R., Caprio, G., & Levine, R. (2012). *Guardians of finance*. Cambridge, MA: MIT Press.

Brierley, P. (2016). Presentation at the conference of the National Institute for Economic and Social Research (NIER) on 18 March 2016. Retrieved from www.niesr.ac.uk/financial-regulation-are-we-reaching-efficient-outcome

Cabo-Valverde, S., Benink, H., Berglund, T., & Wihlborg, C. (2015). Regulatory response to the financial crisis in Europe: Recent developments 2010–2013. *Journal of Financial Economic Policy, 7*(1), 29–50.

De Grauwe, P., & Mongelli, F. P. (2005). Endogeneities of optimum currency areas: What brings countries sharing a single currency closer together? *Working Paper Series*, no. 468, European Central Bank. Retrieved from http://www.ecb.europa.eu/pub/pdf/scpwps/ecbwp468.pdf

European Commission. (1990, October). One money, one market: An evaluation of the potential benefits and costs of forming an economic and monetary union. *European Economy*, vol. 44.

European Commission. (2014). Banking Union: Restoring financial stability in the Eurozone. Memo.14/294, Brussels, 15 April 2014.

European Shadow Financial Regulatory Committee. (2014, November 10). Complexity and credibility in the single resolution mechanism. *Statement*, no. 39.

European Shadow Financial Regulatory Committee. (2017, January 24). Legacy problems as a threat to the Banking Union. *Statement*, no. 43.

Frankel, J. A., & Rose, A. K. (1998). The endogeneity of the optimum currency area criteria. *The Economic Journal, 108*(449), 1009–1025.

Hertig, G., & McCahery, J. A. (2003). Company and takeover law reforms in Europe: Misguided harmonization efforts or regulatory competition? *European Business Organization Law Review (EBOR), 4*(2), 179–211.

International Monetary Fund. (2014). *Global financial stability report*. Washington, DC: IMF.

Kerber, W. (2000). Interjurisdictional competition within the European Union. *Fordham International Law Journal, 23*, 217–249.

Kydland, F. E., & Prescott, E. C. (1977). Rules rather than discretion: The inconsistency of optimal plans. *Journal of Political Economy, 85*(3), 473–491.

Luciano, E., & Wihlborg, C. (2018). Financial synergies and systemic risk in the organization of bank affiliates. Journal of Banking and Finance, 89, (March).

Nouy, D. (2014). *Towards the European Banking Union: achievements and challenges.* Speech at the OeNB Conference, Vienna, 12 May 2014.

Prabha, A. P., & Wihlborg, C. (2014). Implicit guarantees, business models and banks' risk-taking through the crisis: Global and European perspectives. *Journal of Economics and Business, 76*, 10–38.

Romano, R. (2006). The states as a laboratory: Legal innovation and state competition for corporate charters. *Yale Journal on Regulation, 23*(2), 209–247.

Schmidt, R. H., & Spindler, G. (2002). Path dependence, corporate governance and complementarity. *International Finance, 5*(3), 311–333.

Sweeney, R. J., Goldberg, L., & Wihlborg, C. (2007). The Nordea experiment: Evidence from market and accounting data. *Journal of Banking and Finance, 31*(4), 1265–1286.

Sykes, A. O. (2000). Regulatory competition or regulatory harmonization? A silly question? *Journal of International Economic Law, 3*(2), 257–264.

Tower, E., & Willett, T. D. (1976). The theory of optimum currency areas and exchange rate flexibility. *Special Papers in International Finance*, no. 11. Princeton, NJ: Princeton University.

Trachtman, J. P. (2000). Regulatory competition and regulatory jurisdiction. *Journal of International Economic Law, 3*(2), 331–348.

Vaubel, R. (2009). The future of fiscal federalism and the need for global government: A response to Vito Tanzi. *European Journal of Political Economy, 25*(1), 133–136.

Wihlborg, C. (2012). Developing distress resolution procedures for financial institutions. *SUERF Study*, no. 4.

Wihlborg, C. (2017). Bail-ins: Issues of credibility and contagion. *SUERF Policy Note*, no. 10.

Wihlborg, C., & Willett, T. D. (1991). Optimum currency areas revisited. In M. Fratianni, C. Wihlborg, & T. D. Willett (Eds.), *Financial regulation and monetary arrangements after 1992.* Amsterdam: Elsevier.

Wihlborg, C., Willett, T. D., & Zhang, N. (2010). The euro debt crisis: It isn't just fiscal. *World Economics, 11*(4), 51–77.

Willett, T. D., Permpoon, O., & Wihlborg, C. (2010). Endogenous OCA analysis and the early euro experience. *The World Economy, 33*(7), 851–872.

Wyplosz, C. (2006). European Monetary Union: the dark sides of a major success. *Economic Policy, 21*(46), 208–261.

The Question of Trust in EU Criminal Law Cooperation: A Constitutional Perspective

Ester Herlin-Karnell

The European Union is currently facing a number of crises: from the migration and euro crises to the increased threat of terrorism throughout Europe and the political uncertainty regarding the impact of 'Brexit'. According to the Lisbon Treaty, the EU is bound to establish an area of freedom, security and justice for the citizens of Europe. The question is what this promise actually entails? Is the EU really able to ensure the freedom of movement and guarantee that human rights are not violated at the same time as the EU sets out to combat organised crime and security threats such as terrorism? The concept of 'freedom' within the scope of this policy area undoubtedly brings this issue to a head. Due to the passport free zone in Europe (Schengen), the objectives regarding, on the one hand, the freedom of movement and, on the other hand, the fight against crime and terrorism are sometimes in conflict. In other words, the safety and security of one person may entail less freedom for another.

The area of freedom, security and justice has developed into one of the most dynamic legal and policy areas of the EU in recent times. Due to the tough political climate in the EU in the wake of the crises of recent years,

E. Herlin-Karnell (✉)
The VU University Amsterdam, Amsterdam, Netherlands

A. Bakardjieva Engelbrekt et al. (eds.), *Trust in the European Union in Challenging Times*, https://doi.org/10.1007/978-3-319-73857-4_7

one of the core principles of EU free movement based on mutual recognition and thereby trust in other EU member states' judicial systems, that is, that the member states accept judgments and decisions made in other member states, has come under serious strain. The idea of mutual trust can be regarded as an expression of the principle of subsidiary in the EU, that is, that national laws and rules are maintained and that legislation is created at the lowest possible level in the EU without reducing effectiveness (Weatherill, 2016). In this light, it is self-evident that trust between the EU member states is of decisive importance in this area, but it has nonetheless proved difficult to achieve within judicial cooperation since national judicial systems are so firmly based in well-established theories on the rights and obligations of the state and the individual.

It should, however, be stressed that since the Lisbon Treaty came into effect in 2009, judicial cooperation in criminal matters has come closer to other areas of cooperation in the EU and principles established by the Court of Justice of the European Union (CJEU) such as that of direct effect of EU directives and of precedence of EU law over national law. Since criminal law has been one of the policy areas most closely linked to national sovereignty in the member states and since the EU has not been regarded as having a mature system of legal safeguards, this has often constituted an obstacle to the emergence of trust among national authorities of different EU member states. For example, the European Arrest Warrant (EAW) (OJEC, 2002) was often mentioned in terms of an unacceptable EU initiative during the British debate in the run up to the 'Brexit' referendum. The 'no side' claimed, for instance, that British citizens could not be guaranteed a fair trial in other member states.

The aim of this chapter is to explain what is meant by judicial cooperation in criminal matters in the EU and in particular to highlight the importance of trust in the case law of the CJEU (the importance of trust in judicial cooperation in civil matters is analysed in Eva Storskrubb's chapter in this volume). The terms 'trust' and 'mutual recognition' must, however, be understood in their specific contexts, which is why this chapter begins with an explanation of what we as legal scholars have in mind when we use these terms here and why the issue of trust is both important and difficult to interpret (trust in political institutions and trust between people is discussed in Linda Berg's and Andreas Bergh's chapters in this volume). In addition, the chapter discusses the constitutional principles that EU law is based on and that are of crucial importance for judicial cooperation in criminal matters within the EU as well as for the area of freedom, security and justice. This is in turn followed by a discussion on proportionality, solidarity and trust since they hold important functions for the creation of this law and policy area. The chapter does not only include an analysis of criminal law, it also takes examples from asylum and migration law. Finally, there are recommendations for action to be taken by the EU in, for example, describing the potential for using the principle of proportionality in the EU as a constitutional 'right' when mutual recognition fails. This is important not least because Europol and Eurojust (the EU bodies for police and prosecutor cooperation) have decision-making functions all whilst lacking clear guidelines for how individuals can appeal decisions.

EU Judicial Cooperation in Criminal Matters and the Emergence of the Area of Freedom, Security and Justice

The EU area of freedom, security and justice is a relatively new legal and policy area even if judicial cooperation has taken different forms in the EU since the Maastricht Treaty came into effect in 1993 (within the framework of the third—intergovernmental—pillar for Justice and Home Affairs (JHA)[1] as it was known at the time). It was, however, only with the entry into force of the Lisbon Treaty that the idea of creating an area of freedom, security and justice, and extending cooperation in criminal law, became a central issue for the EU. At the same time, the UK and Denmark were quick to set limits to how far the EU could be allowed to impact national law in this area. Denmark, for example, chose not to be included in the cooperation at all, while the UK managed before the 'Brexit' referendum to negotiate an opt-out where the UK itself could decide when and how much it wished to participate in EU cooperation in the area of criminal law and migration-related issues.

The reason why security issues have become core issues in Europe is due to the threats and risks linked to terrorism, cross-border organised crime and the freedom of movement within the EU. 9/11 in 2001 in particular contributed to the rapid development of judicial cooperation in criminal matters within the EU. One of the first EU legal acts adopted in this new wave of judicial cooperation in criminal matters was the EU Framework Decision on the EAW (OJEC, 2002). In practice, with this Framework Decision, the right of decision-making regarding these issues was transferred from the politicians to the courts. The EAW did away with the requirement of double criminality (i.e. that an action must be an offence in both countries in question for it to constitute a crime) for 32 named offences. The EAW also introduced the principle of mutual recognition for prosecutions based on the concept of 'trust' between EU member states. However, for a long time the problem with this was the lack of fundamental common understanding, due to the fact that the member states have comparatively different legislation covering the area in question. It is perhaps self-evident that the mutual recognition of legal decisions in EU member states requires a certain amount of trust between the law enforcement agencies. Yet, this has been rather difficult to achieve in such a sensitive area as criminal law (see e.g. European Commission, 2014a).

Dependence on trust in 'ordinary' EU law is, on the other hand, far from new. After all, it was the classic ruling in the *Cassis de Dijon* case (Case C-120/78), which introduced the principle of mutual recognition into EU law, initially for the free movement of goods, to be later on extended to other areas of freedom of movement. The principle implies that when goods produced in one EU member state are released in the Internal Market, they shall be allowed to circulate freely without cross-border obstacles. The gist of it is that national provisions that limit this freedom can only be maintained if proven to be absolutely necessary for overriding reasons of general interest. Thus 'trust' became a key concept in European integration law. In consequence, it is reasonable to presume that the CJEU's focus on trust in the framework of EU criminal law is to a large extent affected by fundamental EU judge-made principles that regulate the Internal Market.

- *Example*: imagine that member state A suspects that person X, a citizen of another member state, has committed a crime in member state A. This state issues an EAW to member state B where X is now located. Previously, state B was obliged to extradite X only if the act for which X was prosecuted in state A constituted a crime also in state B. This principle of double criminality, one of the sacred principles of international criminal law, has however been abolished with the EAW and state B is instead requested to extradite X to state A without looking into whether the deed X is suspected of having committed qualifies as a crime in its domestic legal system.

All EU citizens have the right to freedom, security and justice. Relevant provisions can be found in Article 3(2) in the Treaty on the European Union (TEU) that establishes that:

> The Union shall offer its citizens an area of freedom, security and justice without internal frontiers, in which the free movement of persons is ensured in conjunction with appropriate measures with respect to external border controls, asylum, immigration and the prevention and combating of crime.

Article 4 in the Treaty on the Functioning of the European Union (TFEU) confirms this by expressly recognising the EU's competence in this area and by clarifying that in order to achieve this aim, the EU shall share decision-making competence in this area with the member states. As regards the area of freedom, security and justice, Article 67 TFEU stipulates EU competence as follows:

> The Union shall endeavour to ensure a high level of security through measures to prevent and combat crime, racism and xenophobia, and through measures for coordination and cooperation between police and judicial authorities and other competent authorities, as well as through the mutual recognition of judgments in criminal matters and, if necessary, through the approximation of criminal laws.

Democratic support is vital as regards the issue of trust in this legal and policy area since it touches upon public law, migration policy, human rights in judicial cooperation in criminal matters as well as the fight against terrorism and organised crime. Schengen cooperation is under extreme pressure and the migration crisis still constitutes one of the biggest challenges that the EU has ever faced. This leads us to ask the fundamental question: what is the actual point of extending judicial cooperation in criminal matters within the EU? Is it about safeguarding security for EU citizens or is it also something above and beyond that? In order to understand why and how EU competence is being broadened to cover basically all traditionally national areas of competence, you have to take a step back and study the constitutional regulations that govern EU law and how the policy areas of the EU are integrated.

Constitutional Principles in the EU's Area of Freedom, Security and Justice

The question of trust in the area of criminal law and in EU law in general is primarily an issue about the trust that exists between national authorities, and between them and the EU institutions. Mutual recognition and trust are strongly linked as the EU has few means of its own to monitor the application of EU law in the member states, apart from, for example, the possibility for the European Commission to fine the member states that violate EU rules and regulations (see also Göran von Sydow's chapter in this volume). Thus the EU is ultimately dependent on its member states fully respecting EU law and trusting each other in this regard. The principle of mutual recognition emanates from the Internal Market and the regulation primarily of goods and the freedom of movement for persons (see also Clas Wihborg's chapter on the EU's banking union in this volume). The principle of mutual recognition entails, for example, that all goods that are legally marketed in one member state can be marketed in another, even if they do not fulfil all the technical provisions in that country—apart from under strictly defined circumstances. The difficulty has been transferring this economic logic to criminal law and security-related issues where human rights are often at stake.

Let me explain this problem by using examples of certain important constitutional principles that represent the core of EU cooperation in this field. If the EU is to have its own criminal law structure, a prerequisite is that it has a developed legal system that guarantees human rights and constitutional principles on legality and the rule of law. In EU law, the rule of law is an overarching principle which captures both legality in a strict sense and the due process of law. It is expressed as a constitutional principle in the EU and is also recognised in Article 2 of the TEU. Accordingly, the Union shall be

> founded on the values of respect for human dignity, freedom, democracy, equality, the rule of law and respect for human rights, including the rights of persons belonging to minorities. These values are common to the Member States in a society in which pluralism, non-discrimination, tolerance, justice, solidarity and equality between women and men prevail.

Central to the rule of law is naturally the idea of the legislator being limited by law so that it does not act beyond its powers. Legal certainty is moreover of decisive importance, bearing in mind the public law nature of the area of freedom, security and justice. Thus, the rule of law is fundamental in this context. However, it was not until the 1980s that the ECJ explained in the familiar case *Les Verts* (Case C-294/83 *Les Verts*) that the rule of law was a constitutional principle for the EU. In the much discussed *Kadi* case (Case C-414/05 *P Kadi*), about the right to judicial review in the context of emergency legislation, the EU had frozen financial assets of suspected terrorists (and thereby implemented UN measures regulating the area). The ECJ did not touch upon whether international law took precedence over conflicting EU law on the right to judicial review but instead established that the EU has its own legal system and referred to 'constitutional principles' in the EU, including the right to a fair trial. In short, the rule of law includes the principles on legality, predictability and clarity. In other words, it must be possible for an individual to know which laws and provisions apply to him or her.

Taking the rule of law and the principle of legality into consideration is a necessary condition for the area of freedom, security and justice. Naturally, the principle of legality constitutes the basis for whether the EU has legislative competence in a certain policy area (Articles 4 and 5 TEU, and 7 TFEU), which is also in line with the principle of conferral. The challenge is to strike a balance between the different parameters for freedom, security and justice all whilst upholding the rule of law. However, the question is to what extent the concept of justice, which in itself is difficult to define, is a constitutional EU axiom as such or rather, an objective for the EU (judging by Article 67 TEU it would seem to be an objective).

The European Commission (2014b) published a policy document on the rule of law in 2014 and this document concludes that this principle is the mainstay of every democracy and the entire workings of the EU. The Commission points out that if the member states' mechanisms for safeguarding the rule of law fail, this may jeopardise also the EU as a legal system. This is because the EU needs to protect this principle as a common value for the Union. It can be said that the rule of law encompasses a broader understanding of the concept of 'justice' or 'fairness' and is thus the fundamental constitutional principle that other EU principles are based on. Hence, the rule of law can be regarded as the foundation on which the area of freedom, security and justice must be built.

As noted above, mutual recognition as a form of integration has developed chiefly through the case law of the CJEU. The reason for this development lies in the fact that the EU has often lacked legislative competence when the member states have not meant for the EU to have legislative powers and have therefore preferred this 'milder' form of cooperation in criminal law. However, at the same time, the absence of a clear definition for how the area of freedom, security and justice should be constructed is a challenge for the prevalence of trust in Europe and what can perhaps be called the constitutional system of the EU that shall guarantee human rights. The question is all the more urgent since the EU, as is well known, has as yet not signed the European Convention on Human Rights (ECHR) and Fundamental Freedoms due to the Opinion of the Court in 2/13 (see Joakim Nergelius' chapter in this volume). The Court implied that if every individual EU member state were, for example, to check whether an EAW also fulfilled the requirements in the ECHR that would have a negative impact on the effectiveness of (and thus trust in) EU law and its application in the member states (Herlin-Karnell, 2013).

The Lack of a Common Yardstick Undermines Trust in Judicial Cooperation in Criminal Matters in the EU

The function of trust is notably the assumption that EU member states trust each other sufficiently not to require further legal guarantees or checks to execute their commitments within the framework of judicial cooperation in criminal matters. As mentioned above, the EAW is perhaps the most well-known example of mutual recognition within the EU in a criminal law context. The EAW system is based on the principle of mutual recognition. This is in turn based on the mutual trust that exists between member states as regards the ability of the national legal orders to ensure an equal and effective protection of the fundamental rights that are recognised in EU law and in particular in the Charter of Fundamental Rights of the European Union. The ECJ has pointed this out on numerous occasions, most recently in *Aranyosi* and *Căldăraru* (Case C-404/15 C-659/15 PPU):

> Both the principle of mutual trust between the Member States and the principle of mutual recognition are, in EU law, of fundamental importance given that they allow an area without internal borders to be created and maintained. More specifically, the principle of mutual trust requires, particularly with regard to the area of freedom, security and justice, each of those States, save in exceptional circumstances, to consider all the other Member States

> to be complying with EU law and particularly with the fundamental rights recognised by EU law.

However, as the Advocate General of the ECJ, Paolo Mengozzi expresses in the *Da Silva Jorge* ruling (Case C-42/11 *Da Silva Jorge*):

> the principle of mutual recognition which lies at the heart of the mechanism behind the European Arrest Warrant cannot conceivably be applied in the same way as it is in the case of the recognition of a university qualification or a driving licence issued by another Member State. [...] The principle of mutual recognition, more specifically where it is applied in relation to a European Arrest Warrant issued for the purposes of executing a sentence, as it is in the main proceedings, cannot be applied automatically but must, on the contrary, be viewed in the light of the personal and human context of the individual situation underlying each request for the execution of that warrant.

As has already been emphasised, criminal law has traditionally constituted a national issue. In the EU, it has therefore for a long time been managed within the framework of intergovernmental cooperation. Criminal law made a first appearance in the EU when the Maastricht Treaty came into effect in 1993. However, the design of the so-called third pillar that encompassed JHA was criticised by the European Parliament at an early stage for a lack of democratic control as well as the very limited possibility for the ECJ to issue preliminary rulings. Thus, several changes to the system were required, not least since proposed EU legal acts rarely led to concrete results.

Why are trust and mutual recognition sometimes considered a problem in this context? Naturally, there are several reasons for this. EU member states have a great deal in common but there are also many differences. It comes as no surprise that the principle of mutual recognition, irrespective of the fact that it is inherently hard to define, has been popular among EU political leaders, since it has been regarded as an effective way to maintain national legislation despite increased European integration. The principle of mutual recognition, where trust is a prerequisite, has long been prevalent within the Internal Market with the free movement of goods, services, capital and people (Peers, 2015). It has gradually been broadened to also apply to the EU's judicial cooperation in criminal matters. The presumption of trust has constituted a way to broaden the competence of the EU when the EU has not had legislative power. The reason is simple: before the

Lisbon Treaty came into effect, the EU had very limited competence to adopt legislation in the area of JHA. Therefore, it was the ECJ that introduced the concept of 'mutual trust' in its case law (Mitsilegas, 2009).

It should be stressed that this concept has fulfilled an important function also in the area of civil law, as probably in all areas of EU law (see Eva Storskrubb's chapter in this volume). In the CJEU, there has often been a presumption of trust and the view that trust must take precedence over contradictory considerations. It is therefore possible to say that the presumption of trust in this area has constituted a quasi-constitutional standard with the purpose of justifying EU measures. The problem is that it remains unclear how to measure and determine trust objectively. The concept of trust has thus always been fairly vague (Jansson, 2013). This lack of conceptual clarity has been regarded as an important deficiency in the EU's judicial cooperation in the area of criminal law.

What about the legitimacy of the issue of trust? How was it possible to broaden the competence of the EU only through the presumption of trust? Similarly, it is unclear whether trust as a legitimising factor in this respect has ever been a part of either national or international criminal law. It constitutes, in other words, a unique European strategy and, more importantly, it seems to be a mechanical translation taken directly from the model of the Internal Market without any underlying research into whether it actually might lead to successful judicial cooperation in the area of criminal law at all. The function of trust in EU criminal law is thus still a mysterious issue. Even if it is important to question whether an integration model that is based on trust is as forceful as tangible legislation, the concept of trust seems to have been used to justify the promotion of the EU project, even if it, from the start, was much too far-reaching and ambiguous. This explains why the CJEU to such a large extent focuses on the effectiveness of the EU's judicial cooperation in the area of criminal law and why only very few cases have been allowed to break the presumption of mutual trust between member states (e.g. as regards the risk of inhumane treatment such as torture).

As has been mentioned previously, the EAW entails that the double criminality for 32 listed crimes has been abolished and replaced by the principle of mutual recognition. The issue is, however, the extent to which mutual recognition can be limited by other legal principles, such as the rules for a fair trial in accordance with ECHR as well as the EU Charter of Fundamental Rights. In the *IB* ruling (Case C-306/09) on the application of the EAW, the CJEU confirmed that mutual recognition is not absolute and that there may be individual aspects hampering the effectiveness of mutual recognition. Moreover, in *Wolzenburg* (Case C-123/08), the issue of whether the possibility to serve the remainder of a sentence in another EU member state was touched upon. In that case, the ECJ pronounced that according to the European Directive (2004, p. 38) on EU Citizenship, an EU citizen must have lived in another member state for five years before being able to enjoy all benefits accorded by the Directive. The Court also established that it lies in their very nature that the requirements regarding the principles of proportionality and non-discrimination shall be observed within the area of EU judicial cooperation in criminal law. The Directive (2004, p. 38) does, however, mean that the five-year rule regarding the right to serve a sentence in the host country resembles restrictions for students receiving study grants.

A driving principle in the area of criminal law within the framework of mutual recognition has been the principle of effectiveness (Herlin-Karnell, 2012). This has, however, entailed certain problems as regards striking the right balance between effectiveness and the protection of human rights. The issue came to the fore in the *Melloni* case (C-399/11) concerning whether a member state may refuse to execute an EAW based on Article 53 in the Charter of Fundamental Rights and the reasoning that the fundamental rights of the person in question had been disregarded according to the national constitution. The article stipulates the following:

> Nothing in this Charter shall be interpreted as restricting or adversely affecting human rights and fundamental freedoms as recognised, in their respective fields of application, by Union law and international law including the European Convention for the Protection of Human Rights and Fundamental Freedoms, and by the member states' constitutions.

The constitutional issue in the *Melloni* case was therefore whether the EU's principle of effectiveness weighs heavier than the rights established in a national constitution. It concerned the validity of a national constitutional principle on the ban on extraditing a person convicted in absentia. The ECJ ruled that the effectiveness of EU law takes precedence over conflicting national constitutions. However, the fact of the matter remains that criminal law is an area where the involvement of the EU may entail drastic consequences for an individual primarily because there is a risk that centralisation may interfere with the protective aspects of national constitutions since these often include a more developed protection of rights for the individual. The Court took the view that the executive legal authority had to postpone its decision regarding extradition of the person in question while awaiting the supplementary information that would make it possible to disregard the existence of such a risk. The Court also stressed that the executive legal authority had to respect the proportionality requirement, as stipulated in Article 52(1) in the Charter, with regard to the limitation of any right or freedom recognised in the Charter.

Still, in the recent *Aranyosi and Căldăraru* case (C-404/15 and C-659/15 PPU) concerning the execution of an EAW, the ECJ ruled that the prohibition of inhuman and degrading treatment as set out in Article 4 of the Charter of Fundamental Rights is absolute in that it is closely linked to respect for human dignity. The Court held that the executing judicial authority must postpone its decision on the surrender of the individual concerned until it obtains the supplementary information that allows it to exclude the existence of a risk of such treatment.

The risk entailed by the centralisation of judicial cooperation in the area of criminal law is thus the loss of the protective mechanisms in procedural law that are ensured through national law but which have been excluded in EU cooperation due to the effectiveness requirement and conflicts between member states. When one speaks of European criminal law, it is easy to gain the impression that it is the result of the general success of the European project. However, seen in a historical perspective, it is quite difficult to speak of Europeanisation of criminal law as a recent phenomenon, bearing in mind that it already is European in so many respects, inspired as it is by the Age of Enlightenment. There are still, however, substantial differences between EU member states' legal systems and traditions. It is these cultural similarities and differences that also make the concept of European criminal law so very complex.

In *The European Agenda on Security*, the European Commission (2015a) notes that people are crossing national borders within the EU more and more, and are becoming increasingly frustrated by the different rules in the EU member states and the inconvenience of various procedures. According to the Commission, this is mainly due to the economic crisis as well as a lack of capacity in certain national legal systems, which in turn undermine the trust the citizens have in the EU project as such. The Commission also points out that the EU needs to develop a common feeling of justice at the EU level that is linked to the broader issue of values and the type of area of freedom, security and justice that the EU is actually striving to build.

Due to a series of problems that have arisen in relation to the EAW, the European Commission has revised the handbook on its implementation in the member states. The Commission points out in the evaluation that an effective implementation of the EAW has been undermined by the fact that people are often wanted for less serious crimes. Thus, the Commission notes that there is a need to apply a proportionality test for the Arrest Warrant in order to avoid misuse. The Commission particularly emphasises that the handbook on the Arrest Warrant must be adapted to meet the requirement regarding proportionality and is taking into consideration the factors that are going to be assessed in conjunction with the execution of an EAW and the possible alternatives before an arrest warrant can be issued. In this way, the Commission hopes to prevent absurd consequences and unreasonable costs.

The Relationship Between Asylum, Migration and Trust in the EU

The questions concerning trust and mutual recognition and confidence in the EU more generally are also central to the very important area of asylum law. As mentioned above, migration law and asylum law are a part of the EU policy area of freedom, security and justice. They are also central to the understanding of criminal law. When the ECJ builds up its case law on trust in this law and policy area, it perceives the different policy areas as connected. In other words, legislation and case law in the area of asylum and immigration are of direct relevance to criminal law as regards the interpretation of the concept of trust in the area of freedom, security and justice. Moreover, administrative sanctions are often used in the area of migration law in relation to what is often referred to as the people who 'stay behind' (i.e. people who, for example, remain in an EU member state after their visa has expired). The relationship with the criminal law system is complicated since many of the procedures in the area of asylum are similar to criminal law and should thus entail the same protection of rights.

The *El Dridi* judgment (Case C-61/11) is particularly instructive in this regard. In this judgment, the Court established that the principle of proportionality shall be observed when EU member states decide to send asylum seekers back to another state. This means that national courts must try the legality of coercive measures, which, for example, include imprisonment and subsequently deportation. Moreover, the national court has the right to refuse to execute a custodial sentence for illegally staying in the country in question when imprisonment is only a punishment before a subsequent deportation.

In the *NS* case (Case C-411/10), also within the framework of asylum law, the ECJ established that if there is reason to believe that there are systematic deficiencies in the asylum procedure in an EU member state (e.g. as regards the transfer of an asylum seeker to another territory), then transferring an asylum seeker to that member state would be incompatible with the EU Charter on Fundamental Rights. According to the Court, there is no doubt that where there is a serious risk that the rights of an asylum seeker may be violated, the member states should have a great deal of discretion and the EU law presumption of trust may thus be broken. This means that under certain circumstances the principle of effectiveness of EU law is overridden and it enables the member state where the asylum application was submitted to examine the application even if the strictly formulated criteria in the Dublin III Regulation are not fulfilled. This is important not least when a state that is supposedly responsible for the asylum procedure is regarded as being less suitable due to the state not taking sufficient consideration of human rights.

In the EU's *Agenda on Migration* from the spring of 2015, the European Commission (2015b) points out that of the deficiencies found in the EU rules on asylum law and migration, it is the lack of mutual trust between member states (in particular, as a consequence of the continued fragmentation of the asylum system) that stands out. According to the Commission, this has a direct impact on asylum seekers, not just for those who 'choose' the host nation but also on public opinion in the EU. The Commission notes that such a system where solidarity in the EU is broken does not benefit trust in Europe but that it is hoped that the new Common European Asylum System (Directive 2013/32/EU) will contribute to increasing trust between the member states. The political agenda is thus ready and prepared; the question is whether the citizens also have confidence in it.

The Principle of Proportionality and Solidarity and Their Role in EU Criminal Law

Even if trust in the EU member states is a rather vague concept, the idea is that it should contribute to enhancing solidarity within the EU. If solidarity is to have any real meaning in a criminal law context, it must be based on common sense of a kind. This is often mentioned in discussions on proportionality. It is here that the idea of proportionality represents the core of constitutional law (see e.g. Klatt & Meister, 2012). Proportionality in an EU context means a line of reasoning based on common sense where the idea of 'suitability' and 'balance' constitute the golden rule on which decisions concerning the desirability of a certain piece of EU legislation rest, determining whether the costs are higher than the actual gains (Craig, 2012).

When the CJEU or the legislator in the EU determines whether a law is proportional, they examine whether the measure is suitable or appropriate in order to achieve a desired result or whether the same can be achieved through a less onerous measure. Proportionality is thus a general control mechanism in EU legislation that is suitable for the assessment of the reasonability of EU measures and the actions of member states when they later fall within the area of application of the EU treaties. Moreover, the idea of proportionality governs the extent to which the member states may be exempt from their duties and obligations under EU law. The principle of proportionality is also an important tool for making decisions concerning whether exercising the legislative competence of the EU is justified. In this respect, every legislative measure must be effective in order to achieve the goal of the competence that has been granted. Finally, the negative impact on other interests must be compensated by the positive impact of EU action in a specific area.

The principle of proportionality has always played a central role in EU law (both legislative and judicial). Naturally, the Lisbon Treaty stipulates that the EU shall respect freedom and justice but also establishes a high level of security within Europe. It is still unclear what this actually entails in practice and how the right balance between these different values can be achieved. The question is rather whether a correct application of the principle of proportionality may function as a correction of the assumption made previously that there was no, or at least very few, limits regarding the principle of mutual recognition in the area of freedom, security and justice. Therefore, it is important that at least non-discrimination and proportionality within the framework of EU criminal legislation are seen as principles that are inextricably linked. The question of trust in EU criminal law must be seen in a broader perspective. As has been explained above, the EAW has played a central role in the emergence of criminal law at the EU level, but as has also been mentioned above, the EU principle of mutual recognition has never been a success due to the lack of trust between EU member states.

The problem is that the area of freedom, security and justice is to a large extent exempt from the rules of proportionality due to the focus on crisis management that has characterised this area, largely shaped as a response to threats and risks linked to terrorism. The EU has felt the need for greater discretion to be able to act rapidly in the fight against crime and terrorism. Hence, for a long time, a proportionality test was ruled out. Now, however, the EAW has enforced such a requirement since this instrument did not lead to the desired consequences. There was talk of absurd cases that were not linked to terrorism but where the same rigid legal examination was applied. This could result in deportation for the theft of a chicken and other less serious offences (Case Ö-430-07, *Biszak*, the Swedish Supreme Court).

In Article 49 of the EU Fundamental Rights Charter that became binding through the Lisbon Treaty, a guarantee was now stipulated for the legality and proportionality of sanctions in a more all-encompassing manner than in the ECHR. However, it is interesting to note that the principle of proportionality can both broaden rights and limit them. Despite this, Article 52(1) establishes certain important exceptions from the application of the Charter in its entirety. This provision clearly stipulates that:

> Any limitation on the exercise of the rights and freedoms recognised by this Charter must be provided for by law and respect the essence of those rights and freedoms. Subject to the principle of proportionality, limitations may be made only if they are necessary and genuinely meet objectives of general interest recognised by the Union or the need to protect the rights and freedoms of others.

It is true, however, that such a limitation is not unique for the EU. Also the ECHR Article 5 includes a similar possibility to subject fundamental freedoms and rights to limitations if these are necessary in a democratic society. The risk is that even if it is of utmost importance to maintain security in a society, the security agenda can easily be manipulated to always suit 'what is deemed necessary in a democratic society'. That is why it is so important that the principle of proportionality is used in a broader sense as a part of the establishment of trust in the area of freedom, security and justice. The explanatory notes also indicate that the reference to general interests that are recognised by the EU includes both the goals mentioned in Article 3 TEU as well as other interests that are protected through special provisions in the EU treaties, given that these limitations actually respond to a general EU interest.

The application of the principle of proportionality has recently been in the limelight in conjunction with the Data Retention Directive, cyber-related crime and the EU's fight against terrorism. In 2014, the CJEU declared the Data Retention Directive invalid in a judgment which received a great deal of attention. The aim of the Directive was to make it possible to collect data in the member states from individuals and subsequently store it for two years, in order to fight crime and terrorism. This applied even if there was no real suspicion of a crime in each separate case. In this case, *Digital Rights* (Case C-293/12), the Court's view was that such a system was in breach of the principle of proportionality and thus also of the fundamental right to data protection as it is proclaimed in the European Charter on Fundamental Rights.

According to the Court, the Directive was far too sweeping and therefore violated, for example, the fundamental right to data protection as stipulated in Article 8 of the Charter. The Court pointed out that the Directive allowed the national authorities to trace data without any tangible suspicion of a crime. Moreover, in *Schrems* (Case C-362/14), the Court established that allowing US intelligence services, on the basis of US law, to scrutinise *Facebook* pages in the EU in order to gain access to the personal data of EU citizens violated the European Charter on Fundamental Rights. This was against current EU legislation and the doctrine of adequate protection (2000/520), adopted in accordance with Article 25 in Directive (95/46) on data protection. According to Directive (95/46), the transfer of personal data outside the European Economic Area (EEA) (which includes all the EU member states as well as Iceland, Liechtenstein and Norway) to a third country is only permitted if the third country provides an 'adequate level of protection'. The European Commission can establish that a third country meets this standard by considering this country's national legislation or international commitments taking all the circumstances surrounding the transfer of data into account.

In this case, the Court declared the Commission's decision concerning the adequate protection of information that had been transferred to the US as invalid and not proportional (Fletcher & Herlin-Karnell, 2016). Perhaps the theory of proportionality might be seen as a necessary step in the fragmented EU where trust must be accepted at a sufficient level in order to facilitate the application of the law in the national courts and authorities. The idea here is also that it is necessary to take the holistic approach and to see an integrated area of freedom, security and justice. The EU machinery holds together since the different law and policy areas are inextricably linked and in order to understand that, broad knowledge of what the EU is and why enhanced cooperation is needed.

The Path to Enhanced Trust in the EU's Area of Freedom, Security and Justice

This chapter has highlighted the issue of mutual recognition and the concept of trust in EU law and its consequences for the area of freedom, security and justice. The main purpose has been to give a perspective on trust which is used as a proxy for mutual recognition in criminal law and how the principle of proportionality may contribute to an improved and more balanced system in the EU. The chapter has also underlined the danger of the 'proportionality test' as it may provide an opening to depart from EU law depending on what proportionality is deemed to mean in an EU context.

Judicial cooperation in the EU started as an experiment in crisis management at a high level and at the cost of adequate protection for the individual. The EU has been under a great deal of pressure: enhanced cooperation is necessary to handle risks and threats linked to terrorism and cross-border organised crime but the member states have not been entirely prepared to abandon their national competence in the area of criminal law. It could be said that the ECJ and the European Commission, which are the strongest drivers of developments in this area, have more recently perhaps adopted a more mature position where mutual recognition is not believed to be on a par with blind trust (see e.g. Nicolaïdis, 2007). It is above all the principle of proportionality that has become increasingly important even if there is a need for greater specification and a clearer definition.

Judicial cooperation in the area of criminal law in the EU is currently in an interim phase and its future in the area of freedom, security and justice is uncertain. The many crises that dominate Europe call on us to take a step back and critically discuss how cooperation should progress. A strong commitment to the rule of law and the protection of human rights must be the guiding principle throughout this law and policy area. Future EU criminal law will therefore to a large extent not only depend on the politics of the EU institutions but also on the level of commitment and understanding among all those who in some way work in this area.

It is therefore more important than ever that the EU and its member states strive towards a coordination of their case law in the area of criminal law bearing the EU Charter of Fundamental Rights in mind. Another important aspect is that the ECJ now emphasises the importance of reasonable trust as well as the importance of common EU values as regards the full protection of human rights. Moreover, it is necessary to strike a balance between the different components that together shape an area of freedom, security and justice as well as EU law more generally. Perhaps 'Brexit', migration crisis, terrorist threats, financial crisis and all the other crises currently affecting Europe will provide an opening for the EU to reformulate its policy principles and to be more determined and robust regarding the values that should guide the EU in its judicial cooperation in criminal matters.

Against this background, I would propose the following brief recommendations for action to the EU. First, the principle of proportionality should be accorded a greater importance in the EU's legislative process and similarly, the ECJ should integrate a proportionality test in its interpretation of the concept of trust as a way of assuring the member states that the EU Charter on Fundamental Rights and the ECHR are the lowest common denominator. Second, the EU must uphold the rule of law even in emergency situations like the fight against terrorism and strive to remedy the democratic deficit in the EU in general and more particularly in the area of freedom, security and justice where the demand for effectiveness often overshadows fundamental rights. Third, European universities offering courses on EU law, as well as bar associations in the EU, should offer specialised courses on EU criminal law and its place in the EU constitutional grid. It is vital that future legal experts and political scientists have proper knowledge of this area as long as the EU remains a project to be taken seriously. I would even claim that adequate knowledge on the prospects and limits of EU cooperation in the field of criminal law is fundamental for trust in the EU.

Notes

1. The second (also intergovernmental) pillar in the pre-Lisbon EU system was the Common Foreign and Security Policy (CFSP) and the first (supranational) pillar was the Internal Market.

References

Craig, P. (2012). *EU administrative law*. Oxford: Oxford University Press.

Directive 2004:38 OJ, L158/77. On the right of citizens of the Union and their family members.

European Commission. (2014a). *The EU Justice Agenda for 2020—Strengthening trust, mobility and growth within the Union*. COM(2014) 144 final, Strasbourg, 11 March 2014.

European Commission. (2014b). *A new EU framework to strengthen the rule of law*. COM(2014) 158 final, Brussels, 19 March 2014.

European Commission. (2015a). *The European Agenda on Security*. COM(2015) 185 final, Brussels, 28 April 2015.

European Commission. (2015b). *A European Agenda on Migration*. COM(2015) 240 final, Brussels, 13 May 2015.

Fletcher, M., & Herlin-Karnell, E. (2016). Is there a transatlantic security strategy? Area of freedom, security and justice law and its global dimension. In M. Fletcher, E. Herlin-Karnell, & C. Matera (Eds.), *The European Union as an area of freedom, security and justice*. London: Routledge.

Herlin-Karnell, E. (2012). *The constitutional dimension of European criminal law*. Oxford: Hart Publishing.

Herlin-Karnell, E. (2013). From mutual trust to the full effectiveness of EU law: 10 years of the European arrest warrant. *European Law Review, 38*(1), 79–91.

Jansson, C. (2013). *Mutual recognition*. Oxford: Oxford University Press.

Klatt, M., & Meister, M. (2012). *The constitutional structure of proportionality*. Oxford: Oxford University Press.

Mitsilegas, M. (2009). *EU criminal law*. Oxford: Hart Publishing.

Nicolaïdis, K. (2007). Trusting the poles? Constructing Europe through mutual recognition. *Journal of European Public Policy, 14*(5), 682–698.

Official Journal of the European Communities. (2002). Council Framework Decision of 13 June 2002 on the European arrest warrant and the surrender procedures between Member States (2002/584/JHA).

Peers, S. (2015). *EU justice and home affairs: Vol. 1 & 2*. Oxford: Oxford University Press.

Weatherill, S. (2016). *Law and values in the European Union*. Oxford: Oxford University Press.

Mutual Trust in Civil Justice Cooperation in the EU

Eva Storskrubb

This chapter deals with trust in the context of judicial cooperation in civil matters, which has been part of the broader European Union project of creating an Area of Freedom, Security and Justice (AFSJ) since the Amsterdam Treaty (Title IV and Article 81 in the Treaty on the Functioning of the European Union (TFEU), see also Storskrubb, 2016a, 2016b). Particular attention is here given to how trust operates when judgments rendered in civil litigation cases move across borders.[1] The principle of mutual trust has emerged as a political goal in EU's AFSJ but it has also been given a normative understanding in the case law of the European Court of Justice (ECJ) on free movement of judgments. How to understand mutual trust and what it actually entails has in recent years become one of the central and most critical issues in the development of the AFSJ. The broader question that the principle raises is whether individual rights can be sacrificed in some cases in order to uphold a fictitious presumption of trust. I argue that the answer to that question might affect the legitimacy of the EU as a whole, beyond the context of the individual case.

E. Storskrubb (✉)
Uppsala University, Uppsala, Sweden

A. Bakardjieva Engelbrekt et al. (eds.), *Trust in the European Union in Challenging Times*, https://doi.org/10.1007/978-3-319-73857-4_8

The political project to create the AFSJ was set in motion with the Treaty of Amsterdam 1999 and entailed deeper integration in judicial matters than its predecessor, Justice and Home Affairs cooperation that had been launched in the Maastricht Treaty in 1993. A plethora of factors provided the impetus for the political project at that point in time. Apart from the desire to bring the EU closer to its citizens and the challenges of the forthcoming enlargement of the Union, there were also perceived threats such as organised crime and irregular migration. It is striking that such threats were identified long before 9/11 or present-day terrorist threats and immigration crisis of 2015. However, this chapter does not deal with EU criminal justice cooperation or EU asylum and migration policy that are addressed elsewhere in this book (see Esther Herlin-Karnell's chapter). Instead, it deals with the third branch of the AFSJ, namely civil justice that pertains to cross-border civil litigation. Examples of such cases are disputes regarding child custody and maintenance, as well as disputes regarding family succession, consumer sales, large deliveries between companies and employment relationships.

Civil justice cooperation in the EU has strong connection with the EU's Internal Market. Facilitating the resolution of cross-border disputes and increased mutual trust among the legal systems of EU member states are considered to enhance legal certainty and thereby to support cross-border trade and growth. The political connection between trust in the legal systems and economic growth is highlighted in the strategic guidelines of the European Council for the AFSJ for 2015–2019:

> The smooth functioning of a true European area of justice with respect for the different legal systems and traditions of the member states is vital for the EU. In this regard, mutual trust in one another's justice systems should be further enhanced. A sound European justice policy will contribute to economic growth by helping businesses and consumers to benefit from a reliable business environment within the internal market. (European Council, 2014)

Hence, this chapter addresses a question of fundamental importance for the EU and not least for the creation of the Internal Market. If trust fails in a context that is so crucial for the EU, this might be an indication of a more deep-seated fragility of the European integration project. But at the same time, it underlines how important it is to continue to nurture trust in civil justice cooperation since it relates to such fundamental aspects of the EU. In addition, it takes time for legal cultures to meet and for trust to be gained. Therefore, if trust is simply presumed, it may be detrimental for the legitimacy of the EU. The issue of mutual trust in civil justice cooperation is hence of crucial importance for the EU today.

The Development of EU Civil Justice Cooperation

In civil justice, the question of mutual trust has been strongly linked to the goal of implementing mutual recognition of judgments. Already the Conclusions of the Tampere European Council in 1999, setting out the first guidelines for the AFSJ, established that mutual recognition would be the 'cornerstone' for EU cooperation in the field (European Council, 1999). In this context, mutual recognition implies that a judgment from one EU member state shall be granted the same effect in other EU member states. If the judgment does not have such an effect, there is a risk that the winning party to a dispute ultimately is unable to realise its rights. In practice, this entails a risk that the judgment creditor is not paid what it is due based on a judgment or that it takes time and monetary resources for the creditor to obtain payment in another EU member state. Mutual recognition is for this reason important for private citizens and corporate actors.

After Tampere, the Council of the EU elaborated a programme for the implementation of mutual recognition of decisions in civil matters (OJEC, 2001). The programme outlined a number of steps and measures to be taken. With respect to measures aimed at supporting mutual recognition, it noted that:

> It will sometimes be necessary, or even essential, to lay down a number of procedural rules at European level, which will constitute common minimum guarantees intended to strengthen mutual trust between the member states' legal systems. These guarantees will make it possible, *inter alia*, to ensure that the requirements for a fair trial are strictly observed. (OJEC, 2001)

Thus, the underlying logic was that for mutual recognition (i.e. the free movement of judgments in the EU) to be achieved, there needs to be mutual trust between EU member states based on some level of common procedural standards protecting fundamental procedural rights and fair trial. Andersson (2005, p. 247) notes that 'the big problem [...] with the principle of mutual recognition [...] is that it requires mutual trust [and] requires in its extreme, that a domestic legal system allows for enforcement of judgments based on procedural rules and ideological values over which the member state has no influence and very little knowledge'. The intermediary exequatur procedure including the possibility to refuse to recognise a foreign judgment on limited grounds such as public policy has traditionally and historically been a general safeguard against unwanted effects of mutual recognition. Thus, recognition in a foreign jurisdiction has always been predicated upon checks and balances, on balancing the public policy of the forum against the rights of private parties (Paul, 2008).[2] The current debate on mutual trust in civil justice in the EU has been triggered by the aim of going further and removing such checks and balances. At the centre of the debate are questions of whether and how far certification procedures, safeguards and grounds for refusal can be removed in cross-border recognition of judgments.

Mutual recognition was imported in the AFSJ from the Internal Market. It has developed as a regulatory integration method over a number of decades in the context of the four fundamental freedoms related to free movement of goods, services, capital and persons (see Articles 5, 28, 45 and 63 TFEU). The free movement of judgments has therefore been called the 'fifth' freedom. Integration of markets has three basic regulatory models: (i) national treatment (host-country rules), (ii) harmonisation (similar rules) and (iii) mutual recognition (home-state rules) (Schmidt, 2007). Under the first alternative, national treatment, the burden on the market participants is high because they have to adapt to different national rules, but the host country keeps its rules and does not have to relinquish sovereignty. It only has to open its borders to participants willing to enter its market and follow its rules (non-discrimination). With the second and opposite alternative (harmonisation) market, participants wanting to enter other markets do not face additional costs but the states have to relinquish sovereignty vertically to the supranational level and can face considerable negotiating costs. Finally, the third option, mutual recognition, can be seen as an ostensibly benign and easy middle ground. The countries do not need to face negotiation costs and companies do not have to face adaptation costs as home-state control means that it suffices to fulfil only one set of national rules, those in the country of origin (Schmidt, 2007).

What is sometimes overlooked is that mutual recognition as a mode of governance does, nevertheless, mean that states relinquish sovereignty albeit horizontally (Nicolaïdis, 2007). The national regulator can no longer ensure the same level of regulation to users within its territory when new and foreign participants enter the market based on their own (foreign) home-state regulation. This means that although mutual recognition may be a simple solution for states and market participants, the end-users, buyers or consumers may face information and other costs due to the diversity. In addition, diversity may fuel regulatory competition, even creating a risk of so-called race to the bottom (see also Clas Whilborg's and Sarkis J. Khoury's chapter in this volume). If diversity is perceived to cause unwanted risks, the legitimacy of the system may be questioned by the users and states held politically accountable (Schmidt, 2007).

Such a development has not been seen as desirable in the EU and, therefore, the EU model of mutual recognition is not pure. It is of crucial importance to note that mutual recognition in the Internal Market has never been unconditional. Restrictions to protect important national rights and values have always been present in the EU treaties and also introduced in the case law, though only insofar as a limitation is deemed to be proportionate. For example, this applied in the famous *Cassis de Dijon* case (see also Snell, 2014). In addition, mutual recognition has not been the sole regulatory method in the Internal Market, it has been used in parallel with inter alia minimum harmonisation and other governance techniques such as administrative cooperation and communication structures (Chalmers et al., 2014; see also Snell, 2016). Mutual recognition has also therefore been called 'managed', meaning that it does not operate in a void but is always related formally to other forms of integration and informally to societal prerequisites such as acceptance and trust (Lavenex, 2007). Nicolaïdis notes that in implementing mutual recognition, a fine-tuned balance must be struck between recognition and the constraints that must be attached to it. Thus, there is an analogous difference between 'blind' and 'binding trust' (Nicolaïdis, 2007).

Notably, mutual trust has also been present as a normative and regulatory concept in the Internal Market. This has been the case in particular, in cases related to the obligation of competent authorities to accept decisions of authorities in other EU member states, inter alia in relation to inspection of goods carried out by authorities in other member states or decisions on social security made by authorities in other member states (Cambien, 2017). However, also in specific mutual trust situations, it has similar to mutual recognition not been an unconditional principle in the Internal Market arena (Prechal, 2017). Rather, Cambien notes that mutual trust or a lack thereof has also affected the regulatory strategy linked to mutual recognition. For example, in the case of provision of services, it occasioned a debated legislation on the harmonisation of rules related to services and in many other pieces of legislation it has been invoked in order to emphasise to need to deepen administrative cooperation or increase transparency (Cambien, 2017).

The major political driver for introducing mutual recognition as a regulatory strategy for the AFSJ at Tampere was the willingness of EU member states to retain sovereignty in the policy fields of civil and criminal justice. However, as the Internal Market example shows, and as EU leaders presumably knew, sovereignty was only superficially preserved because mutual recognition actually entails relinquishing sovereignty—not vertically to the supranational regulator but horizontally to the other national regulators (Lavenex, 2007; Nicolaïdis, 2007). The question has therefore been raised whether mutual recognition (and by implication mutual trust that is considered necessary to support mutual recognition) is the most appropriate regulatory strategy for the AFSJ. It has been asked whether an integration method originally adopted for goods and services is suitable for judgments and justice systems (Schmidt, 2007; Storskrubb, 2016a). The issue becomes more complex in the context of civil judgments because the stated aim in the above-mentioned programme is to remove all barriers to direct enforcement of judgments. This means that it is potentially difficult to combine or calibrate the effects of mutual recognition with other regulatory strategies. The EU thus appears to have chosen to aim for a stricter regulatory model in this context. This choice can cause problems in case mutual trust is not at hand, and it becomes ever more important for the EU to promote but arguably also support the development of mutual trust. Before we turn to analyse the legislative and regulatory framework closer, it is pertinent to provide some additional context and nuance to the development of mutual trust in civil justice.

Mutual Recognition in a Broader International Context

Importing the principle of mutual recognition from the Internal Market arena to the AFSJ is, notwithstanding the critique mentioned above, not entirely far-fetched seen in a broader international context. There are several historical examples of states cooperating to recognise each other's judgments. The pressure to do so has come from international trade long before today's globalisation. The respect and trust, by Whytock (2014) even called 'faith' (or 'comity'), which states have been prepared to accord each other historically in private international law has often been the most far-reaching between closely situated states; geographically, legally, politically or even commercially. Examples of such close regional ties include private international law conventions between the Nordic countries (Jänterä-Jareborg, 2016). Within the EU (at the time the European Community, EC), the then six member states started private international law cooperation among themselves already in 1968, entering into the Brussels Convention. The Convention was intended to support trade and free movement within the EC. Even though there was a clear mutual interest and proximity on many of the above-mentioned levels between the member states, the Convention still included many of the traditional safeguards for recognition and enforcement of judgments including the exequatur procedure and specific grounds for refusal.

In Europe, we have also since 1953 had the European Convention on Human Rights (ECHR). Although the ECHR has not been enacted under the auspices of the EU, it can still be said to provide EU member states with a common value basis with respect to human rights and fundamental freedoms. Hence, it can be seen as a potential basis for a nascent mutual respect or trust amongst the legal systems of EU member states, long before the EU signed its own Charter of Fundamental Rights. Despite these mutually shared values, all EU member states occasionally breach the ECHR. For example, in 2016, the European Court of Human Rights (ECrtHR) found at least one violation in 385 cases related to EU member states. Of course, not all human rights breaches in the EU reach the Court. Thus, it is clear and uncontested that the legal systems of EU member states do not always in practice manage to uphold human rights and there may arise individual cases in which violations occur. In the context of civil justice, the central right is the right to fair trial guaranteed in Article 6 ECHR and also now Article 47 of the EU Charter of Fundamental Rights. A classic example of a violation of the right to a fair trial in the case law of the ECrtHR is when court proceedings are unreasonably long. For instance, Italy has repeatedly been found in the past to breach Article 6 on this basis due to notoriously slow proceedings in Italian courts (Silvestri, 2014).

An early example of presumed mutual trust in civil justice relates to the mutual jurisdiction rules in the Brussels Convention and subsequent Brussels I-Regulation. Among these rules, the so-called *lis pendens* rule determines what happens in case of parallel proceedings in different member states in the same dispute matter. In the wordings of Article 21 of the original Brussels Convention:

> Where proceedings involving the same cause of action and between the same parties are brought in the courts of different Contracting States, any court other than the court first seised shall of its own motion decline jurisdiction in favour of that court. A court which would be required to decline jurisdiction may stay its proceedings if the jurisdiction of the other court is contested.

In case C-116/02 *Gasser*, the ECJ held that no exception could be made to the *lis pendens* rule with reference to the mutual trust that EU member states must accord each other's courts. In this case, the national court first seized was an Italian one, since one of the parties to the dispute had filed a claim before a court in Italy despite the parties having agreed in their contract that the relevant exclusive court to hear disputes between them was to be in Austria. It was considered possible that the proceedings in Italy were brought simply as a procedural tactic (a tactic known as 'Italian torpedo') to delay the matter, since Italian proceedings were notoriously slow and the Austrian court was according to the *lis pendens* rule prohibited from hearing the matter as long as the Italian proceedings were pending (cf. Bogdan, 2007). The Austrian court that was seized second specifically asked the ECJ, whether the fact that Italy was known to repeatedly breach Article 6 ECHR for excessively long civil proceedings coupled with the parties' choice of Austrian courts could be taken into account. However, the ECJ responded negatively with reference to the mutual trust between the judicial systems of the EU member states.

In the most recent reform of the Brussels I regime, a specific exception in the *lis pendens* rule now attempts to address the 'torpedo problem' and protect choice-of-court agreements.[3] Thus, if the same situation arose as in *Gasser* today, the result would most likely not be the same. Nevertheless, the case is still important as an early expression of presumed mutual trust. In a later string of cases (also in the context of the jurisdiction rules of the Brussels I regime), the ECJ has held that a court in a EU member state is not entitled to prohibit a party from bringing a case in the court of another member state (see e.g. cases C-159/02 *Turner* and C-185/07 *West Tankers*). In other words, this means that national courts in EU member states cannot issue anti-suit injunctions that can have an indirect impact on the jurisdiction of courts in other member states.[4] The ECJ emphasises in these cases that the mutual jurisdiction rules of the Brussels I regime are founded on the mutual trust that EU member states have for each other's legal systems. Thereby, the ECJ implicitly imposes on national courts in EU member states an obligation to trust the courts of other member states and their capacity to correctly follow the mutual jurisdiction rules (Hartley, 2015).

Finally, the Brussels Convention already confirmed that national courts of member states cannot review the judgments by courts in other member states and check whether the court of origin has made a correct ruling.[5] The court that has to enforce a judgment can review neither the substantive ruling nor (as a main rule) the ruling on jurisdiction in the judgment handed down in the court of origin in the cross-border enforcement procedure. This has been confirmed also in case law, inter alia in case C-38/98 *Renault v Maxicar* concerning a potential incorrect application of substantive EU law in the court of origin. Although not explicitly referring to mutual trust in these cases but rather to the system and aim of the Brussels regime, it may also be inferred that the system of the Brussels regime itself is based on a certain level of presumptive trust in the courts of other EU member states. The concept of comity in private international law and the earlier case law of the ECJ should be remembered when mutual trust in the context of recognition and enforcement of judgments is analysed below.

The Civil Justice Framework in the EU

The legislative instruments enacted so far in civil justice in the EU imply that achieving true cooperation in this policy area is a gradual process and that intermediate procedures as well as other forms of checks and balances still remain to be established. But before these are discussed, it is useful to briefly reflect on the procedure and underlying interests in civil justice cooperation in the EU. Traditionally, a judgment creditor has after obtaining a judgment in the court of origin and needing to enforce the judgment in another EU member state, for example, due to the fact that the judgment debtor is domiciled in or has assets in another member state, had to address an application for enforcement to a court in the member state of enforcement. The judgment creditor has only been able to proceed to actual enforcement or execution, by applying to the relevant bailiffs or other relevant execution authorities or actors, after obtaining an enforcement order from a court in the member state of enforcement.[6] The application for enforcement, that is, the exequatur procedure, has had certain formal requirements, including traditionally a translation of the judgment to be enforced in an official language of the member state of enforcement. Traditionally, the judgment debtor has at this stage been able to oppose enforcement on limited grounds, so-called grounds of refusal. The grounds for refusal have not changed fundamentally since the Brussels Convention and encompass the following: (i) the judgment is contrary to public policy, so-called *ordre public*, (ii) the judgment was given in default and the defendant was not duly served in sufficient time to enable him to arrange for his defence or (iii) the judgment is irreconcilable with a judgment given in a dispute between the same parties.

Underlying these rules are partly competing interests. The judgment creditor's right to get paid or otherwise realise the rights that it is entitled based on the judgment is naturally a central interest. The creditor's right to an effective recognition and enforcement procedure is also important. Thus, one can say the judgment creditor's access to justice is an underlying interest. But also the judgment debtor may have legitimate procedural interests to protect, in particular, the judgment debtor's right not to face enforcement of a judgment if it was not made aware of the original trial and did therefore not have an opportunity to participate in it. Hence, also the judgment debtor's right to be heard and access to justice is an underlying interest. The recognition and enforcement system should ideally protect both and provide a suitable balance between the interests. In addition, the EU member state of enforcement may have an interest of its own, namely to protect its fundamental values and to not be forced to contribute to enforce a judgment that violates its public policy or is irreconcilable with the prior judgment rendered by its courts. Thus, it is evident that above-outlined grounds for refusal protect, support and balance these competing interests and that the enforcement application procedure allows the courts of the member state of enforcement to address these issues if needed.

The ultimate aim according to the above-mentioned EU programme of mutual recognition (OJEC, 2001) is to remove all intermediate steps in cross-border enforcement of judgments between EU member states. Consequently, the question arises whether the above-mentioned interests are still to be protected and, if so, how. It is clear that the interests of the judgment creditor are advanced in the simplification of cross-border enforcement or institution of direct enforcement. However, there are also benefits at the supranational system level, since the effective enforcement of judgment debts supports the Internal Market. However, it is apparent that the EU member states' own values and protecting the procedural rights of the judgment debtor are more at risk if direct enforcement is implemented. In such a situation, it becomes important to ensure that the court procedure in the original member state guarantees the defendant's right and that the justice systems of EU member states have mutually shared values. If that is not the case, there is a risk of collision between mutual recognition and the procedural rights of the defendant, alternatively the values of the member state of enforcement. It is in that intersection that it becomes apparent that mutual trust is fundamental for mutual recognition. If actual or binding mutual trust is not enhanced rather than simply presumed, there is a risk that the legitimacy of civil justice cooperation in the EU, or at least mutual recognition as a regulatory method for integration, is put into question.

In addition to the flagship regulation of civil justice, that is, the Brussels I-Regulation which pertains to civil and commercial matters generically and has substituted the above-mentioned Convention, a number of other measures including those in the family law field relate to the recognition and enforcement of judgments. These measures, with more limited or specific scope of application, constitute the first arena for the attempts of the EU to further advance mutual recognition. The measures in this group include the Enforcement Order Regulation and the Payment Order Regulation that both concern debt collection of uncontested claims, the Small Claims Regulation that concerns small claims and the Account Preservation Order Regulation that concerns interim attachment of bank accounts.[7] In addition, the family law measures in this group include the Brussels II-*bis* Regulation and the Maintenance Regulation that respectively concern divorce, parental responsibility and maintenance decisions.[8]

To further remove the intermediate procedures that exequatur traditionally encompasses, the specific solutions in each of these instruments have been varied and this fragmented approach has been considered unsatisfactory from the perspective of the users as well as the credibility and functioning of the AFSJ (Linton, 2016; Frackowiak-Adamska, 2015). Some of the instruments abolish the exequatur procedure, others aim to simplify or streamline it. In addition, when removing exequatur, the instruments vary in the way they retain some residual safeguards such as review mechanisms in the original member state with some limited and minimum grounds for refusal in the enforcement member state. Further, some of the instruments include rules on minimum procedural guarantees that are intended to ensure that there is no need to review a judgment in the enforcement state. The most far-reaching instruments in terms of automatic recognition without review mechanism in the EU member state of enforcement is the Brussels II-*bis* Regulation and its rules for judgments concerning the return of unlawfully removed children (Linton, 2016; Frackowiak-Adamska, 2015).

However, the presumption underlying all these instruments is that there is mutual trust in the procedures and actual proceedings in the member state that renders judgment.

The removal of exequatur has also been considered and debated in relation to the flagship Brussels I-Regulation and was one of the key issues in the recent reform of the Regulation (European Commission, 2009, 2010). Two aims have been identified behind the proposal of the European Commission to abolish exequatur in that context, the first aimed to further simplify and reduce formal requirements and the second aimed to remove safeguards and grounds for refusing recognition and enforcement (Kramer, 2011). In the new recast Regulation, eventually, the formal exequatur procedure has been removed. However, it is significant that EU member states were not prepared to go as far as the original proposal of the Commission and the grounds for refusal have been retained, including public policy, as well as a safeguard review procedure in the enforcement member state. The European Parliament rapporteur also noted:

> A member state before which proceedings are brought is entitled to preserve its fundamental values; therefore, equally, it must be the case for a member state in which the enforcement of a judgment is sought (EP Report A7-320/2012).

In addition, there are other civil justice measures including the later adopted Succession Regulation that still require exequatur (Linton, 2016).

It is interesting to note that most far-reaching provisions in terms of automatic recognition, that is, in terms of mutual trust, concern the Brussels II-*bis* Regulation and the return of children decisions (Moraru, 2016). It is also notable that mutual trust appears most difficult to accept and also most sensitive both legally and politically in respect of the guarantee of fundamental rights and potential breaches thereof (Kramer,

2011). If another EU member state does not guarantee the fundamental procedural rights of the parties, should other member states be bound to still accept that procedure? These issues are relevant when we now turn to briefly review the case law.

In the context of criminal justice and immigration, the case law of the ECJ originally emphasised the presumption of mutual trust (see e.g. Lenaerts, 2015), which culminated in opinion 2/13 on the accession to the ECHR which has been hailed as confirming the constitutional nature of the principle (Marguery, 2017). This presumption has come under critique from the perspective of breaches of fundamental rights in individual cases (Mitsilegas, 2012). The ECJ seemed to promote trust and recognition to the detriment of individual scrutiny' (Düsterhaus, 2017, p. 27). However, the ECJ also refers to the fact that control can be relevant in exceptional cases. In addition, more recent case law in the other policy fields have shown a more nuanced approach accepting limits to mutual trust, in particular joined cases C-404/15 and C-659/15 *Aranyosi and Căldăraru* related to criminal justice. More recently, commentators point to the acceptance of limitations to mutual trust and to the ensuing questions that arise as to the scope of such limitations (Prechal, 2017; Lenaerts, 2015).

There are a few relevant rulings of the ECJ also in relation to civil justice. Cases C-292/10 *G* and C-300/14 *Imtech Marine*[9] that concernt the Enforcement Order Regulation have raised questions in relation to both the safeguard procedures and the minimum procedural requirements under the Regulation and demonstrate the sensitive nature of cross-border automatic recognition of judgments. The strong emphasis given by the ECJ to the safeguard mechanisms as a means to support the trust underlying free movement of judgment shows that without such safeguards free movement is not possible. The ruling in joined cases C-119/13 and C-120/13 *ecocosmetics* and *Raiffeisenbank* regarding the European Payment Order Regulation points in the same direction.

Thus, even if both the regulations have removed the exequatur procedure both regulations in addition to safeguard procedures include minimum procedural rules to be fulfilled in the original proceedings. Both the safeguard procedures and the minimum procedural rules are intended to protect the procedural rights of the parties. Hence, one can say that a minimum level of harmonisation complements mutual recognition and supports mutual trust.

Mutual trust has also been dealt with by the ECJ in a string of cases concerning the Brussels I Regulation enforcement regime (C-420/07 *Apostolides*, C-619/10 *Trade Agency*, C-302/13 *flyLAL-Lithuanian Airlines*, C-681/13 *Diageo Brands* and C-559/14 *Rūdolfs Meroni*). The rulings demonstrate that the ECJ places emphasis on that the aim of efficiency behind simplified enforcement rules based on mutual trust. However, the ECJ also holds that efficiency is balanced against the judgment debtor's right to be heard, which is guaranteed by the grounds for refusal as well as the provisions of the EU Charter on Fundamental Rights ensuring the right to a fair trial. The ECJ is careful to explain that enforcement only can be refused on the limited grounds in the Regulation, which are to be interpreted restrictively.[10] The ECJ in addition explicitly emphasises that the enforcement system of the Regulation requires that EU member states trust each other's courts and judicial systems.[11]

Importantly, the ECJ also holds that if the judgment debtor has not been served and has not had the opportunity to prepare its defence in sufficient time, or recourse to an effective remedy, enforcement may be refused.[12] The Court has also confirmed that the national court in the EU member state of enforcement is entitled to carry out an independent assessment of whether the procedure in the original member state has fulfilled the requirements under the Regulation.[13] This guidance remains relevant under the recast of the Regulation, since the grounds for refusal have all been retained. Thus, the 'compromise' result of the reform process as explained above appears to promote continuity and ensure that effective enforcement must be balanced against the rights of the defence. The protection provided by the Regulation hence imposes requirements on EU member states' legal orders. The ECJ has also explicitly held that in applying the enforcement rules, national courts must comply with Article 47 of the EU Charter of Fundamental Rights.[14]

In contrast, a few cases related to recognition and enforcement of judgments on wrongfully removed or retained children under the Brussels II-*bis* Regulation have caused more debate in relation to mutual trust in civil matters. The reason for this is the Regulation's rules on automatic recognition without any residual safeguards in the member state of enforcement. The underlying policy choice in these cases is, in the interest of the child, to give priority to the court and the authorities and courts in the member state where the child was originally habitually resident before being removed or retained. The debate has most recently centred on case

C-491/10 *Zarraga*.[15] The court in the member state of enforcement essentially asked the ECJ whether an exception could be made from the automatic recognition rules in case the child had not been heard by the original member state. Based on the Regulation, the hearing of the child is a requirement for the original member state to be able to issue an enforcement certificate. In addition, the enforcement court noted that to hear the child constitutes a fundamental procedural right.

The ECJ emphasised the system and purpose behind the automatic recognition as well as the mutual trust between EU member state courts and judicial systems in relation to upholding fundamental rights based on the EU Charter. The ECJ further held that it is only in the court system of origin that any such potential problems can be addressed and since measures of recourse were available in the original member state, there was no possibility to refuse enforcement.[16] The case demonstrates that in certain cases of automatic recognition, the trust imposed by the ECJ may be a fiction rather than based on actual trust in the member state of enforcement, which may give rise to opposition against the system itself. Thus, the legitimacy of mutual recognition may be put into question (Requejo Isidro, 2016). At present, the Brussels II-*bis* Regulation is undergoing legislative reform and the European Commission's proposal also seeks to reform the return of children procedures. Automatic recognition is retained, but the proposal introduces a review procedure in the original member state similar to that in the Enforcement Order Regulation (European Commission, 2016; see also Hazelhurst, 2017).

Regulatory Pressures and the Way Forward

The above analysis suggests that the demands on EU member state courts to presumptively trust each other in civil justice matters are high. However, it also emerges that most of the civil justice legislative measures so far include some safeguard mechanisms to mediate mutual recognition, and in those where exequatur has been removed, these safeguards are coupled with a minimum level of procedural harmonisation. Still, among the civil justice measures, the automatic enforcement rules for return of children is the exception and the *Zarraga* case points to the distrust that may arise among national courts in the EU if one court considers that there may be a breach of fundamental rights.

I maintain that the presumption of mutual trust should be linked to actual protection of fundamental rights in the EU. It should be rebuttable not only when there is systematic failure but also in individual cases. Otherwise, it can quickly serve to feed distrust and it is hard to imagine trust enduring if it is only imposed from above 'by decree' (Storskrubb, 2016a; see also Blobel & Späth, 2005; Mitsilegas, 2012). The legislative development in the field of EU civil justice supports the view that building mutual trust is a gradual process. Logically, legislative safeguards uphold trust in the whole system and are not as such a sign of distrust among EU member states. It should only be necessary and possible to successfully invoke safeguards in limited cases. Safeguards are retained to provide redress when there is a failure in an actual case, similar to extraordinary appeal mechanisms in domestic procedural law. A study on the public policy refusal ground in a number of EU civil justice instruments shows that there are not many cases where it is successfully invoked (Hess & Pfeiffer, 2011). Some argue that this demonstrates that the grounds for refusal are redundant; an alternative position is that the grounds for refusal work as they should (Storskrubb, 2011). If a violation of fundamental rights has occurred and not been corrected in the original procedure by no fault of the relevant party, I would argue that it is important that enforcement of the relevant judgment is not possible across the EU.

It is also true that Brussels I-Regulation and the case law of the ECJ place a heavy burden on the judgment defendant (Emaus, 2017). Thus, before removing further barriers to mutual recognition of judgments, it is imperative to examine carefully whether and where limits are still warranted and remain necessary. Such an endeavour should also take into account practice at the local level and whether the safeguards are sufficient, in the context of potential reform or amendment of the enacted civil justice instruments (Requejo Isidro, 2016; Kramer, 2013). Logically, such an analysis does not have to negate improvements to streamline procedures and make enforcement of judgments more efficient. In addition, to clarify and provide a more simplified legislative framework rather than a multitude of measures may be useful (Frackowiak-Adamska, 2015). As already identified in the programme (OJEC, 2001), another avenue for future action is to analyse whether we need further minimum or common procedural standards in the EU. Recently, several projects that could contribute to such an analysis have been initiated by both European institutions and independent actors.[17]

A third avenue is to consider the benefit and impact of additional supporting governance measures, such as judicial training, networks and e-justice (see e.g. Hartnell, 2002; Blobel & Späth, 2005; Storskrubb, 2008). Already in 2009, the European Council placed greater emphasis on such measures, which shows a realisation that mutual trust needs to be supported and cannot be presumed. A lot of work is being done with less visibility perhaps in the academic debate than the legislative and case law development of EU civil justice. It should be noted that the European Commission has set an ambitious goal of enabling 700,000 legal practitioners, half of the legal practitioners in the EU, to participate in European judicial training activities by 2020 through the use of available resources at local, national and European level. In addition, efforts are being made in relation to e-justice coordination among the member states since 2007 when the Council decided to establish a Working Party on e-Justice. Further, since 2009 the EU has had a multiannual Action Plan for e-justice. The European e-Justice Portal, which is hosted and operated by the Commission and was launched in July 2010, is the main achievement so far. In addition, various member states have participated in and are involved in a number of pilot projects that relate to interconnecting their technical justice facilities.

The recent initiatives of the EU institutions on the strengthening of the rule of law are an example of new and broader governance measures and dialogue in the EU on values of our justice systems (Weller, 2015). In this context, the Justice Scoreboards are a particularly interesting development. Published since 2013 by the European Commission, the Scoreboards are a means for the EU to collect information on the justice systems of the member states and to evaluate certain indicators for key components (quality, independence and efficiency) that are considered relevant to achieve an efficient judicial system. The information is collected in the context of the EU's economic term and enables the EU to make country-specific recommendations and have a dialogue with EU member states on procedural reforms when allocating funds (European Commission, 2017; see also Dori, 2015). Considerable critique can be levelled at the methods of collection of information for the Scoreboards and also at the non-transparent manner in which the data is presented (Storskrubb, 2017b). However, two more fundamental criticisms are relevant here. Firstly, there is no apparent dialogue on the components and indicators that the Commission has decided to collect in the Scoreboards as relevant for 'efficient' justice systems. It is regrettable that the Scoreboards have not yet resulted in a transparent dialogue involving all member states on what we perceived as the important components of an efficient justice system and how to address challenges in civil justice at the domestic level. Such a dialogue would be crucial for promoting strategic learning across and between member states (Storskrubb, 2017b). Secondly, in light of the above discussion it would be useful if the Scoreboards could evaluate also the fundamental procedural rights important in the cross-border EU civil justice measures. Efficient justice is important, but it is also important to calibrate efficiency with quality and fundamental rights. The Scoreboards may be considered a start, but a deeper comparative understanding will be necessary to support the development of best practices in EU civil justice to support mutual trust.

All the above suggested avenues can be compared to analogous strategies that have evolved over time in the Internal Market to mediate the consequences of and support for mutual recognition. It should be noted that mutual recognition is in the Internal Market part of an ever-developing multilayered regulatory strategy. The effectiveness of mutual recognition as a governance strategy has its limits, and this has been understood in the Internal Market, most recently in the context of financial regulation (Snell, 2016; Roth, 2017). Thus, the fourth and final avenue for future development is to debate and develop an overall regulatory strategy for EU civil justice. Some scholars, such as Düsterhaus (2015), focus on the avenues that can be pursued by the ECJ. However, although both the ECJ and the domestic courts are very important actors, there needs to be an awareness of the fact that regulatory options, actors and tools interact, complement and support each other. To find the correct mix of regulatory tools is relevant to achieve mutual trust. In particular, it is important to focus on the measures such as training and dialogue between relevant local actors that can support and foster mutual trust.

Notes

1. The term 'civil justice' can also be held to encompass further and broader civil procedural developments in the EU such as the procedural rules for consumer or competition matters, but the focus in this chapter is directed at cross-border civil litigation (Storskrubb, 2017a, 2017b).
2. See also Weller (2015) on the development of recognition of foreign judgments and the tools for retaining control in traditional bilateral or multilateral private international law cooperation.
3. See Article 31 of the Brussels I (recast) Regulation.
4. An anti-suit injunction is issued against the party in question, in personam (Storskrubb, 2016c).
5. See Articles 29 and 34 in the Brussels Convention. In relation to jurisdiction, the court of enforcement may only refuse enforcement if the judgment

of the court of origin conflicts with exclusive grounds of jurisdiction or special protective grounds of jurisdiction has been applied correctly, according to Article 28 of the Convention.

6. Under the system of the Regulation, recognition and enforcement are two separate concepts. Recognition entails that a judgment can be directly invoked before the authorities of another EU member state without any special procedure of recognition being required. Nevertheless, for enforcement, a separate procedure has formerly been required under the Regulation. The grounds for refusal are the same for both. When the term 'mutual recognition of judgments' is used to denote a regulatory method, it may be used in a more generic sense and both concepts may be included.
7. See regulations (EC) No 805/2004, [2004] OJ L 143/15; (EC) No 1896/2006, [2006] OJ L 399/1; (EC) No 861/2007, [2007] OJ L 199/1; and (EU) No 655/2014, [2014] OJ L 189/59.
8. See regulations (EC) No 2201/2003, [2001] OJ L 12/1; and (EC) No 4/2009, [2009] OJ L 7/1.
9. In addition, case *Pebros Servizi Srl v Aston Martin Lagonda Ltd*, C-511/14, has confirmed that the notion of 'uncontested' in the Regulation is to be assessed autonomously.
10. See, for example, case C-470/07.
11. See inter alia case C-681/13 and C-559/14.
12. See case C-470/07.
13. See case C-61/10.
14. See case C-559/14.
15. See also cases C-211/10 and C-195/08.
16. See case C-491/10.
17. The European Law Institute (ELI) and Unidroit commenced a project in 2014 on European Principles of Civil Procedure (see: http://www.europeanlawinstitute.eu/projects/). The European Parliament's Legal Affairs Committee had, at the time of writing, decided to prepare its own report on the project and has also issues an own initiative report on minimum procedural standards. The European Commission has also initiated a study on national procedural laws and practices.

References

Andersson, T. (2005). Harmonization and mutual recognition: How to handle mutual distrust. In M. Andenas, B. Hess, & P. Oberhammer (Eds.), *Enforcement agency practice in Europe*. British Institute of International and Comparative Law.

Blobel, F., & Späth, P. (2005). The tale of multilateral trust and the European law of civil procedure. *European Law Review, 30*, 528–545.

Bogdan, M. (2007). The Brussels/Lugano *lis pendens* rule and the 'Italian torpedo'. *Scandinavian Studies in Law, 51*, 89–97.
Cambien, N. (2017). Mutual recognition and mutual trust in the internal market. *European Papers, 2*(1), 93–116.
Chalmers, D., et al. (2014). *European Union law* (3rd ed.). Cambridge University Press.
Dori, A. (2015). The EU Justice Scoreboard: Judicial evaluation as a new governance tool. *Max Planck Institute Luxemburg Working Paper*, no. 2.
Düsterhaus, D. (2015). Judicial coherence in the area of freedom, security and justice—Squaring mutual trust with effective judicial protection. *Review of European Administrative Law, 8*(2), 151–182.
Düsterhaus, D. (2017). In the court(s) we trust—A procedural solution to the mutual trust dilemma. *Freedom Security & Justice: European Legal Studies, 1*(1), 26–44.
Emaus, J. (2017). The interaction between mutual trust, mutual recognition and fundamental rights. *European Papers, 2*(1), 117–140.
European Commission. (2009). *Green Paper on the review of Council Regulation.* (EC) 44/2001, COM(2009) 175, Brussels, 21 April 2009.
European Commission. (2010). *Proposal for a regulation of the European Parliament and the Council on jurisdiction and the recognition and enforcement of judgments in civil and commercial matters.* COM(2010) 748 final, Brussels, 14 December 2010.
European Commission. (2016). *Proposal for a Council Regulation on jurisdiction, the recognition and enforcement of decisions in matrimonial matters and the matters of parental responsibility, and on international child abduction (recast).* COM(2016) 411 final, Brussels, 30 June 2016.
European Commission. (2017). *The 2017 EU Justice Scoreboard. Communication from the Commission to the European Parliament, the Council, the European Central Bank, the European Economic and Social Committee and the Committee of the Regions.* COM(2017) 167 final, Brussels, 10 April 2017.
European Council. (1999). Presidency conclusions, Tampere European Council, 15–16 October. Retrieved from http://www.consilium.europa.eu/media/21059/tampere-european-council-presidency-conclusions.pdf
European Council. (2014). *Extract from the 26–27 June 2014 European Council Conclusions concerning the area of freedom, security and justice and some related horizontal issues.* OJ C 240/13, 24 July 2014.
Frackowiak-Adamska, A. (2015). Time for a European 'full faith and credit clause'. *Common Market Law Review, 52*(1), 191–218.
Hartley, T. (2015). Anti-suit injunctions in support of arbitration: *West Tankers* still afloat. *International and Comparative Law Quarterly, 64*(4), 965–975.
Hartnell, E. (2002). EUstitia: Institutionalising justice in the European Union. *Northwestern Journal of International Law and Business, 23*(1), 65–138.

Hazelhurst, M. (2017). *Free movement of civil judgments in the European Union and the right to a fair trial*. Springer.

Hess, B., & Pfeiffer, T. (2011). *Interpretation of the public policy exception as referred to in EU instruments of private international and procedural law*. Study commissioned by the European Parliament, PE453.189. Retrieved from http://www.europarl.europa.eu/RegData/etudes/STUD/2011/453189/IPOL-JURI_ET(2011)453189_EN.pdf

Jänterä-Jareborg, M. (2016). The Nordic input on the EU's cooperation in family and succession law: Exporting Union law through 'Nordic exceptions'. In B. Hess, M. Bergström, & E. Storskrubb (Eds.), *EU civil justice: Current issues and future outlook*. Oxford: Hart Publishing.

Kramer, X. E. (2011). Cross-border enforcement in the EU: Mutual trust versus fair trial? Towards principles of European civil procedure. *International Journal of Procedural Law, 2*, 202–230.

Kramer, X. E. (2013). Procedure matters: Construction and deconstructivism in European civil procedure. *Erasmus Law Lectures*, no. 33.

Lavenex, S. (2007). Mutual recognition and the monopoly of force: Limits of the single market analogy. *Journal of European Public Policy, 14*(5), 762–779.

Lenaerts, K. (2015). *The principle of mutual recognition in the area of freedom, security and justice*. Lecture, 30 January 2015. Retrieved from http://1exagu1grkmq3k572418odoooym.wpengine.netdna-cdn.com/wp-content/uploads/2015/02/The-Principle-of-Mutual-Recognition-in-the-area-of-Freedom-Security-and-Justice.pdf

Linton, M. (2016). Abolition of exequatur, all the name of mutual trust. In B. Hess, M. Bergström, & E. Storskrubb (Eds.), *EU civil justice: Current issues and future outlook*. Oxford: Hart Publishing.

Marguery, T. (2017). Je t'aime moi non plus the Avotiņš v. Latvia judgment: An answer from the ECrtHR to the CJEU. *Review of European Administrative Law, 10*(1), 113–134.

Mitsilegas, V. (2012). The limits of mutual trust in Europe's area of freedom, security and justice: From automatic inter-state cooperation to the slow emergence of the individual. *Yearbook of European Law, 31*(1), 319–372.

Moraru, M. (2016). 'Mutual trust' from the perspective of national courts: A test in creative legal thinking. In D. Gerard & E. Brouwer (Eds.), *Mapping mutual trust: Understanding and informing the role of mutual trust in EU law*. EUI Working Paper, no. 13.

Nicolaïdis, K. (2007). Trusting the poles? Constructing Europe through mutual recognition. *Journal of European Public Policy, 14*(5), 682–698.

Official Journal of the European Communities. (2001). *Programme of measures to implement the principle of mutual recognition of decisions in criminal matters*. 2001/C 12/02, 15 January 2001.

Paul, J. R. (2008). The transformation of international comity. *Duke Law and Contemporary Problems, 71*(19), 19–38.

Prechal, S. (2017). Mutual trust before the court of justice of the European Union. *European Papers, 2*(1), 75–92.
Requejo Isidro, M. (2016). On the abolition of *exequatur*. In B. Hess, M. Bergström, & E. Storskrubb (Eds.), *EU civil justice: Current issues and future outlook*. Oxford: Hart Publishing.
Roth, W.-H. (2017). Mutual recognition. In P. Koutrakos & J. Snell (Eds.), *Research handbook on the law of the EU's internal market*. Edward Elgar.
Schmidt, S. (2007). Mutual recognition as a new mode of governance. *Journal of European Public Policy, 14*(5), 667–681.
Silvestri, E. (2014). Goals of civil justice when nothing works: The case of Italy. In A. Uzelac (Ed.), *Goals of civil justice and civil procedure in contemporary judicial systems*. Springer.
Snell, J. (2014). The internal market and philosophies of integration. In C. Barnard & S. Peers (Eds.), *European Union law*. Oxford: Oxford University Press.
Snell, J. (2016). The single market: Does mutual trust suffice? In D. Gerard & E. Brouwer (Eds.), *Mapping mutual trust: Understanding and informing the role of mutual trust in EU law*. EUI Working Paper, no. 13.
Storskrubb, E. (2008). *Civil procedure and EU law: A policy area uncovered*. Oxford: Oxford University Press.
Storskrubb, E. (2011). *Ordre public* in EU civil justice—Lessons from arbitration? In *Festskrift till Gustaf Möller—Juridisk Tidskrift Finland*, no. 2–4.
Storskrubb, E. (2016a). Mutual recognition as a governance strategy for civil justice? In B. Hess, M. Bergström, & E. Storskrubb (Eds.), *EU civil justice: Current issues and future outlook*. Oxford: Hart Publishing.
Storskrubb, E. (2016b). Mutual trust and the limits of abolishing *exequatur* in civil justice. In D. Gerard & E. Brouwer (Eds.), *Mapping mutual trust: Understanding and informing the role of mutual trust in EU law*. EUI Working Paper, no. 13.
Storskrubb, E. (2016c). Gazprom OAO v. Lietuvos Republika: A victory for arbitration? *European Law Review, 41*(4), 578–589.
Storskrubb, E. (2017a). Civil justice: Constitutional and regulatory issues revisited. In M. Fletcher, E. Herlin-Karnell, & C. Matera (Eds.), *The European Union as an area of freedom, security and justice*. London: Routledge.
Storskrubb, E. (2017b). Några tankar om hur EU-rättens tentakler genomtränger processrätten. In *Festskrift till Dan Frände—Juridisk Tidskrift Finland*, no. 2–4 (pp. 360–383).
Weller, M. (2015). Mutual trust: In search of the future of European Union private international law. *Journal of Private International Law, 11*(1), 64–102.
Whytock, C. (2014). Faith and scepticism in private international law: Trust, governance, politics, and foreign judgments. *Erasmus Law Journal, 3*, 113–124.

The Importance of Trust in a Digital Europe: Reflections on the Sharing Economy and Blockchains

Robin Teigland, Håkan Holmberg, and Anna Felländer

In its 2020 Strategy, the European Union describes the importance of actively participating in the digital society. The global market for information and communication technologies (ICT) is rapidly growing beyond €2 trillion, yet only around 25 percent of this demand is fulfilled by European firms (European Commission, 2010). The EU must actively strengthen its role in the development and government of the internet so that the European perspective on issues such as democracy and freedom of expression continues to be ensured. However, in order to become a significant digital player, the EU must establish trust in the digital environment while at the same time it must successfully contend with emerging digital forces that are challenging not only established business models but

R. Teigland (✉)
Stockholm School of Economics, Stockholm, Sweden

H. Holmberg
Uppsala, Sweden

A. Felländer
Stockholm, Sweden

A. Bakardjieva Engelbrekt et al. (eds.), *Trust in the European Union in Challenging Times*, https://doi.org/10.1007/978-3-319-73857-4_9

also the underlying European social model. Basic assumptions regarding value creation and competitive situations along with current regulations are being challenged by globalization, individualization and industry transformations. When existing structures are questioned, new opportunities are also created for EU citizens. The EU has a clear desire to increase value creation opportunities for its citizens, and the question of how digitalization enables this is central to the EU.

In times of change, we tend to stick to the familiar. However, maintaining and protecting traditional industries against the transformative power of digitalization is likely to only slow down economic growth and make the creation of a digital EU difficult. This in turn would make the EU less relevant for its citizens. As with all technological paradigm shifts, old jobs are transformed or made obsolete while new jobs emerge. For example, recent studies in Sweden have predicted that 36–60 percent of the current jobs will be lost during the next 20 years as algorithms and robots are employed to perform an increasing number of tasks (Fölster, 2014). At the same time, new structures for value creation are developing and many of these fall under the umbrella of the 'sharing economy'.

Transactions within five sectors of the sharing economy—housing, transport, household services, professional services and financial services generated a value of €28 billion in Europe in 2015. Looking forward, estimates have been made that the sharing economy can provide the EU economy with an annual increase between €160 billion and €572 billion. With the help of digitalization, the sharing economy enables the replacement of traditional intermediaries with digital platforms that enable a cheaper exchange of customized goods and services generally among strangers.

Digitalization's low transaction costs enable more individuals than ever before to consume, produce and utilize existing resources more efficiently. Furthermore, untapped skills that today are far from entering the labor market can be identified and integrated in society. This elimination of intermediaries also results in the risks that were previously incurred by the intermediary to be transferred to the users of the platform. To mitigate these risks, 'trust' has been designated as the currency of the sharing economy as trust is the critical factor enabling the transactions of goods and services among strangers. What is trust and how can trust be digitized? One solution receiving increasing attention and investment is the digital technology, the blockchain. This technology is the underlying software for the cryptocurrency Bitcoin, and it has been estimated that around $1.5 billion had been invested globally in blockchain startups as of the end of 2016 (Frost & Sullivan, 2017). Furthermore, the total market capitalization value of Bitcoin and other cryptocurrencies is around $170 billion as of October 2017 with Bitcoin at $99 billion and Ether at $28 billion (https://coinmarketcap.com/).[1] This indicates that it is not only startups and venture capitalists that care about the blockchain. This is not too surprising given the fact that the blockchain reduces the need for trust in individuals and institutions through increasing trust in system processes. In a centralized system, the intermediary ensures that process-based trust of the system is maintained. The blockchain allows groups to formalize their processes to reach consensus without a central middle hand. When groups can maintain process-based trust without a central middle hand, new opportunities are created for adapting consensus processes to the needs of different groups, which further enables the continued development of the services the sharing economy can offer.

This chapter focuses on trust and whether blockchain technology can act as a catalyst for the sharing economy in Europe and elsewhere through enabling an increased level of trust among platform users. A sharing economy based on strong trust can create jobs and economic growth in Europe. Below we discuss the development of the sharing economy within the EU before we provide an overview of how trust has so far been digitized. After that, we describe the blockchain and what opportunities it may offer in terms of digitized trust and economic growth. Our goal is to illustrate how the meeting between the blockchain and the sharing economy, two phenomena created by digitalization, forge the conditions for a future Europe.

What Is the Sharing Economy?

The sharing economy is a broad concept that lacks one distinct and common definition. It is sometimes used as a synonym for notions such as the 'collaborative economy' and the 'on demand economy'. One commonly used definition of the sharing economy is that suggested by Sundararajan (2016) as a market where exchanges happen peer-to-peer in a decentralized network. The European Commission states in their agenda from 2016 a more comprehensive definition of the sharing economy, comprising three parts:

> It aims [...] for business models where the business is enabled by sharing platforms which creates an open marketplace for temporary use of goods or services, often provided by individuals. It comprises three different categories of actors: 1) *service providers* who for instance share their assets, resources or competences and can be individuals offering services on a temporary basis or service providers who make it a part of their business; 2) *users* of services; and 3) *intermediaries* who—through their digital sharing platform—consolidate suppliers and users, which enables transactions. The transactions usually do not mean that the good or the service changes its owner, and they can be executed either with or without a profit-making purpose. (European Commission, 2016a)

The sharing economy is not a completely new phenomenon since people always have shared their assets with others. However, during recent decades, some factors have accelerated the development of a more modern version of the sharing economy, such as internet penetration, IT improvements, easier payment systems and the financial crisis (Felländer, Ingram, & Teigland, 2015). The increase in internet usage together with increased usage of new technologies, such as social media, has enabled individual actors to organize themselves both more easily and faster. For example, public groups on social media organize car rides between Stockholm and Gothenburg on an individual basis. This means that the driver receives a portion of their fuel expenses reimbursed while the traveler enjoys a cheaper journey than through traditional commercial actors. Due to the high number of users on social media, the relatively small market for rides between Stockholm and Gothenburg is able to gather a high enough level of supply and demand to function. IT improvements have also led to the possibility of collecting data, which after statistical processing can be used for recommendation algorithms or dynamic pricing that enables supply and demand to determine the price for the good or service. New IT solutions and decreasing costs for digital tools have also resulted in lower costs for entrepreneurs and small- and medium-sized enterprises to initiate sharing economy startups. Many startups today often do not require more than a laptop and an internet connection in the initial stage.

Easier payment systems have also facilitated financial transactions. A functioning payment system is important, and thanks to improved payment systems, the previously negative attitude against online payment has decreased (Felländer et al., 2015). Users have accordingly been provided with a flexible way to pay for the services consumed in the sharing economy. Thereby, more applications are created since the developer does not have to take responsibility for payment but instead can use already existing solutions and therefore focus on developing their own product. Furthermore, the ability to receive income from alternative sources has also been a driving factor in the sharing economy. Being able to rent out one's apartment during the day to startups in need of office space and teaching Spanish on web-based services during evenings are only two examples of how individuals can gain alternative sources of income thanks to the sharing economy.

Possibilities and Challenges for the Sharing Economy in the EU

Demographic and global changes will most likely demand that the populations of EU member states work both harder and longer but foremost smarter. In its 2020 strategy, the EU is focusing on smart growth where innovation and technology enable increased value creation in the Union.[2] At the same time, more Europeans are gaining access to the internet, which increases the possibility to use the sharing economy's services. In 2015, 81 percent of households within the EU-28 had internet, compared to 55 percent in 2007, according to Eurostat. Usage of mobile phones has also increased during the last couple of years and, in 2014, every other person in the EU had mobile internet. However, there are great differences between countries. In Luxembourg and the Netherlands, 98 percent of the population has access to the internet while in Bulgaria only 57 percent have access. Mobile connections also differ within the EU; in Denmark, Great Britain and Sweden, three out of four people have mobile internet while only one out of four has mobile internet in Bulgaria, Italy and Rumania, according to Eurostat.

A European sharing economy offers many benefits. The EU's competitiveness and growth can be strengthened through new sharing economy business models and more flexible work forms. The sharing economy lowers thresholds to the labor market and could increase the matching of labor supply with demand. The development of the sharing economy is most advanced in the local service sector. New business opportunities as well as new types of cooperation between traditional actors and actors in the sharing economy are created. For consumers, the sharing economy leads to an increased supply, reduced costs and new, even individualized, services. In addition, it can result in a more sustainable community, thanks to a more efficient use of resources. However, while the EU states in its European

Agenda for the sharing economy that 52 percent of the EU population in 2016 knew about the sharing economy's services, only 17 percent had used these services at some time (European Commission, 2016a).

To guarantee user rights, both in the role as a consumer and a producer, actors within the sharing economy are attempting to create various self-regulating functions, often through the form of online rating systems, screenings and digital/physical interactions between the different actors participating in the transaction. However, the question is whether this self-regulation is sufficient to protect the users or if the EU and its member states must create supplementary regulations. The sharing economy has, for example, been criticized for flaws in the security consumers and providers are being offered. Transactions take place peer-to-peer, so, for example, how is a landlord supposed to trust that the guest will not destroy their home, and how is the guest supposed to trust that the description corresponds with the actual house or that the key even fits the lock?

Furthermore, a hotel has regulations regarding fire security that apartments do not necessarily have. Who shall be responsible for the safety in the digital transaction: the individual, the platform or the EU and its member states? Questions regarding responsibility and integrity are further complicated when sharing economy principles are combined with what is called 'the internet of things'. Who is responsible for a car accident caused by a self-driving car shared by a group of people and controlled by artificial intelligence? Shall the responsibility be put on the group of people sharing the car, the person who programmed the car or the other cars involved in the accident? Integrity can be threatened since the more people share things, the greater is the risk of unauthorized persons gaining access to sensitive information, a risk that will only increase as more things are connected to the internet.

Regarding risk management, it is still unclear as of the beginning of 2018 as to whether it is the platforms or the users who are responsible for the transaction and the associated transfer of information. Most of the relevant regulations regarding contractual liability are regulated by the EU member states. When a platform should take over the responsibility of a transaction depends on multiple factors, among others its control over the user's transactions. This opens up for increasing responsibility being given to the user. The new distribution of responsibility will not only affect the relationship between user and company but also between user and legislator. Today's consumer laws, which have been created to protect the consumer at the expense of the company, no longer function in the sharing economy of peer-to-peer transactions. How these risks shall be addressed when the consumer undertakes more and more responsibility is to a great extent an open question.

Platform owners see themselves as the middle hand between supply and demand, not as an employer. This makes the lines between consumers and suppliers, employees and self-employers, and professional suppliers of services and private individuals being erased. Sharing economy activities therefore often end up in a gray zone outside national welfare systems. For example, salaries can be auctioned down to unreasonably low levels when there is high unemployment due to the lack of income insurance for the employees. At the same time, platforms make some limitations in their user agreements, and, in some cases, they even determine the price of the good or service being transacted. Management of the transactions is also handled by the platform since there are some requirements a service supplier must fulfill. For example, Uber, the internet-based service for orders and payment of taxi rides and carpools, has detailed instruction videos on how their drivers shall behave. Thereby, in some sharing economy services, middle hands can be considered more similar to an employer than only a matching service.

If one chooses to see the middle hands as an employer, then there are several shortcomings for those supplying the goods or services to the platforms. For instance, these individuals do not have the same means with which to negotiate their rights as those within existing labor unions have. On the other hand, the relationship between service supplier and middle hand is not the same as an employer-employee relationship since a service supplier can offer their services on many platforms at the same time. For example, an individual can rent out their apartment as an office during the day while they drive their car providing transportation or running small errands for others before finishing the day cooking dinner for someone. Having these many jobs on the side makes the relationship between the employer and the employee even more complicated. Even immaterial rights are affected by the sharing economy. When goods and services are shared, so is information. This exchange of information not only includes collaboration but also the creation of new companies, which demands new requirements for the handling of immaterial rights. The software industry has increasingly started using licenses such as the *Creative Commons* license or the *GNU General Public* license that facilitates the handling of immaterial rights in an economy where information is increasingly seen as shared property.

Self-regulation within the sharing economy must also be studied in terms of what consequences might arise if the self-regulating function does not work. For example, at one end of the scale, if an ambulance service were to be based on a sharing economy model, trust in the traditional licensing of the ambulance service (e.g. equipment, education, etc.) would be replaced by trust in the platform by the peers. In this example, the suitability for being an actor in the sharing economy is low since the risk is high that the service may not be provided at a satisfactory level. At the other end of the scale, however, are services within the local service sector, such as lawn mowing services, which are more appropriate for self-regulation. Then there are numerous industries, such as the financial and hotel industries, with a medium to high risk that the service does not work appropriately, and, as a result, where clarity around insurance and a more traditional regulatory framework are needed.

Taxation within the sharing economy has also been a hot topic for debate. Who or what is taxable? How should taxation be performed on platforms that create their own currency or enable bartering, such as when someone is invited for dinner in exchange for the promise of two bottles of wine? Taxation is also interrelated to the question whether a service is professional or not. Within the EU it is not determined by legislation when an individual exactly shall be considered as a professional supplier in the sharing economy, that is, how does one separate professional services from services provided by individuals for individuals? Different criteria are used within EU member states, for example, how one defines the compensation for the service or a threshold value for how much income one can generate. The difficulties of control within the sharing economy and the separation of taxation on business, service or capital leads to yet another obstacle for effective taxation in Europe and elsewhere.

Within transportation, EU member states have tackled the legal framework around, for example, Uber in different ways (see Tables 1 and 2). The perception of maturity for self-regulation is likely to vary in different member states, and in time, simultaneously as different types of insurance solutions are introduced. The Swedish Taxi Inquiry is interesting in this context since it stated that taxi identification is necessary as a control function for the taxi business (SOU, 2016, p. 86). At the same time, the investigation did not want to generalize the requirement of identification and concluded that the formulation of a legal framework must be decided from industry to industry. Estonia is one of the EU member states that has most actively facilitated the development of the sharing economy. Various

Table 1 Examples on how transport services are organized within the sharing economy

	Centralized carpool	*Decentralized carpool*	*Non-commercial carpool*	*Decentralized transport networks*	*Centralized transport networks*
Example	*Car2go, Drive-Now*	*Drivy, Gomore*	*Blablacar*	*UberBlack, Lyft, (UperPOP)*	Taxi companies
Ownership	Platform and vehicles owned by same actor	Platform and vehicles owned by different actors	Platform and vehicles owned by different actors	Platform and vehicles owned by different actors	Platform and vehicles owned by same actor
Operators' profit interest	Powered by profit	All actors have possibility to profit	Platform has a profit interest but not the owner of the goods/services	All actors have profit interests	Business is run with a profit interest
Platform control over relationship vehicle owners with consumers	High	Low	Low	High	High
Communications environment	Digital and physical	Digital and physical	Digital and physical	Digital	Physical (digital communication occurs)
Advantages	Integrated in local transport network: client acts as driver	Already existing fleet of vehicles is used and all actors can have profit interest	Eludes regulations when driver does not have profit interest	Already existing fleet of vehicles is used and all actors can have profit interest	Business is distinctly regulated
Disadvantages	Cost for fleet of vehicles must be carried by one central actor	Service ends up in gray area regarding current regulations	Lack of profit interest makes platform less attractive for drivers	High control of drivers and profit interest often leads to direct conflict with legislature	Legal framework complicates possibility to find drivers. Central actor must finance whole business

Source: SOU (2016, p. 86)

Table 2 Overview of current legal framework regarding transportation services in the sharing economy

	Regulations directed toward the individual	*Regulations directed toward the platform*
Examples of tax regulations	– Manual declaration of business (Finland, 2018)	– Chargeable information is sent directly from platform to tax authority (proposal, Estonia, Lithuania) – Electronic tax receipt (proposal, Estonia) – Platform responsible for tax payments (proposal, Belgium) – Platforms' legal person must have a national registration number (Finland, 2018)
Examples of regulations intended to strengthen consumer safety	– Access to photo of driver and vehicle registration number before journey begins (proposal, Estonia) – Background check and language test of driver (Finland, 2018) – Registration of driver's fingerprints (Austin, Texas)	– Platform responsible for background check and education of drivers (Lithuania)
Examples of income ceiling	– Great Britain allows tax reduction of 2000 GBP with exception of Uber – Business exempted from VAT and tax rate of 10 percent until €5000 (proposal, Belgium) – Non-professional income from sharing economy businesses taxed with 10 percent until €10,000 (proposal, Italy)	
Examples of registration requirements	– Both vehicle and driver must be registered (Finland, 2018)	– Unlimited amount of driver's licenses at company level (Finland, 2018) – Digital platforms must be registered with tax authorities (proposal, Belgium)

(*continued*)

Table 2 (continued)

	Regulations directed toward the individual	*Regulations directed toward the platform*
Examples of other forms of limitations	– Driver must be insured until USD one million (Massachusetts, USA) – Pre-order requirements of travel (New York, USA) – Forbidden to pick up passengers at airport (Massachusetts, USA)	– Forbidden to raise prices during instances of temporary increases in demand (Massachusetts, USA) – Transparency on how prices are calculated (proposal, Estonia; Finland, 2018)
Examples of different actions meant to simplify sharing economic activity	– Individuals with income beneath €5000 do not have to register for VAT taxes (proposal, Belgium) – Taxi insurance not necessary (Massachusetts, USA)	– No limitations on platform for pricing (Finland, 2018)

Source: SOU (2016, p. 86)

actors within the sharing economy have been given support from the Estonian government. Estonia's Prime Minister, Taavi Rõivas, argued in February 2016 that the business models that are prized within the sharing economy not only lead to increased competition but also are well suited for a sparsely populated country such as Estonia and create incentives for people to become entrepreneurs.

The sharing economy is based on the fact that people can accomplish a significantly higher number of transactions than before. A transaction cost can be explained through the information, administration and follow-up needed for a transaction to be conducted. Many platforms actively work with multiple information services for its users to reduce transaction costs. For instance, Swedish Blocket gives people living in Gothenburg who are interested in purchasing a sofa access to qualitative information instead of having to look for a second-hand advertisement or go to a flea market. Other platforms use reviews and grading to enhance information for the user of the services offered, all in order to reduce the cost for the user to find the necessary information for the transaction.

Sharing economy platforms also work on lowering the transaction administration costs. For example, Uber automated the payment process and removed the need of the customer to manually inform the driver of his position or destination, simultaneously as it provided the customer with direct information on the estimated time of arrival. A technical solution that reduced the number of steps in the transaction with decreased administrative costs is the result. To make sure that all parties hold their promises is an expensive and ceremonious process. Sometimes the parties have entered an agreement without really understanding what is required by them, which further complicates the follow-up. Follow-up is expensive, particularly in complex transactions. The platforms also try to simplify the follow-ups with the help of technical innovation. Finally, platforms are also trying to press transaction costs by creating trust around the transaction moment.

Trust in a Digital Environment

Trust is one of the most complex concepts and has been researched extensively across disciplines. Luhmann (1979) describes in his book, *Trust and Power*, that trust is a collective attribute that emerges as different parties interact while Bicchieri and colleagues develop the concept of trust at the individual level and define it as 'a disposition to engage in social exchanges that involve uncertainty and vulnerability, but that are also potentially rewarding' (Bicchieri, Duffy, & Tolle, 2004, p. 286).

Trust can be seen as a measure of confidence or belief that the other party will refrain from opportunistic behavior and behave in an expected manner (Williamson, 1993), thereby fulfilling the trusting party's expectations without exploiting its vulnerabilities (Pavlou & Gefen, 2002). Trust enables relationships that one can neither completely predict nor control (Luhmann, 1979), and without trust, uncertainty would lead to paralysis among people and their society.

With the rise of digitalization, individuals are now able to interact and engage in online social exchanges regardless of distance and any previous relationships. For example, digitalization has enabled virtual teams and organizations, crowdsourcing, e-commerce and, more recently, the topic of this chapter—the sharing economy. However, these online exchanges are generally characterized by a high degree of transaction complexity and uncertainties, giving rise to the need for trust as an enabler (see e.g. Friedman, Kahn, & Ho, 2000; Jarvenpaa, Tractinsky, & Saarinen, 1999; Ratnasingham, 1998).

A considerable amount of research has been conducted on trust in e-commerce transactions, in many ways a forerunner to the sharing economy. The lack of trust in web providers has been found to be one of the main reasons individuals do not conduct online transactions (Hoffman, Novak, & Peralta, 1999) while perceived risk negatively influences an individual's intention to purchase (Jarvenpaa et al., 1999). For one-time transactions, the existence of trust between parties has been found to be particularly important (Gefen & Straub, 2004) with antecedents to trust being the individual's disposition to trust, that is, a general propensity to trust other parties that can influence an individual's initial belief (Jarvenpaa et al., 1999) and familiarity with the website (Gefen, 2000). Even aspects such as nationality influence digital trust. A study of EU's consumers found that while 61 percent of consumers feel safe when purchasing online from a retailer within their country, only 38 percent feel safe when they purchase from a retailer from another EU country than their own (Eurobarometer, 2014).

The research on e-commerce has further revealed that the concept of trust is multidimensional. For example, auction sites such as eBay and third-party aggregators such as Amazon marketplace have led researchers to distinguish between trust in the individual sellers and buyers and trust in the third-party platforms and intermediaries. One of the more interesting findings of research by Hong and Cho (2011) is that consumer behavior in an online marketplace is largely determined by their trust in the well-established, trustworthy intermediary and not by their trust in the individual sellers doing business in the marketplace, that is, trust in the platforms and intermediaries is more important for users than trust in the individual sellers on these platforms. Researchers suggest that this is because intermediaries govern the entire transaction process through a set of rules and structures—communication between buyers and sellers and financial transactions (Hong & Cho, 2011; Pavlou & Gefen, 2002).

This trust in the intermediary platform is a form of institutional trust, which may be the most important mode of trust in business environments that lack familiarity (Pavlou & Gefen, 2002). Institutional trust can be built through structural assurances, which can provide guarantees or safety nets, for example, escrow services, credit card guarantees, legal recourses and regulations (Pavlou & Gefen, 2002; Shapiro, 1987). Turning to the sharing economy, researchers argue that building and sustaining trust in online sharing economy transactions is more complex than in traditional forms of e-commerce due to a number of factors (Hawlitschek, Teubner, & Weinhardt, 2016; Möhlmann, 2016). Among them is the fact that a large number of transactions tend to be one-off transactions among private individuals who are merely coordinated through an intermediary platform, thereby increasing the number of parties involved in all transactions (Hawlitschek et al., 2016; Möhlmann, 2016). Second, even though the matching occurs online, the transaction can occur offline in physical environments, often leading to a social component that cannot be governed by the platform since the transaction parties interact directly, for example, the renting of a room (Möhlmann, 2016). Third, in many cases the object being transacted differs, that is, merely accessed, used and returned and not purchased—a shift from owning to accessing shared goods, leading to the transaction being associated more with services than goods (Bardhi & Eckhardt, 2012; Möhlmann, 2016) and to potentially more interactions between the parties.

Due to these complexities, trust has even been labeled the sharing economy's 'currency' (Botsman, 2012). Hawlitschek et al. (2016) have outlined a conceptual model that differentiates between three substantial variants of trust: trust toward peers (interpersonal), trust toward the platform (institutional trust) and trust toward the product/service underlying the transaction.

Many platform providers in the sharing economy today have developed extensive systems designed to build interpersonal trust, institutional trust and product trust. For example, both suppliers and users are able to review and rate one another and their products (e.g. Airbnb renters and owners) while some platforms enable suppliers and users to gain different status levels (e.g. Airbnb superhost status), as well as to verify themselves through either uploading personal IDs or connecting their identities to social network accounts such as Facebook or LinkedIn. Structural assurances in the forms of escrow services, guarantees and insurance are also quite prevalent, as well as various measures to ensure privacy protection, transaction security and transaction integrity, which have proven valuable in building trust online (Wu, Hu, & Wu, 2010). These structural assurances can serve to strengthen interpersonal trust due to trust transference, that is, when a supplier does not provide any structural assurances but is associated with a platform that builds trust through structural assurances, then trust in the platform is transferred to the supplier (Stewart, 2003).

Despite these extensive measures, limitations to trust-building, such as information reliability, have been found in online environments. For example, users may artificially inflate the trustworthiness of others when writing reviews or giving ratings because they may be friends or because they may not be willing to write negative comments in fear of retribution due to the public nature of the platform (Lauterbach, Truong,

Shah, & Adamic, 2009). This need for trust in the sharing economy has led to a search for new technological solutions. One such technology is the blockchain, which is the underlying software behind the controversial cryptocurrency Bitcoin.

The absence of physical interaction during a transaction makes the ability to build trust between strangers more difficult. The number of potential individuals involved in sharing economy transactions as well as the individuals' limited experience with the various sharing economy platforms further makes the process of building institutional trust difficult. The blockchain holds promise to resolve this situation as it goes beyond the three forms of trust discussed here: interpersonal, institutional and product to system-based trust in which individuals put their trust in the strict formalized and transparent processes used to gain consensus in the underlying system.

Can Blockchain Technology Increase Digital Trust?

In October 2008, an individual or group of individuals under the pseudonym of Satoshi Nakamoto published a white paper on the internet that presented for the first time the idea behind a fully functioning blockchain (Nakamoto, 2008). The paper describes a network of computers wherein every computer has an identical copy of the network's transaction history, that is, a distributed ledger. In order to perform a transaction, a user informs all computers in the network about the pending transaction. The computers verify that the user is the rightful owner of the assets that are to be transacted and, if verified, all copies of the network's transaction history are then updated to include the newly accepted transaction. The true innovation of Nakamoto's paper lies in its solution to how a network of independent computers can reach consensus with respect to its transaction history. Users of the network let their computers compete in solving a very difficult cryptography problem. The first user to solve the problem enforces their version of the transaction history onto the remaining members of the network. A user's possibility to change the transaction history is, therefore, proportional to the amount of computer power that the user controls. However, computer power is not free and in order to compensate users for their work and expenses in reaching consensus, most blockchains are equipped with a digital currency that is used to reward those who solve the cryptography problem.

A shared transaction history also offers the possibility to implement smart contracts on the blockchain, a concept developed by Szabo (1997). Smart contracts offer networks a digital formalization of more complex relationships as opposed to simple monetary transactions. The contract is a set of instructions that enable a blockchain to execute certain actions based on conditions specified in the contract. The fact that the contracts are written in code means that, in theory, they can have the same functionality as other software applications. The fact that a contract has been verified by a blockchain means that the network has reached consensus concerning the state of the contract. For example, in our traditional system if a car is rented out, a contract is written. If needed, this contract can be evaluated in a court of law. In this case, a judge performs the process of reaching consensus on behalf of society. Whenever a medication is prescribed, a doctor performs a consensus process of who is eligible for which medicine. Blockchains offer a reliable way to reach consensus, which creates trust within a community and in its digital environment, which is a major reason why blockchains are considered to be such a promising technology. However, the term 'contract' can be misleading, and it has been pointed out that smart contracts primarily aim at enforcing contract rules while not settling contract breaches (Werbach & Cornell, 2017).

In a blockchain network, all nodes have access to all information. This architecture enables nodes to come and go without affecting the system. Also, in order to eliminate the network, all nodes have to be eliminated. However, the fact that all nodes have access to all information enforces the need to encrypt sensitive user information. There are concerns about privacy protection in blockchain networks. For example, in the context of Bitcoin, analyzing the transaction history has been shown to offer possibilities of identification (Fleder, Kester, & Sudeep, 2014). The possibility to identify users turns blockchain-stored data into personal data and, as such, falls within the scope of the general data protection regulation (GDPR) (European Parliament & the Council, 2016). This could cause several problems since the GDPR enables users to demand that their data be deleted. This, in turn, would bring into question the immutability of a blockchain's transaction history. Furthermore, the immutability of the transaction history has not yet received a legal interpretation. This creates uncertainty concerning blockchain-regulated ownership. The possibility to edit the transaction history is often connected to the amount of computer power that the user is able to offer the blockchain network.

There are three overarching types of blockchain protocols that have been developed to achieve consensus: 'proof-of-work', 'proof-of-stake' and 'proof-of-authority'. Consensus protocols that are based on computer power are called proof-of-work protocols. The possibility to edit the transaction history can also be connected to a user's exposure toward the network's digital currency, and these protocols are called proof-of-stake protocols (BitFury Group, 2015). Proof-of-stake protocols create a more cost-efficient consensus mechanism. However, it is easier to manipulate the consensus process either by bribing or by simply being a large stakeholder (Bentov, Gabizon, & Mizrahi, 2016). The third consensus protocol is proof-of-authority, where a predetermined number of members are in charge of forming network consensus. These networks are called 'private blockchains' and are considered easier to regulate due to the limited number of users that can edit the transaction history. A common way to compensate nodes that perform the work necessary to reach consensus are transaction fees as well as the creation of a newly minted currency. Bitcoin has a predetermined number of coins, which makes Bitcoin a deflationary network. However, there are also inflationary networks as well as blockchain networks without a cryptocurrency.

The architecture of a blockchain is of importance to the EU since it affects both economic and regulatory activity. Is it possible to regulate a completely open and distributed blockchain? Furthermore, how will the economic activity be affected by a deflationary compensation mechanism? Closed blockchains are considered easier to regulate; however, they could also jeopardize democratic values as well as trust. Bitcoin is the oldest blockchain and has an open architecture, wherein a user's possibility to edit the transaction history is weighted with respect to computer power. Ethereum is also an open blockchain and has a similar architecture to Bitcoin. However, Ethereum implements a more advanced programming language than Bitcoin, which makes it more suitable for smart contracts. There are several blockchains that are already being developed and Table 3 provides an overview of some larger blockchain initiatives.

Blockchains and the EU

At only nine years old, blockchains are a young phenomenon but are being rapidly developed, often in sectors that are central to the EU. For example, the technology could potentially improve healthcare systems

Table 3 Overview of different blockchain actors based on platform access and transactions processed by the platform

		Who do I trust to maintain a truthful record?			
		Central authority	*Group of known actors*	*Group of some known actors*	*No one*
What kind of relations are regulated by the platform?	Ownership of on-platform assets	Central Bank, Commercial Bank	R3CEV	Ripple	Bitcoin
	Ownership of off-platform assets	Custodian Bank	Hyperledger	Ripple	Colored Coins, Counterparty
	Obligations and rights arising from agreement	Clearing House	Eris	Ripple	Ethereum

Source: Richard Gendal Brown, R3CEV

due to its use of encrypted communication. Blockchains could also be used to improve auditing as well as increase financial participation within societies due to low entry barriers (European Parliament, 2016; UK Government Office for Science, 2015). Transparency in public decision processes can be improved and, as a consequence, increase citizen trust in public institutions. Smart contracts are thought to improve the protection of critical infrastructure against cyberattacks. Also, reaching the '5 × 5' goal of reducing global transaction costs to under 5 percent within five years is expected to be improved through the blockchain technology. The large gap between expected and actual sales tax revenues within the EU could also potentially decrease with improved economic control (European Parliament, 2016). One of the biggest challenges in reaching the EU 2020 goal of further innovation is to improve as well as simplify regulations relating to patent and copyright laws (European Parliament & the Council, 2013). At the same time, blockchain-based companies are offering customers the possibility to upload files on the blockchain in order to get a time-stamped proof of ownership. This time-stamped document can be used in future disputes concerning immaterial ownership. Furthermore, organizations are offered a complete and unified transaction history, resulting in new opportunities for improved auditing and accounting. For example, the 'Big Four' professional consulting firms Deloitte, EY, PwC and KPMG are all early adopters of the technology (NEWSBTC, 2017). Blockchain technology is even used to improve digital identification by companies like Cambridge Blockchain LLC, which is developing an identity software with several leading global financial institutions (Medium, 2017). The possibility to implement a European document of identification would further strengthen the European digital market. This single document could potentially replace many of the passwords that people use today and could potentially increase digital security within the EU.

There are several blockchain companies actively seeking to further develop the sharing economy. For example, some companies are developing solutions for the distributed storage of files, where ordinary persons can rent out available disk space, offering a storage solution that is often cheaper than their traditional equivalence. The distributed architecture offers completely new ways of value creation for European citizens while also offering consumers an alternative to established producers. There are several examples of blockchain companies trying to increase trust in the sharing economy. For example, one blockchain-based company is working to solve the problem of insurance companies that are not insuring third-party players in the sharing economy and another is developing digital locks controlled by a blockchain with the goal of becoming the future infrastructure of the sharing economy. Blockchains could also connect different services with each other, thereby making trust gained in one platform accessible in another platform.

Allianz, one of Europe's largest insurance companies, has already started to use smart contracts to improve their settlement processes. However, when smart contracts are implemented in more complex situations, the EU will have to deal with the ever increasing complexity problem. The increased digital trust that blockchains are believed to generate can quickly disappear when smart contracts become more and more dependent on organizations and experts outside the control of the blockchain. This complexity problem is considered to be one of the biggest challenges that blockchains face today and is further highlighted by the smart contract's lack of remediation. For example, Werbach and Cornell (2017) point out that present legal systems will probably see an increase in the demand for remediation due to an increased use of smart contracts. This will require the EU to develop a deeper understanding as to how blockchain technology is used and what functionality it fulfills.

While blockchain technology enables increased economic activity as well as a more efficient bureaucracy, the technology also offers new opportunities for money laundering and other forms of criminal activities such as financing terrorism. This has encouraged the Financial Action Task Force (FATF) of the G7 group to recommend that all EU member states put the same regulatory demands on currency exchanges that deal with digital currencies as they do on those that deal with fiat currencies (FATF, 2015). The European Commission also recommends that virtual currencies be included in existing directives concerning money laundering and the financing of terrorism. Those that control access to digital currencies should be considered responsible and be treated as existing financial institutions (European Commission, 2016b). However, the European Banking Authority points out that including digital currency exchanges in the present regulatory framework forces those exchanges to obtain separate permission for each country where their services are offered (European Banking Authority, 2016). This would lead to large administrative costs since digital currency exchanges are global actors. The European Parliament has noted in resolution 2016/2017 (INI) that too harsh a regulation could jeopardize the development of blockchain technology. At the same time, regulation could quickly become necessary since the technology is implemented in critical infrastructure.

The EU sees several opportunities with blockchain technology. But how active are the different member states and what role should the EU play in this process? The UK and The Netherlands are the two countries that invest the most in blockchain technology (Hilerman, 2016). Both countries have a well-developed financial sector, which could explain their prominent position. Since 2008, Estonia has been storing medical records with the help of blockchain technology with over a million citizens now able to store their medical history on a blockchain. This is considered to increase patient safety as well as reduce medical fraud (Aru, 2016; Palmer, 2016). Estonia has also shown interest in launching their own digital currency called *estcoin* (Korjus, 2017). Poland has a national digitalization plan that describes a willingness to improve financial security through blockchain technology (Kastelein, 2016). The German-based company, BlockCharge, is working on a blockchain-based solution for electricity distribution in the context of electric cars (Tual, 2016). Sweden has explored the possibility of using blockchain technology in registering land ownership in a collaboration between the Swedish government and the companies Chromaway and Kairos Future (Kempe, 2017). Bitcoin is highly volatile and the price can often change between the time of order and the time of purchase, and Safello, another Swedish company, is an example of a financial service that enables their customers to lock the Bitcoin price at the time of ordering in order to reduce the effect of Bitcoin's volatility. However, if a user decides to use Safello, they need to verify their identity before they can purchase Bitcoins. This demand of identification is in line with the regulatory framework proposed by the European Commission (European Commission, 2016a). However, legal demands in a digital context are often hard to enforce and there are already various services, such as mixing services and tumbler that offer users the possibility to not connect their identity with a specific financial transaction.

Finally, outside of the EU, Russia has banned several cryptocurrency websites in an attempt to make it more difficult for normal users to use cryptocurrencies (Raza, 2016; Silver, 2017). China has banned Initial Coin Offerings (ICO), which are a form of fund-raising often used by blockchain startups (Acheson, 2017), and the US Securities and Exchange Commission has ruled that, regardless of the form of currency being used and regardless of a firm's stateless status, if the product is offered to American investors, it is bound to US security laws (U.S. Securities & Exchange Commission, 2017). On the other hand, the Singapore Monetary Authority has stated that they will not regulate cryptocurrencies (Amin, 2017). Blockchain technology is a global phenomenon and when the EU develops its position with respect to blockchain technology, it is also developing its position within a global digital society.

A Future Digital Partnership for the EU

The European sharing economy can help create new jobs in several different ways. Blockchain technology enables the development of a sharing economy with increased levels of trust and security, a key factor in order to create new jobs. A consequence of the sharing economy is that risk is moved from the traditional middleman to the user. This means that the more users a platform has, the more perceived trust it is able to generate. Blockchains also enable networks to use formal consensus processes instead of traditional middlemen. When the blockchain is used as the underlying infrastructure for cryptocurrencies, traditional banks are being replaced by a machinery of trust. This same technology can be used in other areas. However, in order to create new business opportunities within all areas of the sharing economy, blockchain technology needs to be further developed as well as implemented.

By monitoring technical development, the EU can adjust regulatory frameworks in order to enable economic growth. The EU has already created an initiative called the European Observatory on Blockchain Technologies in order to better understand the new technology (European Commission, 2017). The EU has even started to develop a Financial Transparency Gateway that, through blockchain technology, seeks to offer reliable financial information about companies within the Union (Higgins, 2017). Implementing blockchain technology could lead to increased trust in EU institutions and, at the same time, improve digital integrity given its prevalent use of encrypted data. Access to anonymous systems does, however, create new opportunities for tax evasion and other criminal activities. It also becomes harder to protect workers and consumer rights within the sharing economy if more and more information is being encrypted. To ensure that new technology is developed in a way that serves European citizen, the EU needs to become a user, a financier and a developer of the technology. The creation of a single digital market with new opportunities for value creation is a necessity if European societies want to benefit from the process of digitalization. The sharing economy and blockchain technology are being developed as a response to the lack of integrity, trust and low transaction costs—all problems of the digital economy. EU officials seem to share this view, which creates opportunities for the EU to enter into new digital alliances.

To simply apply existing regulations on emerging digital phenomena jeopardizes the creation of a single digital market. The integration of the sharing economy into the European regulatory framework needs to be achieved through cooperation. The EU and its member states need to understand how regulatory frameworks can both help and destroy these new phenomena. However, those who develop services based on sharing economy strategies as well as blockchain technologies need to understand the responsibility that the EU has in relation to its citizens, and they must help the EU to ensure this responsibility within a digital context. Actively developing a new digital society requires member states to make joint decisions on how they want to see the technology evolve. For example, a decision must be made if the EU wants to establish a global standard for the technology. A uniform standard would facilitate the communication between organizations and authorities. However, a premature standardization could lead to the implementation of suboptimal technologies and monopolistic situations could arise. The EU should also decide whether the Union should encourage open instead of proprietary source code and if this will guide how research and development funds are distributed. The European Parliament has already expressed its willingness to support projects based on open source code as this is considered to promote both democratic and economic values. Open source support becomes a distribution policy tool when access to information is becoming increasingly valuable.

In a private blockchain, only a predetermined number of nodes are able to edit the history. Private blockchains offer increased integrity and simplified regulation as well as reduced energy consumption. At the same time, private blockchains reduce ordinary citizens' ability to participate. This makes it more difficult to create digital environments characterized by both trust and democracy. Public blockchains will contribute to the EU's economic and democratic visions and they should therefore be supported. The negative description that the sharing economy sometimes receives in the media (e.g. how drivers and companies try to escape taxes as well as how the platforms take advantage of their users) should be nuanced with descriptions that focus on how actors in the sharing economy contribute to growth and sustainable development as well as the inclusion of weak social groups, all of which are intermediate goals in the EU 2020 strategy (European Parliament & the Council, 2013). As Bitcoin and blockchain technology start to produce lasting positive results with respect to economic development, the description of these phenomena should change to focus less on illegal trade and money laundering and more on robust digital systems as well as increased trust in the digital environment. This would, in turn, facilitate further development of these technologies. Success stories of individuals and companies from the sharing economy and the blockchain sector should be told in order to inspire others to explore these areas.

Furthermore, there is no systematic measure of the value that is created within the sharing economy, which further complicates the communication of sharing economic effects. Uniform approaches for measuring sharing economic activity should be developed, especially when it often adds to or completely overtakes current economic activity. Meanwhile, measurement is often complicated by the fact that many activities lack a monetary value, such as couchsurfing, while other activities cannot be measured by changes in GDP, such as renting a room on Airbnb.

The ongoing transformation highlights the labor market's urgent need to offer fast retraining and re-education when jobs disappear due to digitalization, automation and blockchain implementation. At the same time, higher education must prepare to respond to this need, and the governments of the EU member states should actively advocate the use of platforms offering Massive Open Online Courses (MOOCs). Courses in future subjects such as blockchain technology should be given priority. In parallel, new certification programs and platforms should be designed to enable individuals to verify the completion of MOOCs. This would increase mobility within the European labor force as well as increase the possibilities of finding internet-based work. Finally, since the sharing economy is a global phenomenon, workers in the EU will have increased chances of finding online jobs with overseas companies.

The sharing economy has the potential to increase economic growth when individuals can sell their time, products and services on a global market. Traditional forms of employment are challenged when individuals can earn an income through several sources such as renting out rooms, offering catering services or selling services through digital platforms. Most current regulations that target the labor market are based on the perception that individuals either are employers or employees—something that is not optimal in a sharing economy. Regulation must be reviewed so that it does not prevent people from participating in the sharing economy. For example, many English sole proprietors are subjected to a penalty tax based on a rule that originates from the early twentieth century that was originally intended to encourage people to leave home to take on factory work. EU member states should encourage citizens to explore opportunities for value creation while facilitating organizations that make this value creation possible in a safe environment.

Blockchain technologies are able to reduce the importance of nationality in the relationship between consumers and companies. The need to rely on a specific company has disappeared and it is now enough to trust the blockchain. As a consequence, entry barriers to business opportunities and trade are reduced, which not only strengthens the EU's internal digital market but also, we might even say, European democracy. EU member states must work for parsimonious regulations with respect to the sharing economy and blockchain technology. For example, transport services within the sharing economy show that European regulations differ considerably, with some countries increasing the regulatory burden while others are reducing it. Various regulations within the EU can lead to further imbalances in growth and labor market characteristics. Also, the ability to handle the continued digitalization and automation of society are adversely affected. We have developed the following recommendations for the EU based on our research:

1. Expand the EU Blockchain Observatory and Forum into a lab where different blockchain networks and applications can be tested and developed while learning from each other, with a specific focus on sharing economy applications. For example, examine whether a standardized blockchain should be implemented within the EU or if different industries should develop their own. Enabling trial and error in the development phase is of great importance in order to detect risks associated with the technology.
2. Develop EU regulations enabling flexible control structures in order to not risk the robustness and reliability of blockchain technology nor hamper the sharing economy.
3. Open a dialogue with the US and other non-European countries on regulatory issues.
4. Strengthen the confidence in blockchain technology within the EU through a broad and in-depth analysis of the possibilities of blockchain technology as well as its challenges, for example, the possibility to improve welfare systems with increased institutional trust as a result, with a particular focus on the sharing economy.
5. Provide all EU citizens access to high-speed internet; this can be one of Europe's most important democratic issues and is necessary for the EU's single digital market to become a reality.
6. Explore the opportunities to implement sharing economy principles and technologies in the field of energy efficiency.

Notes

1. The number of blockchain initiatives by major institutions has increased from 22 in the third quarter of 2015 to 34 in the fourth quarter of 2015 to 25 in the first quarter of 2016. Today there are more than 80 financial and other institutions in the R3CEV consortium to develop the Corda blockchain for the financial market and more than 150 organizations supporting the development of Hyperledger.
2. See more information about the Europe 2020 strategy on the European Commission's website: https://ec.europa.eu/info/business-economy-euro/economic-and-fiscal-policy-coordination/eu-economic-governance-monitoring-prevention-correction/european-semester/framework/europe-2020-strategy_en

References

Acheson, N. (2017). China's ICO ban: Understandable, reasonable and (probably) temporary. Retrieved October 28, 2017, from https://www.coindesk.com/chinas-ico-ban-understandable-reasonable-probably-temporary/

Amin, H. (2017, October 24). Singapore won't regulate cryptocurrencies, Central Bank chief says. *Bloomberg*. Retrieved October 28, 2017, from https://www.bloomberg.com/news/articles/2017-10-24/singapore-won-t-regulate-cryptocurrencies-remains-alert-to-risk

Aru, I. (2016). Estonian government adopts blockchain to secure 1 Mln health records. Retrieved October 28, 2017, from https://cointelegraph.com/news/estonian-government-adopts-blockchain-to-secure-1-mln-health-records

Bardhi, F., & Eckhardt, G. M. (2012). Access-based consumption: The case of car sharing. *Journal of Consumer Research, 39*(4), 881–898.

Bentov, I., Gabizon, A., & Mizrahi, A. (2016). Cryptocurrencies without proof of work. *Lecture Notes in Computer Science (including subseries Lecture Notes in Artificial Intelligence and Lecture Notes in Bioinformatics)* (pp. 142–157), 9604 LNCS(240258).

Bicchieri, C., Duffy, J., & Tolle, G. (2004). Trust among strangers. *Philosophy of Science, 71*(3), 286–319.

BitFury Group. (2015). Proof of stake versus proof of work. Retrieved from http://bitfury.com/content/5-white-papers-research/pos-vs-pow-1.0.2.pdf

Botsman, R. (2012). The currency of the new economy is trust. *TED Talks*. Retrieved from https://www.ted.com/talks/rachel_botsman_the_currency_of_the_new_economy_is_trust

Eurobarometer. (2014). E-communications and the digital single market. Retrieved from http://data.europa.eu/euodp/en/data/dataset/S2062_84_2_438_ENG

European Banking Authority. (2016). *Opinion of the European banking authority on the EU Commission's proposal to bring virtual currencies into the scope of Directive*. (EU) 2015/849 (4AMLD).

European Commission. (2010). *Europe 2020: A strategy for smart, sustainable and inclusive growth*. COM(2010) 2020 final, Brussels, 3 March 2010.

European Commission. (2016a). *A European agenda for the collaborative economy*. COM(2016) 356 final, Brussels, 2 June 2016.

European Commission. (2016b). *Proposal for a directive amending Directive (EU) 2015/849 on the prevention of the use of the financial system for the purposes of money laundering or terrorist financing and amending Directive 2009/101/EC*. COM(2016) 450 final, Strasbourg, 5 July 2016.

European Commission. (2017). *A connected digital single market for all*. COM(2017) 228 final, Brussels, 10 May 2017.

European Parliament. (2016). *European Parliament resolution of 26 May 2016 on virtual currencies*, 2016/2007(INI). Provisional edition (pp. 1–4).

European Parliament & the Council of the EU. (2013). Establishing Horizon 2020—The Framework Programme for Research and Innovation (2014–2020) and repealing Decision No 1982/2006/EC. *Official Journal of the European Union, 2010*(1291), 104–173.

European Parliament & the Council of the EU. (2016, March). Regulation 2016/679 of the European Parliament and the Council on the protection of natural persons with regard to the processing of personal data and on the free movement of such data, and repealing Directive 95/46/EC (General Data Protection Regulation). *Official Journal of the European Communities, 2014*(2014), 1–88.

FATF. (2015). Guidance for a risk-based approach to virtual currencies. Retrieved from http://www.fatf-gafi.org/publications/fatfgeneral/documents/guidance-rba-virtual-currencies.html

Felländer, A., Ingram, I., & Teigland, R. (2015). *The sharing economy: Embracing change with caution*. Stockholm: Entreprenörskapsforum.

Fleder, M., Kester, M. S., & Sudeep, P. (2014). Bitcoin transaction graph analysis. *arXiv:1502.01657* (pp. 1–8).

Fölster, S. (2014). *De nya jobben i automatiseringens tidevarv*. Stockholm: Stiftelsen för Strategisk Forskning.

Friedman, B., Kahn, P. H., & Ho, D. C. (2000). Trust online. *Communications of the ACM, 43*(12), 34–40.

Frost and Sullivan. (2017). The 2017 global blockchain startup map. Retrieved from https://ww2.frost.com/news/press-releases/frost-sullivan-identifies-2017-global-blockchain-startup-map/

Gefen, D. (2000). E-commerce: The role of familiarity and trust. *Omega, 28*(6), 725–737.

Gefen, D., & Straub, D. W. (2004). Consumer trust in B2C e-commerce and the importance of social presence: Experiments in e-products and e-services. *Omega, 32*(6), 407–424.

Hawlitschek, F., Teubner, T., & Weinhardt, C. (2016). Trust in the sharing economy. *Die Unternehmung: Swiss Journal of Business Research and Practice, 70*(1), 26–44.

Higgins, S. (2017). The EU is building a 'financial transparency gateway' with blockchain. *CoinDesk*. Retrieved October 28, 2017, from https://www.coindesk.com/eu-developing-prototype-blockchain-platform-public-company-data/

Hilerman, G. (2016). State of blockchain Q1 2016: Blockchain funding overtakes Bitcoin. *CoinDesk*. Retrieved October 28, 2017, from https://www.coindesk.com/state-of-blockchain-q1-2016/

Hoffman, D. L., Novak, T. P., & Peralta, M. (1999). Building consumer trust online. *Communications of the ACM, 42*(4), 80–85.

Hong, I. B., & Cho, H. (2011). The impact of consumer trust on attitudinal loyalty and purchase intentions in B2C e-marketplaces: Intermediary trust vs. seller trust. *International Journal of Information Management, 31*(5), 469–479.

Jarvenpaa, S. L., Tractinsky, N., & Saarinen, L. (1999). Consumer trust in an internet store: A cross culture validation. *Journal of Computer Mediated Communication, 5*, 1–35.

Kastelein, R. (2016). Polish government makes plans to explore blockchain. *Blockchain News*. Retrieved October 28, 2017, from http://www.the-blockchain.com/2016/06/24/polish-government-makes-plans-explore-blockchain/

Kempe, M. (2017). The land registry in the blockchain. https://chromaway.com/papers/Blockchain_Landregistry_Report_2017.pdf

Korjus, K. (2017). Estonia could offer 'estcoins' to e-residents. *Medium*. Retrieved October 28, 2017, from https://medium.com/e-residency-blog/estonia-could-offer-estcoins-to-e-residents-a3a5a5d3c894

Lauterbach, D., Truong, H., Shah, T., & Adamic, L. (2009). Surfing a web of trust: Reputation and reciprocity on couchsurfing.com. *Computational Science and Engineering, CSE'09. International Conference, 4*, 346–353.

Luhmann, N. (1979). *Trust and power*. Chichester: John Wiley & Sons.

Medium. (2017). 21 companies leveraging blockchain for identity management and authentication. *Medium*. Retrieved October 23, 2017, from https://medium.com/@LetsTalkPayments/21-companies-leveraging-blockchain-for-identity-management-and-authentication-d09d88e3a4bf

Möhlmann, M. (2016). Sharing economy: Building trust in P2P online marketplaces. *New York Computer Science and Economics Day*. New York.

Nakamoto, S. (2008). Bitcoin: A peer-to-peer electronic cash system. *Bitcoin.Org*. Retrieved from https://bitcoin.org/bitcoin.pdf

NEWSBTC. (2017). The 'big four' audit firms and their contribution to blockchain technology. Retrieved October 23, 2017, from http://www.newsbtc.com/2017/07/07/big-four-audit-firms-contribution-blockchain-technology/

Palmer, D. (2016). Blockchain startup to secure 1 million e-Health records in Estonia. *CoinDesk*. Retrieved October 28, 2017, from https://www.coindesk.com/blockchain-startup-aims-to-secure-1-million-estonian-health-records/

Pavlou, P. A., & Gefen, D. (2002). Building effective online marketplaces with institution-based trust. In *Proceedings of the 23rd International Conference on Information Systems* (pp. 667–675). Atlanta: Association for Information Systems.

Ratnasingham, P. (1998). The importance of trust in electronic commerce. *Internet Research, 8*(4), 313–321.

Raza, A. (2016). Current state of Bitcoin in Russia. *The Merkle*. Retrieved October 28, 2017, from https://themerkle.com/bitcoin-in-russia-2/

Shapiro, S. P. (1987). The social control of impersonal trust. *American Journal of Sociology, 93*(3), 623–658.

Silver, A. (2017). Russia to block access to cryptocurrency exchanges' websites. *The Register*. Retrieved October 28, 2017, from https://www.theregister.co.uk/2017/10/10/russia_to_ban_cryptocurrency_exchanges/

Statens Offentliga Utredningar. (2016). *Taxi och samåkning—i dag, i morgon och i övermorgon*. SOU 2016:86.

Stewart, K. J. (2003). Trust transfer on the world wide web. *Organisation Science, 14*(1), 5–17.

Sundararajan, A. (2016). *The sharing economy: The end of employment and the rise of crowd-based capitalism*. Cambridge, MA: MIT Press.

Szabo, N. (1997). Formalizing and securing relationships on public networks. *First Monday, 2*(9). Retrieved August 28, 2016, from http://pear.accc.uic.edu/ojs/index.php/fm/article/view/548

Tual, S. (2016). Blockchain energy P2P sharing project Share&Charge going into live Beta. *Medium*. Retrieved October 28, 2017, from https://blog.slock.it/blockchain-energy-p2p-sharing-project-share-charge-going-into-live-beta-ad4e069e79d

UK Government Office for Science. (2015). *Distributed ledger technology: Beyond block chain*.

U.S. Securities & Exchange Commission. (2017). *Report of Investigation Pursuant to Section 21(a) of the Securities Exchange Act of 1934: The DAO, 21(81207)*.

Werbach, K. D., & Cornell, N. (2017). Contracts Ex Machina. *Duke Law Journal, 67*, 1–57.

Williamson, O. E. (1993). Calculativeness, trust, and economic organization. *The Journal of Law and Economics, 36*(1), 453–486.

Wu, G., Hu, X., & Wu, Y. (2010). Effects of perceived interactivity, perceived web assurance and disposition to trust on initial online trust. *Journal of Computer-Mediated Communication, 16*(1), 1–26.

Trust and Crises in the EU: Exit, Voice and Loyalty

Göran von Sydow

The European Union has been in a state of crisis for several years. Several subsequent crises have come one after the other: the euro crisis, the refugee crisis and most recently 'Brexit'. The Union's leading representatives seem to have been deeply affected by the grave situation. The President of the European Council, Donald Tusk, spoke in September 2016 about the EU being in an 'existential crisis'. In the same month, the President of the European Commission, Jean-Claude Juncker, also painted a dark picture of the state of the Union:

> Never before have I heard so many leaders speak only of their domestic problems, with Europe mentioned only in passing, if at all. Never before have I seen representatives of the EU institutions setting very different priorities, sometimes in direct opposition to national governments and national Parliaments. It is as if there is almost no intersection between the EU and its national capitals anymore. Never before have I seen national governments so weakened by the forces of populism and paralysed by the risk of defeat in the next elections. Never before have I seen so much fragmentation, and so little commonality in our Union. (Juncker, 2016)

G. von Sydow (✉)
Swedish Institute for European Policy Studies, Stockholm, Sweden

A. Bakardjieva Engelbrekt et al. (eds.), *Trust in the European Union in Challenging Times*, https://doi.org/10.1007/978-3-319-73857-4_10

Juncker's bleak picture illustrates a state of severe tensions in the EU. Tensions between the EU member states, between member states and EU institutions and between the electorate and the elected. In a nutshell: the Union seems to have entered into a phase of diminishing trust.

The concept of trust is hard to pin down and it may seem as if we tend to notice its absence much more than its presence. The antonym of trust is distrust. The synonyms are fairly wide-ranging: confidence, assurance, reliance, faith, hope, belief. In relation to the European integration process, the related concept of loyalty also seems relevant. Rothstein emphasises that personal loyalty depends on how we perceive and anticipate the loyalty of *other* persons (Rothstein, 2005). In cooperative situations, we make judgements about how we believe the others are going to act in the future. The EU has evolved into a comprehensive cooperation in which the member states are becoming increasingly embedded with each other, but the EU is not (yet) a state. European integration is asymmetric in relation to the 'what' and the 'how' of cooperation. Due to this embeddedness and interdependence, however, a certain degree of loyalty and trust has been considered essential to the survival of the EU in its present form. Mutual trust is also necessary between the member states and the supranational level.

There are various ways to approach the problem of trust in the EU. In this chapter, I focus mainly on trust between EU member states and between member states and EU institutions. One cannot, however, ignore the degree of trust that exists between citizens and their representatives (see Linda Berg's chapter in this volume). The EU is not structured as a federal state; it is rather a far-reaching process of integration that transforms the member states (see e.g. Bickerton, 2012). Although democracy remains primarily national, the EU project is profound and imposes considerable demands for loyalty. In earlier stages of the integration process, the asymmetric relationships between power and accountability could be upheld through a 'permissive consensus' that relied on the trust of citizens in their national leaders and the often uncontroversial nature of EU policies (Lindberg & Scheingold, 1970). As the EU has become increasingly involved in politically contested issues and policies while political leaders have found it ever more difficult to mobilise support, the conditions for cooperation in the EU are changing (Hooghe & Marks, 2009). Protests against the austerity policy in the wake of the euro crisis, opposition to the refugee policy, 'Brexit', national opposition to EU free trade agreements with the US and Canada, are all signs of a heightened level of conflict and possibly an expression of rising mutual distrust of one another and of the European integration project as such. As a result, national leaders are finding themselves squeezed between loyalty to the EU and responsiveness to their own voters.

European integration is becoming increasingly politicised, which raises questions about what basis for legitimacy can bolster the long-term sustainability of the system. For this reason, this chapter is devoted to a discussion of the EU's legitimacy problem that brings the relationship between *exit*, *voice* and *loyalty* to the fore as being of fundamental importance to the function and survival of political systems. The euro crisis with focus on the troubles in Greece, the British impending exit from the EU and the EU's management of the refugee crisis are analysed through the lens of this conceptual triptych. These dramatic events also have bearing on what future European integration is heading for, in that all of these can be considered *systemic crises* for the EU. A distinct retreat to nationalism can be seen in the light of the surfacing antagonisms and the widespread suspicion that EU member states seem to entertain about each other's loyalty. The antagonism within and between the member states is, of course, obvious in the case of 'Brexit' but also in relation to opposition in some EU member states to participating in the common refugee policy and to cooperation in the euro zone. How does one compel greater loyalty from the member states to adhere to decisions once made? What is the right balance between exit and voice to instil loyalty? The concluding discussion focuses on the EU's future constitutional policy choices and the prerequisites for restoring trust.

Trust and Loyalty in the EU

In spite of the supranational elements of the EU, democracy remains national. This formula for coexistence is expressed in an 'informal pact of confidence'. This takes place in terms of a 'living constitution' in the EU, where the member states remain loyal to the Union and where the supranational elements are exercised with respect for national democracy (Gustavsson, 2014). During the euro crisis, attention was brought to signs that the pact of confidence was beginning to crack and that national recalcitrance can be interpreted as an expression that EU countries no longer trust that the balance between common and national interests is being appropriately struck. Article 4 of the Treaty on European Union includes both the second paragraph, which addresses respect for national identities, and the key principle of 'sincere cooperation' (Article 4(3) TEU). Together, these balance each other as regards loyalty to the supranational Union from the member states' perspective and respect for the member states' national identities from the supranational Union's perspective. The conflicts surrounding the EU refugee policy in recent years serve as a good example of how the limits of the pact of confidence are being tested. This applies both to the EU member states that are resisting coercive European actions aimed at forcing solidarity through hierarchical governance and to the member states that support the established policy and whose loyalty to the system is at risk of eroding if joint responsibilities and regulatory compliance fail to materialise.

It was in hopes of what practical cooperation would lead to that French Foreign Minister, Robert Schuman, composed the by now famous text calling for a united Europe. In the Schuman Declaration of 9 May 1950, it was stated that 'Europe will not be made all at once, or according to a single plan. It will be built through concrete achievements which first create a de facto solidarity.' Seen from an academic perspective, Haas described the integration process as 'the process whereby political actors in several distinct national settings are persuaded to shift their loyalties, expectations and political activities towards a new centre, whose institutions possess or demand jurisdiction over the pre-existing national states' (Haas, 1958). But do these conditions of shifting loyalties apply today?

It seems that the deeper cooperation within the EU reaches, the greater the demands on trust becomes. Somewhat pointedly, one might ask: are the euro crisis, 'Brexit' and the refugee crisis pushing the EU towards becoming more like a real state or are these crises rather the beginning of a process in which the EU is falling apart? Just as the euro crisis revealed the weaknesses of the unfinished European structure, the latest developments show that the EU's specific, soluble formula for cooperation is sensitive to severe stresses. Having a common monetary policy but no common fiscal policy gives rise to tensions. The refugee crisis highlights the dilemma of free movement within the EU but without having fixed external borders or common refugee policy. 'Brexit' lays bare the fundamental uncertainty about where the EU begins and ends, which in turn begs the question of what loyalty can be demanded and by whom. Is the choice between taking 'the great leap forward' towards the building of a federal state or dismantling that which has been achieved thus far getting closer? Those who advocate a leap forward suggest this could achieve better balance between power and accountability and argue that this could restore trust. Those who instead consider this to be a perilous path argue that the fundamental prerequisites for taking such a step do not exist and that trust would instead be severely damaged. Promoters of a sort of in-the-middle muddle-through perspective emphasise that even though the EU is facing severe stresses in which trust and loyalty will be challenged, integration will nevertheless proceed in small steps.

The loyalty of the EU member states can thus be seen as a manifestation of trust, and yet political leaders need to be responsive to public opinion in matters that have become increasingly politically sensitive. The three disruptive challenges—systemic crises—for the EU referred to above can all be, I contend, regarded in the light of the concepts of *exit*, *voice* and *loyalty*. These concepts have been used by scholars including Stein Rokkan when he studied state formation and nation-building processes in Europe (Rokkan, 1970). Interaction and balance between how difficult it is for political entities (people, social actors, territories, states) to exit a context and what opportunities for political influence exist are central to this typology, in which loyalty is seen as a mediating factor. If the balance between exit controls and voice channelling is distorted, problems of loyalty (and trust) will ensue. The evolution of the EU should not be regarded as a classical state formation process, but the issues that the EU nowadays has become increasingly involved in impinge on matters related to core state powers. Over time, the scope of European integration has expanded and extended into policy areas that are more politically controversial (De Wilde & Zürn, 2012). Taken together, this puts sharper focus on the basis of the legitimacy of the Union.

A State in the Making?

The hybrid nature of the EU as something more than a strictly intergovernmental organisation but less than a federal state offers a particular challenge. If one were to regard the European integration process as an endeavour to engage in state formation, it can be useful to analyse it by applying the concepts of exit, voice and loyalty. When Stein Rokkan wrote about the emergence of the nation state, he was inspired by Albert O. Hirschman's classic book *Exit, Voice and Loyalty: Responses to Decline in Firms, Organizations and States*. Put in simple terms, Hirschman's theory seeks to explain how we behave in response to decline. Should one leave, object or acquiesce? Aimed at categorising alternative ways of reacting, Hirschman introduced the concepts of exit, voice and loyalty. Exit entails switching suppliers, organisations, states or parties. The cost of exit—as for entry—varies with the associated sanctions or the cost of outside options. If you are unhappy with the country you live in, you can choose to emigrate, but this will result in costs: economic (you must find another means of support), political (you might need to become a citizen of a new country) and cultural (you must probably learn a new language). If you are unhappy at work or in a relationship, you will face similar calculations. Instead of exit, you can choose voice, that is, to attempt to affect your situation. The higher the cost of exit, the more reason to instead seek to influence the content of the policy or the organisation (Hirschman, 1970). Hirschman does not, however, give a clear definition of loyalty (Bartolini, 2005). Loyalty is instead an intermediate category used when individuals consent to or accept something they feel strongly about and which is perhaps an important part of their identity. Loyalty thus becomes an expression of internalised boundaries.

Rokkan developed Hirschman's essentially economic model of individual behaviour into a macromodel of state formation. From this perspective, state formation involves limiting opportunities to exit a territory by establishing and upholding boundaries. This refers to boundaries in a wider sense than purely territorial: that is, also military, legal, economic, cultural and political boundaries. The legal, cultural, economic and political systems of the various European territories are also differentiated through boundary building, which lays the foundations for the differences between Europe's nation states. According to this perspective, European history can be read as a process aimed at making all of these boundaries coincide within the framework of one (nation) state. From Rokkan's point of view, loyalty becomes the mechanisms and structures that hold the parts together. Loyalty becomes a system-building component based on identity, solidarity and trust.

But it is important to remember that the differentiation in which various overlapping systems in Europe are gradually separated and result in the nation state is a process that spans several centuries (see e.g. Tilly, 1992). European history can be interpreted through the boundaries that are created and removed. Again, boundaries refer to not only physical border controls but also political-administrative, legal, economic, cultural, military and linguistic boundaries. The state controls the costs of entry and exit and how citizens and organisations can influence policy. Importantly, state formation precedes both nation-building and democratisation. In the often turbulent processes leading up to the birth of modern democracy, the nature of external boundaries is profoundly important. In peaceful state formation processes, the absence of conflicts about boundaries is beneficial to creating the right balance in order to control exit and the voice of the citizenry. When democracy collapses, for example, during the interwar period in Europe, the balance is skewed (Rokkan, 1970; Flora et al., 1999). Unsettled boundaries were replaced with border conflicts, wars and oppression, causing the nation state in several places in Europe to take on its most destructive form as of yet.

Is examining the balance between exit control and voice channelling in today's EU a productive approach to understand how the EU as a political system is developing? By illustrating what this balance looks like in relation to a few contemporary examples, this chapter sheds light on the EU's present constitutional challenge. The EU thus entails an internal lowering of boundaries, at least partially, and a weakening of differentiation between its member states in the EU territory. But is the EU a kind of state formation? Well, not really. The EU is instead another form of cooperation where new, hard external borders are not being built and where the member states have chosen to retain several central functions while still delegating authority to the EU when and where necessary to solve common problems. The gradual enlargement of the EU and the close relationships to neighbouring countries have also blurred the Union's external boundaries. Territorial boundaries will remain unclear due to 'Brexit'—and this also depends on what 'boundary' one is referring to. The external boundaries are porous and the 'height' and 'strength' of internal boundaries vary between different types of policy areas in the EU. The EU has strong regulatory mechanisms but only in certain areas, a strong judicial system but weak central administrative power and weak military and fiscal policy capability (Bartolini, 2005). In spite of these limitations, the integration is of such importance that we can, like Bickerton, talk about a profound transformation of member countries by which they are transformed from *nation states* to *member states*, a development that the states themselves are pushing for (Bickerton, 2012).

Free movement within the EU is driving deeper cooperation because it is utterly apparent that problems become common and the same then goes for potential solutions. The EU member states, however, have not chosen to give the EU more power to decide over matters they perceive as close to their own sovereignty. The central path through which democracy works in the EU is still at the member state level, which is also where it derives its legitimacy. Bartolini has applied Rokkan's theory on state formation and nation-building to the EU in his work on the borders and boundaries of Europe and its 'peculiar' form of state formation. Bartolini argues that the EU's 'political production' is not commensurate to the loyalty that can be summoned from countries and citizens. There is only weak system-building capacity in the EU. The weak political structures and the lack of a common European identity become a significant hindrance to the supranational level's capacity to compel results and support for decisions. Bartolini is, however, highly sceptical of attempts to democratise the EU from the top down because the political structures needed to lend meaning to a supranational European democracy do not exist (Bartolini, 2005).

It is also notable, however, that the multitude of opportunities for partial exit (i.e. choosing to opt-out of certain areas of the cooperation) make the issue of legitimation in the EU different to a situation where there is stronger control of exit options. Genschel and Jachtenfuchs (2016) have studied how European integration within 'core state powers' has developed over time. They determine that there is steady growth of formal authority in the EU over core state powers (e.g. coercive power, public finance, public administration). In contrast to historical examples of federalism, where nationalisation of the core state powers triggered an institutional, territorial and political *consolidation* of the emerging state, the integration within the EU of these powers of EU member states is instead linked to institutional, territorial and political *fragmentation*. Unlike the creation of the Internal Market, the integration of core state powers is not being driven by business interests but by national elites and (constraining) expressions of public opinion. Genschel and Jachtenfuchs conclude that the integration of core state powers is leading to deeper integration but, ironically enough, less federation. The differentiation that arises is not of the ilk where the EU is moving at clearly different speeds, although the euro zone is a form of distinctly deepened cooperation; instead, the boundaries are blurred and overlapping in policy-specific forms of 'variable geometry' or 'Multispeed Europe'. Genschel and Jachtenfuchs argue that, contrary to the expectations of the Euro-federalists, this type of integration is not contributing to 'an ever closer union' and a more federal Europe but is instead driving Europe's populations apart and fragmenting the EU, territorially and institutionally. The more the EU is involved in policy areas that define the state, the clearer it becomes that there are enduring differences between the EU and a state. But there is one difference here that is based on whether the EU builds its own *capacity*, which tends to lead to politicisation and fragmentation, but this does not seem to be the case when the EU devotes itself primarily to *regulatory* activities.

Legitimacy and Voice in a Multilevel Polity

Beyond the overarching narrative of the European integration process as a way to prevent large-scale wars in Europe, the traditional way to legitimate the EU has been linked to higher efficiency gains. Common EU regulations have made it possible to demonstrate the benefit of integration in relation to effectiveness. Scharpf describes how the EU's capacity ultimately lies in generating 'output legitimacy', while the EU's structure does not offer the same alternatives when it comes to 'input legitimacy' (Scharpf, 1999). The EU is still based on the idea of conferral of powers, where the EU member states are the masters of the treaties and democracy chiefly remains with them. Because there is no effective means of exercising accountability at the supranational level, there is also no effective democratic input side. Such a link would, in Scharpf's view, be required if it were to pursue policies of a redistributive nature. Removing barriers to trade in order to create an efficient Internal Market, however, is doable based on a purely output-oriented logic of efficiency (Scharpf, 1999).

In the early 1970s, Lindberg and Scheingold identified the 'permissive consensus', meaning that citizens of EU (then European Economic Community (EEC)) member states could accept the transfer of power to the European level with no consequent implication that the supranational Union (then Community) was democratic or that there were any opportunities for demanding accountability at the European level (Lindberg & Scheingold, 1970). The democratic deficit, which can in its most condensed form be described as an asymmetric relationship between power and accountability, could be accepted because citizens had a high degree of trust in their national leaders. In addition, the matters regulated at the European level were of a technical nature and rarely concerned redistributive aspects. Today, Hooghe and Marks are describing a post-functionalist integration where permissive consensus has been replaced by a 'constraining dissensus' (Hooghe & Marks, 2009). A few decades ago, the low political salience of EU policies and issues among the European electorates gave political elites wide scope to drive EU integration onwards. But as the policies and issues addressed within the framework of the EU have become increasingly politicised and have come to encompass matters that are traditionally the subject of political conflict and domestic policy competition, a constraining popular opinion has emerged in many EU member states.

The potential for political mobilisation against the EU is a 'sleeping giant' that can be awoken by increasing the salience of the issues dealt with by the EU (van der Eijk & Franklin, 2004). There is a distinct pattern of discrepancy between public opinion towards the EU and the election results of parties representing a similar point of view. The electorates in most EU member states have tended to vote for political parties that are more positive towards the EU than the electorates are. The explanation for this discrepancy of opinion presented in the research often has to do with the relatively low importance of EU issues in eyes of the voters when they go to the polls (von Sydow, 2013). When the EU project involves issues of a more politically sensitive nature, mobilisation may ensue. This mobilisation of opposition is facilitated by its linkage with other matters related to boundaries, such as immigration, multiculturalism and free trade (Kriesi et al., 2012). Combined, these issues form a new dimension in politics, exploited primarily by radical right-wing populist parties. These parties inject a high dose of establishment critique into their political messages. National leaders find their scope of action restrained when they must take a clearer stance in relation to public opinion in EU matters.

And yet, there are obvious difficulties with how interaction with the electorate should take place in the EU and as regards EU issues. Mair contends that there is a problem in that the EU tends to have a depoliticising effect. The internationalisation of decisions shrinks the scope of national decision-making. This can obscure political cleavages and alternatives. If classic opposition politics cannot be channelled, there is risk that this will instead be replaced by system-critical opposition. This is driven by the political 'void' that is created when political leaders use the EU to avoid being held accountable and when discussions of political deliberations are not held in public when they involve EU issues, and when a far-off 'Brussels' is used as a scapegoat for (often self-inflicted) problems (Mair, 2013). Mair succinctly concludes that 'Political opposition gives voice. By losing opposition we lose voice, and by losing voice we lose control of our own political system' (Mair, 2007, p. 17). Mair essentially argues that since we cannot organise opposition *in* the EU, we instead organize opposition *to* the EU (ibid.).

This has to do, at least in part, with the special constitution of the EU, in that the Treaty for the European Union does not clearly differentiate between the form of EU policy and its content. Constitutions commonly regulate, first and foremost, *how* we make decisions and not *what* decisions can or cannot be made. Naturally, there are restraints imposed by the rule of law but, in general, the will of the people should influence the direction of policy. The EU treaties tend to lock the political output of the Union to a particular policy outcome (von Sydow, 2014). This constitutional lock-in of policy direction also makes things considerably more difficult for those who suggest that the EU should be politicised and that there should be more political conflict surrounding the question of which EU we would like to see in the future. It is hard to foresee that such a genuine political arena for political competition and accountability can become a reality within the framework of the current constitutional order in the EU, even though one can argue that small steps were taken in this direction during the European Parliament election in 2014 when, for example, party groups put forward candidates for the President of the European Commission before the election (i.e. the so-called *Spitzenkandidanten*) (Hix, 2006).

In the absence of a means for the national parties to handle the EU dimension within the frameworks of representative democracy, a need is thus emerging to manage these conflicts and tensions in other ways, including referendums. Holding referendums tends, however, to politicise rather than depoliticise the EU question. In subsequent elections, this benefits parties that are highly critical of the EU (von Sydow, 2013). Because mainstream parties and other social elites usually support the EU, a conflict between the 'people' and the 'elites' is shaped. Referendums can thus be considered as a way of dealing with the lack of a functioning electoral linkage in the EU. In addition to the difficulty of 'squeezing' the EU dimension into traditional conflict structures on the national level, such as the left-right scale (and the EU's tendency to split parties internally), referendums can also be used for tactical reasons. For example, when the former British Prime Minister David Cameron promised a referendum on UK membership in the EU (ahead of the 2015 general election), his intention was to isolate the national (and for him, the primary) voter arena from the EU issue, in a bid to win the election. It did not exactly work out according to the plans, to say the least. However, in terms of exit, voice and loyalty, British voters were afforded an opportunity to use their voice to make an exit from the EU. Although this did not occur within the framework of representative democracy but instead via a referendum.

No Exit, Limited Voice, But Pressure to Stay Loyal in the Euro Crisis

The euro crisis, that has been ongoing for several years, shows that there does not seem to be any exit from the monetary union, or at least that the cost would be high. At the most critical points of the Greek crisis, a voluntary or forced exit ('Grexit') seemed imminent, but the price of allowing a member country to leave has obviously been judged to be far too high. Trust has been put under pressure as a consequence. The countries most severely affected, such as Portugal, Ireland, Italy, Greece and Spain, have been castigated for inadequate regulatory compliance and other shortcomings. The leading countries in the euro zone, Germany in particular, have had credibility problems in their arguments, however, since several of them were the first to breach the common regulations—without sanctions (see Clas Wihlborg and Sarkis J. Khoury's chapter in this volume).

In addition, the euro countries have gone above and beyond what is stipulated in the TEU no-bailout clause and the crisis management measures have brought several institutional and political reorganisations that transfer further decision-making power to the EU level. This makes the legitimacy concerns partially different. Scharpf argues that declining trust in the EU is a consequence of the increasing politicisation of the issues combined with the inability to find a legitimate way to exercise power at the EU level. There is no functional means of creating the input legitimacy that would be needed to strengthen legitimacy and the political system of the EU does not seem able to generate output legitimacy either (Scharpf, 2015).

Antagonisms between EU member states surfaced and trust between them was damaged during the euro crisis. White describes how a kind of state of exception emerges in crisis, creating a situation in which drastic actions can be implemented under a coercive logic (White, 2015). Often, these actions are such that go beyond, or outside, the rules laid down in the EU treaties. Meanwhile, Mény sees the emergence of a kind of 'executive federalism' whose flawed democratic qualities make it unsustainable in the long term. In a regime where political alternatives are 'locked-in' under the mantra that 'there is no alterative' (TINA), the options available to the electorate are severely limited (Mény, 2014). Müller describes this state of affairs as a European tragedy in which populism will grow if political leaders are unable to give any better reason for policy than the TINA mantra (Müller, 2016). In this way, populism and technocracy are mirror images of each other. The populist logic claims that there is only *one* authentic will of the people (and that the populist leader is the best equipped to interpret it). To technocrats, on the other hand, critique of the current economic and political order in the EU is seen as expressions of irrationality, since in their view there are only a few ways in which economic growth and political stability can be achieved. Both of these polar opposites can be seen over the course of the crisis.

Especially in the EU countries worst hit by the crisis, there is limited political scope for politicians who are aiming to adhere to agreements to even suggest far-reaching changes. The prime examples of this lock-in of political alternatives were seen in Ireland and Greece when lenders, represented by the so-called Troika (IMF, ECB and the European Commission), demanded loyalty from both governing parties and opposition parties in order to effectuate loans. When voters later go to the polls, it is not unlikely that they will feel a certain measure of powerlessness. When there is no alternative among the mainstream parties, there is a certain allure to aligning with the parties that have often expressly dismissed governing responsibility and instead unilaterally emphasised responsiveness, listening and channelling opinions (Mair, 2011).

Seen from the electorate's horizon, it also seems that what constitutes potential political alternatives is determined somewhere else, outside of national/electoral borders. Consequently, the pushback against a unilateral emphasis on accountability is also directed at the EU. Within the EU, the member states are expected to be loyal to the agreements they have signed. The qualitative difference in the current situation in the euro zone is that decisions bound by common respect and commitments are so extensive and that they concern areas often surrounded by a high level of national political conflict. One could say that the regulations that have sprouted up around the common currency were intended to have a built-in barrier against political 'irresponsibility' (i.e. not so strict fiscal and monetary policies). The problem is that increasing criticism of this arrangement is evident in the choices of the electorate. In fact, the limited scope of action can encourage system-critical opposition because that which was intended to create trust between elites at the European level has actually created distrust of the EU at the national level.

During the crisis, former Belgian minister and political scientist Paul Magnette (later Minister-President of Wallonia and, in 2016, the leader of the opposition against the EU-Canada trade agreement) asked the rhetorical question 'Who is Olli Rehn?' (Schmidt, 2015, p. 102). The context was that Rehn (then the European Commissioner for Economic and Monetary Affairs) had given a stern warning to the Belgian government that they must further cut the national budget or face sanctions. At the time, the relatively recently installed Belgian government had just cobbled together a comprehensive savings package after protracted negotiations among many parties in the fragmented Belgian party system. Was the Commission now going to override that which the national parliamentary system had, with considerable difficulty, managed to push through? Magnette's rhetorical question stemmed from frustration over the asymmetric relationship between power and accountability. If the national governments, to a great extent, implement policy that was actually decided elsewhere, by non-elected EU officials, who are the electorate supposed to hold accountable? And through which electoral arena?

Greek voters have gone to the polls repeatedly during the gruelling years of crisis, but the impression is that voters might not primarily want to hold their national politicians accountable for the policy they have pursued. A referendum on whether to accept the conditions of the bailout package for Greece was held in July 2015. The outcome was a clear rejection of the conditions (61 percent of the voters said 'no'). This was a way for the Greek government to raise its voice against the lenders. Ultimately, however, the Greek government chose loyalty to existing agreements and to implement the policy dictated in the deal with the troika. The complex arrangements that control policy frameworks in the euro zone offer few opportunities for the system to respond to the demands of the electorate. The voice of a single member state's public cannot unilaterally change the direction of the EU. Combined with what seems to be no option to exit the euro (due to the high costs associated thereto), all that remains is to attempt to generate loyalty in a rule-based manner in the face of the political and economic bonds created by the common currency.

'Brexit': Voicing to Exit, But at What Cost?

A majority of the British voters that voted on 23 June 2016 supported the option that the UK should leave the EU. With a turnout of 72 percent, 52 percent of those who cast their vote opted for the UK to exit the EU (out of the entire electorate roughly about 38 percent voted to leave and 34 to remain). The British process for implementing its exit from the Union has thus begun in practice. The path provided by the EU treaty was taken with the triggering of Article 50 by Prime Minister, Theresa May, in March 2017. In the case of the UK, the balance between voice and loyalty has alternated over time during the four decades of British EU membership. Finally, the British voters chose exit instead. The country already enjoyed several opt-outs from the EU's common policy, which can be considered as examples of 'partial exit'. Prior to the 2016 referendum, the British government used its voice to negotiate a new agreement with the EU. One issue that was an important matter of principle to the British was the implications of EU treaty's wording on an 'ever closer union'. The British criticism can be seen as a matter of what future loyalty can be demonstrated towards a system perceived as being in a state of constant evolution. Even on the 'remain side', voices were heard that the EU of today is not the same EEC that the UK once joined. Linked to the question raised in the introduction to the chapter about how trust is created out of expectations about the future behaviour of others, one can interpret the British trust in the EU as very conditional indeed. In the agreement with the EU negotiated in February 2016, the British government successfully negotiated a concession saying the country did not have to be part of 'an ever closer union'. In return, several other EU member states considered this to be disloyal and detrimental to the trust between them. But this assurance alone was not enough to persuade the majority of British voters to choose to remain in the EU in the referendum a couple of months later.

An 'exit clause' in the EU did not exist until after the Treaty of Lisbon (and Article 50 TEU) entered into force. It was inserted as a way of emphasising the international basis of the EU and that delegation of political power to the Union can be revoked. Because the delegation of authority is so comprehensive and the commitment to be part of the EU is so demanding, there must arguably be a way to revoke this. This discussion intensified in connection with the Maastricht Treaty in the 1990s, and the German Federal Constitutional Court's opinion on the treaty, in which the idea of the legitimation of transfer of power to the EU as a sort of 'provisional arrangement' was extensively argued. Article 50 TEU can be read in parallel with the preceding Article 49, which sets out rules for membership 'Any European State which respects the values referred to in Article 2 and is committed to promoting them may apply to become a member of the Union.' Once a state has been admitted to the Union (which must be approved by all EU member states), the rules of the club must be followed. If a member state does not like it, it can notify its intention to withdraw and there is thus an exit. If the application of Article 50 turns out to be successful in the British case, this could be taken as a pretext for that a member state can in fact 'take back control' and that the existence of a door by which the member state can leave clarifies the commitments of EU membership.

But taking back control, as promised by the Brexiteers, may prove much harder than first anticipated. It seems that the British government prefers regained national sovereignty over other desirable objectives, such as economic growth and prosperity. The EU has made it clear that any splitting of the free movement of goods, services, capital and people is out of the question and thus indicates that negotiations between the EU and the UK are going to end with a hard exit from the EU and that the new relationship will be considerably less extensive than what the UK enjoys today as being a full member of the Internal Market. Thus, there is an exit from the EU, which eliminates the demand for loyalty. But lack of participation also begs the question of what voice the UK and its citizens are giving up by leaving the important decision-making arenas to which they have thus far had access.

Between Voice and Loyalty in the Refugee Crisis

Beyond 'Brexit' that is being negotiated and the 'Grexit' that did not materialise, the EU is confronting several other major crises. Particular tensions have arisen surrounding the handling of the refugee crisis in 2015 and its aftermath. The crisis has laid bare the incompleteness of free movement of people within the EU with no fixed external borders. The Schengen system has for all intents and purposes been sidelined due to the lack of common management of the refugee situation. Further steps are being taken gradually to establish a clearer, common external border, by means including strengthening the capacity of the EU's border authority, Frontex. What is also obvious is that the refugee situation has sparked an intense and contentious discussion between the member states as to whether the EU can and should have joint responsibilities for resettling refugees within the Union. Vocal dissent, especially by several of the Eastern EU member states (such as Hungary, Poland, Slovakia and the Czech Republic), include objections to decisions made by the European Council on a system of mandatory quotas to reallocate 160,000 refugees in Italy and Greece to the other member states (see also Bo Petersson's chapter in this volume). The countries that voted against the proposal in the Council are clearly not willing to accept the outcome. Slovakia requested a review of the decision by the European Court of Justice (ECJ), and the Hungarian government held a referendum on the issue in October

2016. Opposition in the form of voice is thus being used by these EU member states in several ways.

Meanwhile, those who supported the deal argue that it is unreasonable to criticise a decision made in accordance with the current rules of the EU. The Nordic countries have encouraged the European Commission to take action and Swedish Minister of Justice, Morgan Johansson, remarked in an interview with *Dagens Nyheter* in September 2016 that 'If you are a member of an organisation, you have to follow the organisation's rules. Otherwise, you cannot be a part of it. We cannot have a system where members can pick and choose which rules they will follow' (Dagens Nyheter, 2016). The conflict highlights the tension that arises when one or more EU member states oppose decisions and refuse to implement them. A unique feature of the EU, compared to purely international organisations, is that there is scope for applying majority voting in the Council. If the Commission's role as the watchdog of common rules, the precedence of EU law over national law, the role of the ECJ as interpreter of the law in disputes, as well as the power to fine member states in infringement proceedings, are all taken into account then it is clear that the EU has a relatively powerful enforcement arsenal at its disposal.

Other EU member states have either encouraged the opening of infringement proceedings, threatened to find ways to punish recalcitrant member states by attempting to withdraw funds from the EU budget or to open a process in accordance with Article 7 TEU on the breach of the Union's values. As in other situations when the fundamental values of the Union as set out in Article 2 have been challenged, the mechanisms provided in Article 7 have appeared too draconian (hence, the sobriquet 'the nuclear option') and the requirement for unanimity far too difficult to meet. Nevertheless, the presence of Article 7 in TEU, along with the new proceedings for safeguarding the rule of law in the member states, is a step towards ensuring that the EU has instruments at hand when the member states do not live up to the Union's values as established in Article 2. Failure to live up to the values can be considered disloyal to the EU (see Joakim Nergelius' chapter in this volume).

What should the EU do to compel loyalty from the member states in cases where they really do not want to give it? The Hungarian Prime Minister, Viktor Orbán, used a referendum to further strengthen his negotiating position vis-à-vis the EU. A crushing majority of those who voted (98 percent) supported the Hungarian government's position, which was to vote no to the proposal that the EU should be able to force Hungary to accept refugees without the approval of the Hungarian National Assembly. But the outcome of the referendum was declared invalid due to the low voter turnout of 43 percent. The EU member states that supported the decision on mandatory quotas contend that the decision was made in a valid process. But the problem of how the EU should handle the issue remains. As said, there are certain ways and means available, but the nature of the issue is not only legal, political concerns must be considered as well.

When European Commission President, Jean-Claude Juncker, dealt with the issue of solidarity in the refugee policy in his State of the Union address in 2016, he said, '[W]hen it comes to managing the refugee crisis, we have started to see solidarity. I am convinced much more solidarity is needed. But I also know that solidarity must be given voluntarily. It must come from the heart. It cannot be forced.' There is no explicit reference to the mandatory quotas in Juncker's remarks, but the address is still open to the interpretation that the President of the Commission does not believe that Brussels can hierarchically force loyalty and solidarity from EU member states. One way of interpreting this conciliatory attitude is that it is an expression of the 'informal pact of confidence' mentioned at the beginning of the chapter and of that the European Commission does not believe it has sufficient legitimacy to coerce loyalty through hierarchical governance. The risk is that it would inflame the conflict and that the recalcitrant countries would instead choose to exit the EU. At present, however, it does seem as if the wayward countries have judged the cost of exit to be far too high.

The unilateral opposition to adhering to the EU treaties' demand for loyalty of individual member states may present a risk of undermining the collective trust among all member states, which would have systemic consequences. The dynamics of the tensions arising from the management of the refugee crisis are somewhat different than those of both 'Brexit' and the euro crisis. The refugee crisis not only involves member states' opportunities for voice in relation to the loyalty that is expected of them, but it also risks effecting fundamental issues related to boundaries, both national and European. As Genschel and Jachtenfuchs (2016) show in their study of the European integration of core state powers, this has been possible because the member states that did not want to participate could choose 'opt-outs'. The demand for solidarity on the refugee issue seems to disallow this because it would impact the system as a whole. Now, opinions are instead being voiced that flexibility is the only reasonable way to resolve this conflict.

Another aspect that Genschel and Jachtenfuchs emphasise is that the Europeanisation of core state powers is taking place primarily via regulation and not capacity-building (Genschel & Jachtenfuchs, 2016). The solution to the refugee crisis that, for the moment, seems the most favoured among European leaders involves securing the external borders of the EU. This would seemingly require more extensive European capacity-building, which the member states might find more difficult to justify than creating common regulations. Management of the refugee crisis is inciting obvious tensions as regards trust in the EU. The perspective of the countries opposed to a common EU policy in the area is that it would undermine national democracy and lead to deep distrust of the EU. On the part of those who argue that the EU needs to act in solidarity, there is peril that if joint responsibility is not taken this also risks fomenting distrust of the EU. If the European Commission does not take action against the refractory member states, there is risk that the other member states will begin to distrust the motives for the actions of the supranational institutions and ask why they themselves should be loyal when the Commission, on some other matter, opens infringement proceedings against them. If the solution to this conflict lies in some kind of 'flexible solidarity', there is risk that an attitude towards the EU, by which the member countries can cherry-pick (or, in terms of the concepts of exit and voice, engage in repeated partial exit from EU policy areas they do not like), will be entrenched. This could damage trust in the system as such. With no mandatory requirements for loyalty and low costs of (partial) exit, the issue of legitimacy in the EU becomes less problematic, but it also seems reasonable to believe that the benefit of cooperation would decline substantially (perhaps even to the point where citizens start asking what is the point of cooperating at all).

Balancing Exit, Voice and Loyalty: Ways to Restore Trust

Wavering trust between the EU member states has been discernible during the crises of recent years. The member states are also demonstrating insufficient trust in and loyalty to the supranational Union and thus also European integration as such. Behind this lies a lack of public trust in European integration and in elected representatives. Due to the absence of full democracy at the EU level, mandates for political action and accountability occur primarily within the framework of national democracy (Gustavsson, 2009). Insufficient citizens' trust of elected representatives is thus an underlying factor when one approaches the Union's state of declining trust. Paradoxically, this is occurring in a context where the challenges the EU is facing seem to require the EU to assume more 'state-like' characteristics. The EU version of state formation, however, differs from the processes in which the European nation states emerged. The integration in recent decades has in many respects involved areas that encompass the core state powers, but the EU has not become more federal as a result. Instead, it is institutionally fragmented and territorially differentiated. The euro crisis, however, has entailed stronger European control over economic policy and the refugee crisis has increased pressure to build up stronger external border control, increase joint responsibility and increase common decision-making.

Going back to the issue of the state of balance between exit controls and voice channelling within the EU, it follows from the arguments above that it varies in different policy areas. The outcome of the British exit from the EU will probably further clarify the cost (in the wider sense) of exit. Regardless of the cost, the exit option exists, and this is important as a matter of principle. That path thus exists for those member states that no longer can or want to be loyal for other reasons, such as the refugee issue. In relation to the common currency, the cost of exit seems considerably higher. This should then lead to a more fundamental discussion of how channels of voice can be found within the framework of the euro zone and a more symmetric relationship between power and accountability. A federal structure for the euro zone would rectify the vague confusion of powers that leads to de-politicisation and difficulties with demanding accountability at the appropriate level. From this perspective, a clear division of authority should be made so that voters more clearly understand what is decided at what level and that they can demand accountability from elected representatives at the level decisions are actually made. From a federalist perspective, trust in the European project can be regenerated in this way. A clearer, constitutionally established division of competences could break the policy lock-in if the political content was 'de-constitutionalised' at the same time. In this way, genuine political competition among various political alternatives could materialise at the EU level but only within the framework of the issues that belong at the EU level. The aim would be to make it clearer to the electorate which issues should be discussed and what accountability demanded at the European and national levels, respectively.

But there is also ample reason to argue that the conditions for a functioning democracy at the European level simply do not exist. A big leap forward assisted by institutional reforms could damage trust and give rise to even greater, and potentially more destructive, opposition. The crises of recent years indicate rather that the boundaries of policy commitments at the EU level must be set in better proportion to the loyalty that can be mobilised in the member states. Others argue that this can be done through a clearer division of competences that might entail a re-nationalisation of certain competences. From this perspective, the constraining national interests should gain wider scope and the EU would, in this scenario, become more of a 'flexible union'. The member states would have more latitude to pick and choose the parts they want from the cooperation and accountability at the national level would be clearer. This would also be a way to manage the national differences in the EU of 27 member states. In this model, the member states would be involved only where they want to be. National leaders would thus feel they had a clearer mandate from their voters in connection with further delegation, whereupon trust could possibly be restored. It should be noted, however, that it can be argued that the EU's historical success has relied on precisely the opposite. That is, the common regulations, package solutions and compromises are what have made the EU into a cooperative project of its current magnitude and without these arrangements, it is possible that trust in the project would be further undermined.

The point I want to emphasise here is that regardless of whether one recommends a leap forward or some other solution, it is imperative to think critically about the capacity of representative democracy to channel conflicts in an interwoven and multilevel polity. The insufficient trust in the EU can, at least partially, be interpreted as an expression of uncertainty about where power and influence are exercised and how we manage conflicts that pertain to matters involving both *where* decisions should be made and *what* decisions should be made. The 'locking-in' of the areas of political conflict described in the chapter have a tendency to make the politicisation of the EU into an expression of pure voice rather than a political conflict with multiple courses of action within the framework of representative democracy. Whether one believes the solution lies in a more effective system for political conflict and accountability at the EU level or in the capacity of national democracies to manage EU issues, this issue is central to correcting the problems of trust in the EU. In the light of growing populism and nationalism, it is imperative that actors endeavouring to defend the European project find a formula for establishing trust among the electorate. The often-cited technocratic rationality obviously does not suffice. Instead, it should be possible to combine accountability and responsiveness without obscuring relevant conflicts by means of depoliticising techniques. At the same time, it is a major challenge of constitutional policy to find a formula that balances demands for constitutionalism, democracy and effectiveness in a complex and intertwined political system such as the EU.

If the current formula is to endure—high demands for loyalty to decisions made at the EU level while democracy remains national—it needs to be based on the premise that national democracy is capable of managing the conflicts that arise between loyalty to the EU and responsiveness to the electorate. In times when the forces of populism are gathering strength, it is easy to see how a shift in favour of responsiveness to public opinion at home. This could make it more difficult to re-establish trust in and loyalty to the common project. If trust is based on expectations about the future behaviour and loyalty of others, political developments in several EU member states, involving populism and nationalism, present a particular challenge. If we do not trust that others will uphold key principles, there is risk that our own faith in the system as a whole will be undermined. If, moreover, the supranational Union does not have adequate means at its disposal to stop a march away from constitutional democracy in the member states, there is risk that trust will diminish even further.

One way of solving this problem is to have clear principles and values, as well as procedures for managing breaches of these principles and values. But it must also be even more clearly stressed in public debate that as long as democracy remains primarily national, the capacity of the EU to compel loyalty—in politically sensitive and controversial matters—will have its limitations. It thus will not suffice, as some political leaders claim, for the EU to return to simply 'deliver' desirable output. Emphasising effectiveness on the output side is not enough to ensure an increase in trust in the EU again, quite simply because the challenges the EU is confronting today are of a politically controversial nature and thus demand another form of legitimation. It would be a mistake for political representatives at the national and EU level to not take these matters seriously, and a first step in the right direction would be to facilitate a comprehensive debate about the future of the EU that is directed at and yet aims beyond the dichotomy between federalisation and re-nationalisation.

References

Bartolini, S. (2005). *Restructuring Europe: Centre formation, system building and political structuring between the nation-state and the European Union*. Oxford: Oxford University Press.

Bickerton, C. J. (2012). *European integration: From nation-states to member states*. Oxford: Oxford University Press.

Dagens Nyheter. (2016). De nordiska länderna ökar trycket på Ungern, 2016-09-10. Retrieved from https://www.dn.se/nyheter/sverige/de-nordiska-landerna-okartrycket-pa-ungern/

De Wilde, P., & Zürn, M. (2012). Can the politicization of European integration be reversed? *JCMS: Journal of Common Market Studies, 50*(1), 137–153.

Flora, P., Kuhnle, S., & Urwin, D. W. (Eds.). (1999). *State formation, nation building and mass politics in Europe: The theory of Stein Rokkan*. Oxford: Oxford University Press.

Genschel, P., & Jachtenfuchs, M. (2016). More integration, less federation: The European integration of core state powers. *Journal of European Public Policy, 23*(1), 42–59.

Gustavsson, S. (2009). Putting limits on accountability avoidance. In S. Gustavsson, C. Karlsson, & P. Persson (Eds.), *The illusion of accountability in the European Union*. London: Routledge.

Gustavsson, S. (2014). The need for legitimate opposition and protectionism. In O. Cramne & S. B. Hobolt (Eds.), *Democratic politics in a European Union under stress*. Oxford: Oxford University Press.

Haas, E. B. ([1958] 2004). *The uniting of Europe: Political, social and economic forces 1950–1957*. Notre Dame, IN: University of Notre Dame Press.

Hirschman, A. O. (1970). *Exit, voice, and loyalty: Responses to decline in firms, organizations, and states*. Cambridge, MA: Harvard University Press.

Hix, S. (2006). *Why the EU needs (left-right) politics? Policy reform and accountability are impossible without it, in, politics: The right or the wrong sort of medicine for the EU?* Paris: Notre Europe.

Hooghe, L., & Marks, G. (2009). A postfunctionalist theory of European integration: From permissive consensus to constraining dissensus. *British Journal of Political Science, 39*(1), 1–23.

Juncker, J. C. (2016). Speech on the State of the Union, Strasbourg, 14 September 2016. Retrieved from https://ec.europa.eu/commission/state-union-2016_en

Kriesi, H., Grande, E., Dolezal, M., Helbling, M., Höglinger, D., Hutter, S., et al. (2012). *Political conflict in Western Europe*. Cambridge: Cambridge University Press.

Lindberg, L. N., & Scheingold, S. A. (1970). *Europe's would-be polity: Patterns of change in the European community*. Eaglewood Cliffs, NJ: Prentice Hall.

Mair, P. (2007). Political opposition and the European Union. *Government and Opposition, 42*(1), 1–17.

Mair, P. (2011). Bini Smaghi vs. the parties: Representative government and institutional constraints. *European Union Democracy Observatory*, no. 22. Florence: European University Institute.

Mair, P. (2013). *Ruling the void: The hollowing of western democracy*. London: Verso Books.

Mény, Y. (2014). Managing the EU crises: Another way of integration by stealth? *West European Politics, 37*(6), 1336–1353.

Müller, J. W. (2016). *What is populism?* Philadelphia, PA: University of Pennsylvania Press.

Rokkan, S. (1970). *Citizens, elections, parties: Approaches to the comparative study of the processes of development*. Oslo: Universitetsforlaget.

Rothstein, B. (2005). *Social traps and the problem of trust*. Cambridge: Cambridge University Press.

Scharpf, F. W. (1999). *Governing in Europe: Effective and democratic?* Oxford: Oxford University Press.

Scharpf, F. W. (2015). No exit from the euro-rescuing trap? In V. Schneider & B. Eberlein (Eds.), *Complex democracy: Varieties, crises, and transformations*. New York: Springer Verlag.

Schmidt, V. A. (2015). The Eurozone's crisis of democratic legitimacy: Can the EU rebuild public trust and support for European economic integration? *European Commission Discussion Paper*, no. 15.

Tilly, C. (1992). *Capital, coercion, and European states*. Oxford: Blackwell Publishing.

van der Eijk, C., & Franklin, M. (2004). Dimensions of contestation in European elections. In G. Marks & M. R. Steenbergen (Eds.), *European Union and political conflict*. Cambridge: Cambridge University Press.

von Sydow, G. (2013). *Politicizing Europe: Patterns of party-based opposition to European integration*. Stockholm: Department of Political Science, Stockholm University.

von Sydow, G. (2014). Parties and politics of opposition in the European Union. *Polish Quarterly of International Affairs, 23*(1), 69–82.

White, J. (2015). Emergency Europe. *Political Studies, 63*(2), 300–318.

Index

A. Bakardjieva Engelbrekt et al. (eds.), *Trust in the European Union in Challenging Times*, https://doi.org/10.1007/978-3-319-73857-4

The manufacturer's authorised representative in the EU is Springer Nature Customer Service Centre GmbH, Europaplatz 3, 69115 Heidelberg, Germany. If you have any concerns regarding our products, please contact ProductSafety@springernature.com

Printed and bound by CPI Group (UK) Ltd, Croydon, CR0 4YY
30/09/2026
02225653-0008